The Electronic Pirates

DIY crime of the century

**John Chesterman
and Andy Lipman**

R

**A Comedia book published by
Routledge**

A Comedia book
First published in 1988 by
Routledge
a division of Routledge, Chapman and Hall
11 New Fetter Lane, London EC4P 4EE

Set in 10/11½ pt Imprint, Linotron 101 by J&L Composition Ltd, Filey, North Yorkshire
Printed in Great Britain by The Guernsey Press Co Ltd, Guernsey, Channel Islands

British Library Cataloguing in Publication Data
Chesterman, John
  The electronic pirates: DIY crime of the
  century. —— (A comedia book).
  1. Copyright. Law
  I. Title   II. Lipman, Andy
  342.64'82

ISBN 0–415–00738–0
ISBN 0–415–00739–9 Pbk

Comedia
Series editor: David Morley
The Electronic Pirates

New technologies, photocopiers, videos, tape-recorders, and computers have blown a gaping hole into the old ideas of copyright. John Chesterman and Andy Lipman question how secure the fortress of mass culture and big business really is when faced with the cunning and curiosity of the electronic guerillas.

Their book looks at the enormous scale of worldwide piracy, in print, tapes, videos, and computer software. It uncovers the shady and dangerous world of the electronic pirates, and its parallels with international drugs dealing and terrorism. It looks at how the battle against the outlaws is fought – the enforcers, the changing law, and new methods of 'control', such as taxes on tapes. And it explains the intricacies and inconsistencies of the copyright law itself.

The Electronic Pirates will intrigue students of information technology, communication, and media studies. It will interest criminologists and those working in legal studies, as well as computer buffs.

John Chesterman is a science historian and full-time writer and journalist. Andy Lipman is a lawyer and journalist. He was Video Editor of *City Limits* magazine and legal consultant to the Independent Film and Videomakers Association. For the last two years he has been series producer of Channel 4's 'The Media Show'.

Whereas the Improvement of Knowledge, the Progress of Civilization, the public Weal of Community and the Advance of Human Happiness greatly depend on the Efforts of learned and Ingenious Persons in the various Arts and Sciences ... the principal Encouragement such persons can have to make great and beneficial exertions of this nature must exist in the Legal Security of the Fruits of their Study and Industry ... there being no property more peculiarly a Man's own than that which is produced by the Labour of his Mind.

(Copyright Law, State of Massachusetts, 1782)

Contents

Part four: **The future**

Abbreviations

Technological abbreviations and jargon

ATM	Automated Teller Machine (cash dispenser)
DAT	Digital Audio Tape
DBS	Direct Broadcast Satellite
DES	Data Encryption Standard (by US cipher system)
EBU	European Broadcast Union
ETF	Electronic Telephone Fraud
FORSCOM	Forward Readiness Strategic Command (US)
GSP	General System of Preferences (trade agreement)
MAC	Multiple Analogue Components (broadcast system)
MCTL	Military Critical Technologies' List
PAL	Phase Alternation Line (broadcast system)
PIN	Personal Identity Number
PKN	Public Key Notorization (cipher system)
RAM	Random Access Memory (computer storage)
ROM	Read Only Memory (programmed microchip)
SCOMP	Secure Communications Processor (computer)
SECAM	Sequential Couleur à Mémoire (broadcast system)
STD	Subscriber Trunk Dialling
TNC	Transnational Corporation
VCR	Video Cassette Recorder

Copyright enforcement agencies and pressure groups

APG	Anti-Piracy Group (UK)
BIVA	British International Video Association
BMI	US royalty collecting society
BPI	British Phonographic Industry
BVA	British Videogram Association
CIB	Counterfeiting Intelligence Bureau
CICI	Confederation of Information and Communications Industries (UK)
CISAC	International Confederation of Societies of Authors and Composers

CLA	Copyright Licensing Agency (UK)
CRG	Computer Reform Group
DPSO	Data Processing Service Organizations (US)
FACT	Federation Against Copyright Theft
FAST	Federation Against Software Theft
FLAPF	Federación Latinoamericana de Productores de Fonogramas y Videogramas (South America)
FPRA	Foreign Publications Reprinting Association (Korea) (pirate association)
GOSH	Guild of Software Houses
GVU	West German copyright enforcement agency
IFPI	International Federation of Phonogram and Videogram Producers
JAPIG	Joint Anti-Piracy Intelligence Group
MCPS	Mechanical Copyright Protection Society
MPAA	Motion Picture Association of America
MPEAA	Motion Picture Export Association of America
MU	Musicians' Union
NFVA	National Federation of Video Associations
PA	Publishers' Association
PPL	Phonographic Performance Limited
PRS	Performing Right Society
RIAA	Recording Industry Association of America
SACEM	French composers' association
SPAM	Society of Producers of Advertising Music
TMG	Tape Manufacturers' Group
VCPS	Video Copyright Protection Society
VTA	Video Trade Association

Part one
Copyright

1

The party of the first part

Do you think I could buy back my introduction to you?
(Groucho Marx, in *Monkey Business*)

According to film legend, when the Marx Brothers were making their classic comedy *A Night In Casablanca* they received a hostile letter from a rival studio, demanding that they change the title. It came from Jack L. Warner, the head of Warner Brothers, who threatened them with legal action if they persisted in using the word Casablanca, because it was linked in the public mind with his own highly successful film starring Humphrey Bogart and Ingrid Bergman.

Groucho replied that the Marx Brothers had been in vaudeville longer than Warners had been making films, so if they continued to use the word 'Brothers', *he* would sue *them*.

They never heard from Jack Warner again.[1]

As in many stories about copyright and piracy, it was the film studio, and not the original artist, who was seeking redress – and it was hardly surprising that Warners thought they owned Casablanca. In view of the contract their legal department had devised, they could be forgiven for thinking they owned Morocco.

The film was originally based on a play called *Everybody Comes to Rick's*, written by a New York scriptwriter, Murrey Burnett, in 1940. At the time when Warners bought it, they paid a record fee of $20,000 for the rights to his unpublished manuscript, and Burnett must have thought he had a good deal.

Unfortunately, he failed to appreciate the small print, because the contract contained a watertight clause giving the studio all rights, 'of every kind and character whatsoever', to his creations – the cynical loner with a soft centre immortalized by Bogart, Ingrid Bergman's character, Isle (called Lois in the play), and Claude Raines's character, Captain Renault.

Burnett was forbidden to write about them, to create sequels, or to make use of them in any way. His characters no longer belonged to him, and he was forced to watch them being exploited by others, in advertisements and vulgar imitations. It is only recently, a lifetime later, that he has been able to seek justice, and the return of his property, in the courts. Now aged 72, Burnett has finally started a $60 million suit against Warner Brothers, not only for a slice of the royalties from the uninterrupted television and cinema screenings, but for the right to write about them again.[2]

It isn't the only form of exploitation likely to befall classic Hollywood movies like *Casablanca*. Films of this sort, which include *King Kong* and *Gone with the Wind*, are prime targets for the pirate video trade (which we describe later), and the companies are losing a fortune in distribution rites.

Nor, it seems, are they immune from the commercial scams of legitimate distributors, like the new breed of 'recycling merchants' who buy up the rights to 'golden oldies' from the studios, and re-release them with computer-added colours and jazzed-up soundtracks. A version of Fritz Lang's *Metropolis* was recently reissued in this way, with a disco backing that would have horrified the director; and predictably a 'painted' version of *Casablanca* has been promised. Woody Allen and Sidney Pollack, on behalf of outraged film buffs, are leading the protest lobby to ban it.

But they seem to be fighting a losing battle; and much to their dismay, in 1987 the US Copyright Office ruled that these tinted editions could actually be claimed as 'original' works. So that when they are shown on television or sold as video cassettes, the promoters can collect the royalties, and the original creators are disinherited.[3]

The saga of *Casablanca* illustrates two of the main themes in this book: the extraordinary range of things which can be copyrighted – and pirated – and the extraordinary range of people who end up 'owning' them.

The idea of buying imaginary characters from their creator is one of the more bizarre aspects of copyright, but a fairly common one, and their original authors are often aggrieved at the way they are treated. Murrey Burnett's zeal for justice after forty years was prompted by the success of Dashiel Hammett, who signed 'the same stupid contract' for the *Maltese Falcon*, and found his private detective, Sam Spade, sent out on other movie assignments beyond his control (and even, ignominiously, a television commercial for lager). After years of legal wrangling, Hammett managed to obtain his dues from the extended life of his character. Now Burnett has hired the same lawyer and is hoping for similar success in retrieving what he signed away as a young man.

The proprietors of fictional characters do not take kindly to clones of their properties, as Warner Brothers (yet again) proved when they took the US television network ABC to court over its series *The Great American Hero*. The show featured a caped crusader with X-ray vision who bore a remarkable similarity to Superman. Warners claimed it was a direct steal of their own superhero, who continues to earn the studio a fortune from movies and merchandising tie-ins.

As it turned out, the Manhattan federal judge who tried the case decided that ABC's prodigy may have looked the same, but had an entirely different personality. He was a bumbling character who gave the show a different 'feel' and 'concept' to Warners' original and therefore did not infringe their copyright. Warners have appealed.[4]

Even such desperate ploys as giving a fictional favourite a sex-change have failed to dent the proprietorial instinct of the owners. Dexter Films, for instance, found this out to their cost when their film *Queen Kong* had an injunction slapped on it by RKO and the De Laurentis Corporation – the commercial parents of *King Kong*.[5] In defiance of the writ, Dexter tried to smuggle the film out of the country. RKO's lawyers complained that what had originally been described as 'gorilla warfare' was beginning to look suspiciously like 'monkey business'.

Claiming to have been present at the conception of a screen legend – especially one from another planet – appears similarly fraught with danger. Take the example of the Los Angeles woman who demanded $750 million from the profits of Steven Speilberg's *E.T.*, claiming it was based on her one-act play *Lokey from Maldmar* which she had submitted to Universal Studios in 1979. It was tough when she found out (from Speilberg's lawyers) that *E.T.* had originally been developed, not at Universal, but at Columbia Studios. It was a nice try, though.

Back on earth, the worst aliens that artists encounter frequently turn out to be their managers. The record industry has a long record of management monsters, as the Beatles discovered with their rotten Apple company.

It took nearly twenty years, after all, for Reginald Dwight, alias Elton John, to retrieve the royalties on the 136 songs which, in 1967, he signed over to his publisher, Dick James, for a £350 down-payment and a £15-a-week retainer. In the following years Elton John saw his songs notch up more that £200 million in record sales, but claimed in court that the money due to him had been diverted into subsidiaries of the main publishing company, depriving him of royalties.[6]

He got them in the end. Which is more than can be said for 'The Singing Nun', who quickly discovered that getting them in the first place was something of a mixed blessing. In 1978 the ex-Dominican nun, who became a world-famous performer with her hit record 'Dominic-nic-nic', received a summons from the Belgian Inland Revenue to pay four million francs in overdue tax on royalties from her records. She hadn't a cent to pay it with, because she had donated all her income from records and recitals to convents and other Christian charities.[7] Sometimes you cannot even give your creations away. The characters of Murrey Burnett and the songs of Elton John are 'intellectual properties'. Using them without their owner's consent is theft; and commercially exploiting them without permission is piracy. Or is it?

In the music business, which as one of the main victims of electronic piracy spends almost as much on litigation as it does on promotional hype, the theft of 'intellectual property' takes place at every level. The pirates steal the profits of the record companies, the record companies 'creatively account' for the royalties of the artists, and the artists themselves steal each other's music. There is nothing surprising in this, since the whole development of art is based on borrowing and handing on ideas.

There are only so many arrangements of eight basic notes, and they have all been tried. Every tune and every chord has been played before by someone, somewhere. Beethoven lifted tunes from Mozart. Verdi quoted from Schubert, and, as the music critic Philip Hope Wallace remarked, '"Under The Spreading Chestnut Tree", is no more than a syncopated version of "Rock of Ages".'[8]

Yet, by law, each melody is uniquely copyright, and even unintentional copying is an offence, even if it consists of only four notes.[9] George Harrison found this out to his cost when Motown producer Phil Spector successfully sued him for 'unconscious plagiarism' over the similarity between 'My Sweet Lord' and Spector's 'He's So Fine'. More recently, the rock songwriters Walter Becker and Donald Fagan of Steely Dan were charged by jazz musician Keith Jarrett with appropriating material from one of his jazz pieces in their successful *Gaucho* album.

One of the more determined modern litigants is Yoko Ono, who was recently forced to defend her song 'I'm Your Angel' on the Lennon–Ono album *Double Fantasy*. The publishers of the 1928 classic 'Makin' Whoopee' claimed that her song was 'largely copied from and substantially similar' to their own.

Yoko Ono has the distinction of bringing one of the most unusual copyright actions in history, to protect a track entitled 'Silence', consisting of three minutes' silence, on her album *Shaved Fish*. The defendants in this case had added insult to injury by preceding their version with a 'Rehearsal for the Silence', consisting of coughing and scraping chairs.[10] Fortunately, there are limits to what can legitimately be claimed as intellectual property, and Ono lost. Had she won, it is interesting to speculate whether two minutes fifty-nine seconds of nothing would also have been an infringement.

The only comparable case of legal lunacy concerns not records but films. In 1984 the Russian film agency, Sovexport, protested to the

Institute of Contemporary Arts, in London, over the showing of Sergo Pavadjanov's film *The Colour of Pomegranates*. The film had been made in 1969, and at the time the Soviet and Iranian censors had cut out twenty minutes. However, the film was later banned altogether for political reasons. All mention of it was prohibited in the press, and the director was thrown in gaol.

When the pirated version was shown at the ICA, Sovexport threatened legal action, claiming that they had not given permission. Chris Rodley of the ICA summed up the situation when he said, 'I imagine they are very upset, but what rights can they have over a film they say never existed?'[11]

It is surprising that there are not more actions for plagiarism in the pop world, given that the limited language of pop is constantly using and reusing similar melodies and harmonies in pursuit of chart hits. Even discounting recent complications caused by music synthesizers and 'sound samplers' (where other people's recordings be fed in and processed to whatever degree of 'adaptation' is required), the values of copyright custom seem strangely out of date. Any 'recognizable' melody is a rule-of-thumb guide to what is sufficient for copyright protection – and the only defence is to *prove* that you never heard the original.

Musical compositions can turn out to have the most unlikely owners. For instance, every time The Internationale is sung by the comrades in East Germany, the royalties go to a capitalist firm in West Germany, owned by Herr Hans Beierlein, who bought the rights from the song's original French owner in 1975 for £1,818.[12]

The anthem of international socialism is a profitable commodity, just like the early songs of the Beatles, purchased in 1984 by the American pop star Michael Jackson, after outbidding Paul McCartney himself for them. They become commodities, no longer linked to their original creator, but with a life – and a value – of their own.

This can have odd consequences, as the South Australian Film Corporation discovered when they learned that the American performing rights to 'Waltzing Matilda' were owned by the US firm of Carl Fisher. Fisher had the cheek to offer to sell them back to them for $1 million. The poet Banjo Patterson, who wrote the lyrics nearly ninety years ago and still lives in Winton, Central Queensland, was unaware of the original sale, which must have taken place in the 1930s.[13] Australian Prime Minister Bob Hawke, in response to the national outrage, said jokingly that he would 'ring Ron about it'.[14]

What's in a name?

Of course, it is not only literary and musical works which are copyright. Maps, plants, timetables, recipes, chemical formulae, computer software, and bacteria – anything which has been devised by human ingenuity, any kind of information which could be described as 'intellectual property', can be bought and sold under the laws of copyright.

For instance, people feel as protective about emblems as they do about anthems. In 1981 the Irish Export Board sued a West German dairy company for displaying the shamrock on its products. Unfortunately, although St Patrick is supposed to have used the shamrock leaf to explain the Holy Trinity to the pagan Irish, it is not actually the national symbol. That happens to be the Irish harp.

So is it possible to copyright a folk tradition? In this case the court thought not, but the exploitation of what is called the 'ethnic repertoire' is now so extensive that UNESCO is holding a series of conferences to decide how to protect this collective form of art and music. In the meantime, it is much easier to copyright real flowers than symbolic ones. In the UK new varieties automatically have fifteen years' protection under the Plant Varieties and Seeds Act 1965. The first case of 'pirate flowers' was brought to court by the British Association of Rose Breeders in 1979 and concerned the duplication of Harry Wheatcroft's Alexanders, Apricot Silks and Blessings at a Southend nursery.[15]

Curiously enough it has long been possible to patent organisms, provided you can claim to have bred a new species. New strains of yeast, for instance, were patented in the nineteenth century, and genetic engineering is creating a host of new 'designer bugs', which are owned and marketed by their creators. New legislation is proposed to cover this area, so it may soon be possible for an individual to own both a disease and its cure, not to mention the chemicals used to alleviate the side-effects, and even the flowers by the patient's bedside. The design of more complex organisms (which will be possible in the next few decades) raises an interesting moral issue, which could be described as the Frankenstein Question.

To put it bluntly, whatever its origins, when it comes down to it, does a living creature have a right to its own identity?

It is even possible to copyright a single word, provided you can claim a special association with it. The question was debated in the British courts in 1977, when that bastion of English culture, the Oxford Dictionary, which has been published since 1928, was challenged by Robert Maxwell's Pergamon Press, which proposed to publish its own *Oxford Dictionary*. This was a reasonable enough proposal, because the company happens to be based in Oxford; but the Oxford University Press thought otherwise and stood by its right to exclusive use of the town's name.

Pergamon lost its battle in the Court of Appeal because, although words like 'Oxford' and 'Dictionary' can be used by anyone, when they are put together, said the judges, 'the value of the name is almost beyond measure'.[16] (Normally attempts at unfair competition like this are dealt with under the law of 'passing off', rather than copyright legislation.)

More recently, the Standard Oil Corporation found that its newly invented name, Exxon, was not entitled to protection despite there having been research, skill, and imagination employed in its creation. To justify its recognition as an original literary work (the definition of copyright in these cases), it must have 'qualities and characteristics in itself, if such a thing is possible ... rather than merely as an invented word'.

The judges distinguished another invention, Lewis Carroll's 'Jabberwocky' in Alice's adventures *Through the Looking-Glass* (1872), because it was protected by the copyright in the whole book. However, they abstained from taking any firm decision on 'Supercalifrajilistickexpialidocius', the subject of an earlier, furious legal battle between Life Music Corporation and Wonderland Music Co. in 1965.

Parodies necessarily sail close to the wind when it comes to defending originality against claims of infringement. It wasn't enough, for instance, for Wellingtons Ltd to copy the label of a bottle of Schweppes Indian Tonic Water and simply change the name to 'Schlurppes'. The brand leaders in carbonated water were not amused.

A related, but far more serious, problem is the widespread counterfeiting of goods and forgery of brand names, where trademark and patents legislation plays its part, along with copyright, in the protection of intellectual property. For example, forgeries of Dunlop Maxply tennis-rackets made in Taiwan recently found their way into British Home Stores and the House of Holland chain. So meticuluous was the craftsmanship, they even bore a forged inspection number stamped under the grip, where only professionals would look for it.

A police raid in West Germany unearthed 10,000 fake bottles of Johnny Walker, bearing a counterfeited Distillers label but containing an inferior brand of whisky. And Levi Strauss once agreed to a £250,000 out-of-court settlement againt the City of London firm Nolton Management after accusing them of conspiring to sell three million pairs of fake jeans, again made in Taiwan.[17] Brand-name piracy of this kind is on the increase, and such goods often infringe both industrial design copyright and artistic copyright in their labels.

But perhaps the most embarrassing – and still unresolved – example of product forgery were the counterfeit albums of EMI records which were discovered for sale on the shelves of their own Oxford Street shop. The explanation for this was the sale-or-return practice whereby local record shops could send unsold discs back to EMI for a refund. While most traders stuck to the rules, some were ingenious enough to return 'unsold' counterfeits, which got recycled back on to the store's own racks.[18]

The case illustrates the close, almost symbiotic, relationship between the pirates and the system they exploit. Like parasites and their host, predators and prey, the one cannot exist without the other. They reflect each other like mirror images, responding to the same tides of taste and fashion; and in a world where we increasingly buy the image rather than the product (and copies are indistinguishable from the original), it can be difficult to tell them apart.

Copyright or patent?

There are two ways to protect intellectual property. Broadly speaking, an artist or writer can establish ownership of their works by *copyright*, and inventors protect their devices by *patent*. There are two basic requirements in each case. They must be original, and they must be recorded in some material form, such as a text, recording or blueprint. Brilliant ideas in the bathtub do not count, nor do speeches or live performances if the words exist only in the person's mind.

From then on the systems are very different. Any functional device can be patented, from a plant to an atom bomb. (Though, in the case of the atom bomb, this did not offer much protection, because the documents presented to the London Patent Office were prepared by an *émigré* German scientist, Klaus Fuchs, who immediately gave copies of them to the Soviets – probably the most important example of piracy in history.)

On the other hand, copyright is owned quite independently of the physical object that reproduces it. It involves the concept of *intellectual property*, which is usually defined as 'literary, dramatic, musical, or artistic works', though it is flexible enough to cover street-maps and painting-by-numbers.

The most important difference from the artist's point of view is that copyright is automatic, whereas patents are not. The process of patenting a design is expensive and protracted. It may take a year or more before it is properly protected, and by then it may be out of date, but in the long run it offers better protection. Copyright is taken to start at the moment of creation – and, in Britain at any rate, it is not necessary to publish or register the work first – but it is more difficult to enforce. The difference between them is often illustrated in this book by the difference between 'software' and 'hardware' – and the disputed boundary which has developed between them.

In the field of scientific research, patentable designs must involve an 'inventive step' which is not already obvious to others. Pure discoveries, theories, and mathematical methods are not patentable as such; they must be translated into practical applications. Nor are schemes for performing mental tasks or simply presenting the information in an original way. Where the creativity is in the expression of ideas, or aesthetic qualities, protection can be sought only through copyright. This raises particular problems with computers, where the 'literary' work may consist of nothing more than the way that information is arranged in the machine.

A few years ago there was a considerable controversy over whether computer programs should be protected by patents (which the computer companies lobbied hard for) or by copyright. It was finally decided that copyright was more appropriate, if only because the issues raised by computers would confuse the patent laws still further. They had no idea of the problems they were letting themselves in for.

2

Whose copyright is it, anyway?

All the so-called 'higher' forms of labour – intellectual, artistic and so on – have been changed into commodities and have thereby lost their old sanctity. What great progress it was to have the whole regiment of parsons, physicians and lawyers defined solely in terms of their commercial value!

(Karl Marx and Friedrich Engels, *Werke*, vol. VI, 1979)

The notion that creative ideas are treated as property – 'intellectual property' – which can be bought and sold like any other commodity, may seem odd and even confusing to many people. Yet its obscure principles are as fundamental to modern society as the invention of money.

The concept includes patents for new inventions, trade-marks, industrial design, and copyright. In particular it is the eighteenth-century system of copyright upon which the modern mass media, scientific research, and electronic information networks all ultimately depend. None of them could have developed without the 'currency' of copyright, regulating the trade in 'products of the mind', protecting the investment in 'cultural works', and dividing the profits according to 'royalty' percentages. From the *Star Wars* movies to 'Star Wars' military research, the bottom line is copyright.

When does an idea become intellectual property? The simple answer is when it is *recorded* in an original, unique way. Ideas themselves belong to no one. Like fresh air and sunshine, ideas are there for the taking. What is legally protected is not what you say, but the way you say it.

If only it were that simple in practice. For, in fact, the line between an idea and its expression can be a hard one to draw. The protection of intellectual property is often a tightrope walk between competing interests. On the one hand are society's needs for the widest possible dissemination of ideas and facts – indeed, all forms of knowledge – and on the other are the rights to privacy and society's desire to encourage creativity by ensuring that creators benefit from their work. Copyright attempts to balance those interests, although, as Elton John and Murrey Burnett discovered, the threat to the artist's rights does not always come from the public.

The paradox of copyright is that it seeks to protect the interests not only of the original creators, but of the commercial exploiters as well – the investors, publishers, producers, and distributors, and all the 'middlemen' between.

Where have all the garrets gone?

Many people retain the romantic myth that copyright is there to protect the lonely, starving artists – their only defence in a cruel world and the last resort to earn a crust of bread. But in the world today there have been many changes which have eroded that protection and altered the status of the individual creator. The media systems on which they depend for a living, to whom they sell their copyright, and which are virtually their employers, are themselves changing. The rise of vast multinational conglomerates and the introduction of new technology are undermining the creator's role, even in established industries. And the situation is compounded by the spread of piracy, which is eroding the traditional means of distribution and beginning to threaten the whole structure.

Ironically, the artist has become an almost peripheral character in this cultural drama. The battle to preserve and extend copyright may still be waged in the name of the author, but it is the corporations that stand to win or lose.

In today's world of publishing, mass media, and the commercial exploitation of scientific research, only a very few authors, inventors, and composers can actually earn a living from their royalties. For the vast majority, if they are lucky enough to get a commission or advance at all, must, in order to survive, learn to operate under the same conditions as other employees – servicing a cultural and information production line whose objectives or methods they have no means of affecting.

Today's environment for creators – be it for films, records, television programmes, or computer software – is likely to be one of collaboration and team-work. A combination of technical and creative skills is required, and the identification of individual 'authorship' gets increasingly blurred. At the same time, the reliance on sophisticated machines like video-editing suites and music synthesizers is breaking down the traditional distinction between 'technicians' and 'artists'. Who, then, owns the copyright?

In many cases, too, artists and scientists are required to enter contracts of employment or engagement in which the rights to their intellectual and creative efforts are assigned to their employers without further ado.

It can seem at times as if original ideas are no more than the raw material for the chain of cultural merchandise that spreads across the globe, a minor element in the vast communications and marketing network which prefers the cloned best-seller and the tested television format to anything new. Nowadays it is market research and ratings, and not the inspiration of creative minds, that determine next week's products on the shelves and screens.

In this perspective, the real control of the channels of distribution, and access to the means of production, lies outside the ambit of copyright, in the state's regulation of broadcasting and freedom of information, in the economic power of the media and technology corporations, and in the political strategies of government.

Is it catching?

The copyright principle (at least in the non-communist world) presumes a free market economy. As technology has developed new ways to use copyright material, attempts have been made to maintain the link between the creator and the eventual use (like the number of copies of a record sold, or the amount of airplay on the radio it receives) by the payment of royalties. As we shall see, this is no longer viable in the conventional way – or it is becoming at best an increasingly abstract calculation; this is due to the nature of the new technology and to the new and unprecedented scale of piracy.

This may seem a rather sweeping scenario, but these two themes – the scale and variety of piracy, and the nature of the new technology – run throughout this story, and it is necessary to stand well back to get them in perspective. Many of our definitions and assumptions will have to be revised, because the rise of electronic piracy is not a series of isolated phenomena but the symptom of a much larger process of change. It raises questions we have never asked before, and introduces new rules and players to the game.

For instance, it is no longer realistic to assume that individual authors and composers can match the bargaining power of the conglomerates, or compete with the complicated organizations that make up today's cultural industries. This fact alone explodes one of the commonest myths propounded by the defenders of copyright.

Bizarre and entertaining anomalies crop up from time to time, but we are not directly concerned with the age-old 'rip-offs' between artists, agents, and distributors. That practice is as old as time. Newton and Leibnitz nearly sued each other over the invention of algebra; and if you go back far enough, Plato's works were pirated by one of his students, Hermodorus, who wrote down his speeches and took them to Sicily to sell. This was frowned on at the time, but it was just as well that he did so, because the 'bootleg' copies provide one of the few surviving sources of Plato's material.

The story of the electronic pirates, on the other hand, is about something new, a process that technology has only recently made possible and which attacks the very core of the operation: the *distribution* of information. This is a challenge which affects artists, middlemen, and the transnationals alike, but has not yet been properly understood or evaluated by any of them.

There are two protagonists in the story. On the one hand are the pirates, the millions of people in every country in the world who now have the means of reproducing books, tapes, and records (or any kind of information) for themselves. On the other are the information brokers who supply it. We return to the nature of these transnational corporations later in the book, but it is important to remember, while reading the evidence, that it is these centralized organizations, in the last analysis, which decide what form information should take, what it should cost, and who should have it.

At home (in Europe and North America), they see themselves as part of the social system, an established hierarchy alongside the government, military, and industrial complexes, with unquestioned authority to control the flow of news, information, educational material, and entertainment. The government may pay for the schools and textbooks, but it is the publishers who decide what is taught, in the same way that RCA decides what music we listen to, and Reuters or the BBC decide what news we receive.

The role of large corporations abroad is more ambiguous. On the whole they prefer to see themselves as bringing the benefits of an advanced culture to the poor and deprived – though the export of the English language and western values could just as easily be described as cultural imperialism.

This immense concentration of power and influence is not sanctioned by any democratic process. Corporations are not 'necessary' in the way that governments and legal systems are. No one voted them into existence. They are straightforward commercial organizations which manufacture and process a commodity, and their power resides in one simple fact: they are the only ones with the resources to *manufacture* the products – books, films, and records – and to *distribute* them around the world. On both counts, the pirates now represent a serious threat.

Instead of controlling the lines of distribution, from the source to the consumer, corporations now see their products disappear in a mass of duplicates as soon as they are released. Their markets are evaporating. The established chains of command, from manufacturer to wholesaler to retail outlet, are disintegrating. The channels of informaton are leaking, spilling their contents far and wide, as words, ideas, and music multiply like a virus.

The occasional newspaper stories about the losses due to piracy are only the most obvious sign of the malignancy. The repercussions go well beyond the complaints of record companies and film studios. The analogy with a new disease, or crime, may be oversimplifying the problem; but it puts piracy into the same category as two other phenomena which have developed over the same time-scale, with equally disruptive effects, which, as we shall hear, are often described in the same terms: terrorism and drug-trafficking.

The parallels between them are striking. Like a disease, all three have mutated so rapidly that it has proved impossible to halt their growth or even to slow it down. In each case, they have spread around the world like an epidemic, attracting large sums of money and developing international organizations, which involve the connivance of authorities at the highest level.

There is another characteristic they have in common. In the absence of any consensus, or international co-operation, the battle against them is waged by the same weapon: propaganda. As a result, whether it is designed to blur the distinctions between 'terrorists' and 'freedom-fighters', or between 'hard' and 'soft' drugs, expediency will inevitably rule at the expense of logic or consistency.

Like most of the important changes in history, electronic piracy has not come about as the result of political theory or armed struggle. No one planned it, or even realized it was happening until it was too late. It came about, as most revolutions do, as a by-product of technology – in this case the invention of five particular machines, whose function is to copy, or transmit, information.

The *tape-recorder*, the *video cassette*, and the *photocopier* make it possible for almost anyone to duplicate almost anything at will. The *computer*, in its mass-produced form as PC (personal computers) or micro, is used to copy software, and since it contains copyright material in its design, it can itself be 'pirated' or 'cloned'. The fifth machine is the *telephone*, which is certainly the oldest, and may yet be the most important, of them all. This is because it allows anyone who owns a computer to gain access to the whole electronic communicatons system.

The original designers could hardly have foreseen that telegraphy would become the key to unlock the world's secrets, but that is the nature of technology. The railways, for instance, began with a machine for pumping out mine workings; and the computer itself was originally designed as a means of calculating the trajectory of artillery shells.

The first president of IBM, Thomas J. Watson Sr, once estimated that computers were so expensive that the world would never need more than 'about a dozen' of them. In fact, in the last twenty years the spread of these apparently harmless copying machines has shaken the information and media industries to their roots. Computers are not only destroying their distribution systems, but challenging the assumptions on which their power is based.

3

The information dossiers

The subject of this book is information in all its forms — a curious abstraction that is almost impossible to define. It is something that can be stolen without depriving the owner of it, a commodity which can be extremely valuable, and yet falls outside the normal political and social definitions. The technology is information technology. We are in the middle of what has been described as the 'information revolution', but what exactly is *information*?

Most of the people whose views and attitudes are expressed in this book assume that information is a possession, a form of property that can be bought and sold in the market-place, like any other.

But Alvin Toffler, in his book *Previews and Premises* (1984), makes it clear that we are dealing with something new and entirely different in kind:

> If I own a share of IBM (which I don't), what do I really care about? What do I own? I don't care a rap about Yorktown Heights, the land on which IBM has some buildings. I don't care about its plants in San Jose, California, or Bogota, Columbia. What I really care about is the organised information it controls.
>
> My property is doubly abstracted from reality. A share of IBM is a piece of paper — a symbol. And beyond that, it's a symbol not of hardware or real estate. It's a symbol of other symbols inside people's heads.
>
> Info-property is distinct from 'real property' in that it is not finite. I can use it, and you can use it, at the same time. And, in fact, the more people who do use it, the more information is likely to be generated.
>
> So property isn't what it used to be when Marx and the early Socialists built their theories on it.
>
> This is a fatal contradiction. Private property has been the defining characteristic of capitalism. Now, suddenly, the essential property transforms from symbolic to meta-symbolic, and from finite to non-finite in character. And that contradicts the very notion of property, which has been based on its scarcity and materiality.

It is because of this that in this book we have tried to avoid the traditional forms of political analysis. Anyone who expects a Marxist dialectic along the lines of Marcuse or Gramsci will be disappointed.

It is not that their language is inadequate, it is just irrelevant. The traditional arguments are still used, of couse, by both sides, and it is necessary to record them as accurately as possible. But then, as Toffler warned, 'Property remains an obsession for many, despite the fact that new developments make ideological goulash out of old economic theories – capitalist and socialist alike'.

The new polemics have yet to emerge, and when they do they are (sadly) more likely to come from the New Right rather than the Old Left. In the meantime, we must make do with the facts and leave the interpretation to others. And the facts about electronic piracy are startling enough.

The layout of the book

In part two of the book, we present 'dossiers' on the various forms of piracy, with as much of the evidence as we could condense into them without producing statistical indigestion. We describe how piracy has affected the different media, from print and sound recordings to the film and video industries, computers, and broadcasting; and we show how it has evolved in a variety of ways in different parts of the world.

There are four different areas where the phenomenon (or disease, or crime, according to your point of view) has taken root – four distinct zones, as separate as continents, inhabited by different characters, with different backgrounds and motives. In each case there is a different system under attack.

The first is very close to home: the office or place where you work, or a normal living-room in an ordinary home of the sort where you may well be reading this book. In this domestic environment it is unlikely that anyone has committed a crime worse than parking offences. It's the sort of home you can find in every town and suburb in the western world.

The piracy here is almost innocent: photocopies of teaching materials from school, buying a cut-price video from a friend at work, making a tape of your favourite LP to play on the car stereo. Small-scale and relatively harmless, but when it is repeated a thousand, or a hundred thousand, times a day, everywhere, it can bankrupt a multinational corporation.

The second zone is the electronic world outside the home, the global communications system that enables you to phone a relative in Australia, or watch the world's weather patterns from outer space each night on television. The pirates who attack this network of cables, microwave beams, and broadcast frequencies are experts, or skilled amateurs, who know exactly what they are doing. They are few in number, but they play for high stakes, and the damage that even one of them can do is immense, because the information is so concentrated and valuable.

The third area is, literally, the Third World: the populations in the underdeveloped countries, hungry for education and technology, and hypnotized by the cultural glamour of Europe and America. This is the market for the professional pirates, who exploit it with ruthless efficiency on a world-wide scale. They regard it as a business, like any other business, a matter of supply and demand. Their motive is profit, and morality doesn't come into it.

These are the main kinds of piracy which appear and reappear throughout the book, occasionally overlapping but never dependent on each other. They just happened to have occurred at the same time; if you took one away, the others would remain.

And the fourth? Well, the fourth is an altogether different and more sinister continent, where events are reflected as in a dark mirror, and all the arguments are turned upside down. It is a continent that stretches from the Berlin Wall to the Pacific, from Saigon to the Arctic, where copyright belongs to the state, and the only function of the mass media is propaganda. There is no secret about this. Lenin publicly declared that it should be so, and it has been ever since.

The dossiers in part two contain technological information as well as other details. In fact, the machines which make piracy possible are so important to the story that we described how they came to be invented and how each idea was exploited. In their own way, the stories are like parables of piracy.

Later on, in part three, we describe the efforts to find a technological solution, by setting machines against machines, sealing the electronic leaks, and producing 'copy-proof' material. If the problem was created by science, it seems reasonable to assume that scientists could design their way out of it. But the difficulties they encountered were another indication that the problems, like the machines themselves, are very different from anything that has gone before.

In part four we move on to the social implications and the struggle to find a legal or political solution to the problem. Here, too, the nature of the information raises issues which have never surfaced before. For instance, how do you enforce a law when the entire population is breaking it? Do the traditional laws even apply to the situation? How do you restore international control in a world where every country has a different legal system? And ultimately, is it more realistic to sanction piracy than to apply sanctions against it?

Finally, we try to give an overview of the situation (a rather optimistic claim under the circumstances). When the time-scale of these events is only fifteen or twenty years, and in some cases less than a decade, it is impossible to forecast their outcome with any accuracy. They are unfolding at such speed and in so many places that the most we can realistically do is report what is happening from our point of view.

It is not the only interpretation. Each character in the drama has a different perception of events. The institutions regard it as a hiccup in world trade; the radicals see it as a revolution. Scientists describe it as the birth pangs of the 'wired society', and doomsday theorists identify the first symptoms of Armageddon. There is no historical viewpoint, because it is not yet a history. All one can say with any certainty is that it has only just begun; and by the time it is over, the world will be a very different place.

The signs that something was happening first became obvious in the late 1960s. By 1984 not even the US Office of Technological Assessment could miss the writing on the wall:

> Just as the public became readily accustomed to photocopying books, journals and other printed materials, so it is now learning routinely to copy films, discs and tapes and to make unauthorised copies of electronic data.
>
> Software creators, producers and providers call this 'stealing'; some software users call it 'sharing'. Thus there is a growing gap between the theory of intellectual property law and its practice.
>
> This gap is likely to widen in the next several years, potentially challenging the legitimacy of the law and creating significant problems of enforcement.

This book is about that gap.

Part two
The pirates

4

The photocopiers

In the early Sixties, the IBM Corporation had an opportunity to invest in and gain control of a struggling new venture with an untested concept. They studied it and turned it down. The new venture, so disdainfully rejected by the computer giant, was the concept brought to fruition by Xerox – the photocopy.

(Jacques Valee, *The Network Revolution*, 1982)

At 3.00 p.m. on 28 September 1984, 104 officers of the Hong Kong customs and excise department carried out simultaneous raids on twenty-seven premises in the city. The date was significant because it was the start of the academic year, and the raids were designed to uncover a large-scale piracy operation specializing in reprinting western textbooks. The authorities seized 1,300 finished copies and more than 30,000 printed sheets, along with 647 original textbooks and twenty-two binding machines. They also seized – and this is what made the whole operation possible – sixty-nine *photocopying machines*, mostly from small booths in Hong Kong's crowded street markets.[1]

The Chinese, who originally invented the movable type that made printing possible, are now pioneering labour-intensive, decentralized electronic book piracy. The rise of this phenomenon around the world has paralleled the spread of cheap printing methods such as photo-typesetting (which allows a book to be photographed, page by page, directly on to a printing plate) and the photocopier (which makes even this unnecessary). The effect of this innocent technology has been astonishing.

It is from the invention of printing in Germany in 1436 that the origins of 'copyright' can be traced, on the reasonable assumption that there could be no 'right' to produce 'copies' until there was a way of making them in the first place. For the first 500 years, 'bootleg' editions of books and sheet music were the main forms of copyright infringement; but the development of Victorian technology, the width of the Atlantic, and the spread of literacy on both sides of it gave the piracy business an enormous boost in the nineteenth century. Figures such as Mark Twain, Gilbert and Sullivan, and Charles Dickens were constantly involved in litigation over illegal copies of their work.

The early pirates were more of a nuisance than a threat. Printing and binding a book are an expensive business. Even with modern technology such as offset lithography, it requires presses and heavy equipment, and over the years lawyers have ensured that the chances of getting away with it are slim.

But electronics has changed the nature of piracy, as it has changed everything else. Not only the technology, but the nature of the market, the scale of the operation, and even its location have altered out of all recognition. In 1967, when piracy was still a traditional 'craft', it was costing the international book trade about £1 million a year. In 1977 the figure was up £100 million and rising fast. By 1983 it had escalated to £500 million, with British publishers alone losing £75 million a year. By 1986 this figure had almost doubled, with UK losses at about £150 million and one publisher, Macmillan, claiming an individual loss of over £3 million.

In less than twenty years the sheet music industry was almost destroyed, the once-profitable educational market had been decimated, and piracy had become a major source of income for several Third World countries, such as Singapore and Indonesia. It was not so much a crime as a shift in the world's trade balance.

The photocopier had a lot to answer for. Unlike most inventions, it had been the brain-child of one man, a young American lawyer named Chester Carlsen, who developed the basic principles, built the machines almost single-handed, and, most unusually, managed to hang on to his patents and to die a millionaire on the profits. He originally trained as an engineer but lost his job with the Bell Telephone Co. during the Depression and had to tramp the streets of New York in search of work. He was eventually taken on by an electronics firm, P. R. Mallory & Co., where he worked in the patents department. He took a law degree in his spare time and set about his life's work.

Carlsen was determined to find a cheap way of reproducing documents. Photography was too expensive, and anyway the field had been thoroughly exploited, so he turned to the relatively unknown principle of electrostatics. He spent months studying the work of the Hungarian physicist Paul Selenyi, and when he was sure he could adapt it to his purposes he rented a second-floor apartment in Astoria, which he fitted out as a makeshift laboratory. It was here, on 22 October 1936, that the first photocopy was run off.

Carlsen patented the techniques of what he called *xerography* (or 'shadow writing') and set out to sell them to an indifferent world. No one was interested; it was a classic case of a brilliant idea that goes unrecognized, of people being unable to see what they are looking at.

Between 1939 and 1944 Carlsen's idea was turned down by more than twenty companies.

Still hanging on to his patents, he eventually signed a contract with the Batelle Memorial Institute, a non-profit research organization in Ohio. Even then it was another three years before they entered into an agreement with a small photographic paper firm called Haloid to develop a prototype.

The first commercial photocopier went on sale in 1949, but the early models were dirty and complicated to operate. Sales were slow, and rival systems, such as Eastman Kodak's wet process and 3M's Thermofax, had appeared on the market. However, Haloid regained their lead by introducing the first fully automatic system in 1955; and in 1959, twenty-one years after he had invented the process, Carlsen saw his dream come true with the first push-button, plain-paper copier.

It was called the *914* (because it took paper up to 9 in × 14 in), stood 4 feet tall, weighed 648 lb, and could manage only seven rather messy copies a minute. But it now stands in the Smithsonian Museum's hall of fame alongside the first telephone and light bulb. In 1961 Haloid changed their name to Xerox, and their shares were quoted on the New York Stock Exchange.

Carlsen's refusal to license his patents to other manufacturers was to land the company in trouble because, on his death in 1968, Xerox were plunged into the longest and most expensive trial in US history. But in spite of competitors, like Smith Corona, snapping at their heels and charges of illegal monopoly by the Federal Trade Commission, business boomed. While they defended their copyright on a device that infringed other people's, they continued to export their subversive machines to every corner of the world. It was an ironic situation.[2]

Xerox eventually lost out. In 1978 they were found guilty of anti-trust law violations and had to pay out more than $200 million in compensation. At the same time, the world was beginning to wake up to the effects of the copier revolution.

Among the first to feel the wind of change were the sheet music publishers, when the sales of music parts to schools and orchestras began to dry up. Many of these firms went out of business, and there was no doubt in their minds about the cause.

In 1979 the president of the Music Publishers' Association announced, 'The catalogues are a quarter the size they were ten years ago, when photocopiers really began to spread. Unless something is done, there is not going to be any music to copy'. The following year, with losses now amounting to £6 million a year, they decided to make an example of some pillars of the establishment. Wolverhampton

District Council were sued for copying orchestral parts in 134 schools, where more than 15,000 photocopies were discovered.[3] A few months later, Oakhampton school followed them into the dock and paid out £4,250 in damages.

'The schools end up breaking the law in sheer frustration,' explained David Jones, the musical adviser for Warwickshire. 'If you are doing three separate pieces, eight or nine minutes of performance can cost you £100 – and the school's music department only has £200 a year to spend.'[4]

The same simple but ruthless economics applied to the supply of textbooks, especially in universities. Educational publishers woke up to the alarming fact that they were losing £20 million in the UK alone. There were 100,000 machines in daily use, on which 200 million pages were being illegally copied each year. There was one in every library, every club house, and every school in the country.

The situation was similar in the United States, though more commercialized. In 1981 a group of seven US publishers took on Gnomon, a chain of photocopying shops in New Haven, Cambridge, and other university towns in New England. The evidence showed they were so well organized that they were offering students a range of 9,000 photocopied pages, from 300 books, by 100 different publishers – for 2 cents a sheet.[5]

There were more cases the following year, including three which were settled out of court. The Association of American Authors sued ten faculty members of New York University and an off-campus copying centre for pirating a whole range of books, from Truman Capote's *In Cold Blood* to *The Implications of Projective Identification for Marital Interaction*.[6]

The professional villains were not slow to see the possibilities. One of the best-sellers of 1980 was *The Big Dummy Guide*, which cashed in on the popularity of CB radio. It sold a million copies in the USA, but when the publishers launched it in Britain they found the market had already been flooded with 100,000 copies at half the trade price.[7]

In 1980 a bizarre ring of book pirates, run by the Neiman family, was uncovered in Pennsylvania. They had been systematically copying famous – and presumably dead – British authors, by photocopying the pages of their books, binding them in imitation leather and selling them for $25 each. Unfortunately many of their victims, including Veronica Wedgwood and J. B. Priestley, were alive and very annoyed.

'They are a monstrous crowd,' fumed Priestley.

But the pirates were unrepentant. 'Who is this Dame Wedgwood, and what's she fussing about?' asked Mark Neiman. 'How the hell does one find out where this guy Priestley lives? Don't you realize that it costs 10 bucks to write a letter?'[8]

Apart from organized piracy, in any of the thousands of stationery shops across the USA and Europe it cost less than 10 cents to photocopy a page of any document from a magazine article to a research manuscript. Most offices had one, major companies had hundreds. But it was impossible to estimate how much of their use was innocent, and how much of it infringed copyright.

It was this dilemma which led some countries, starting with the USA and West Germany, to introduce compulsory licences for the use of photocopiers (for whatever purpose) in government and commerce. A fee is paid for every copy that is made, and a proportion of the resulting fund is redistributed to publishers. The British government has since followed suit, and the UK Copyright Licensing Agency (with the Publishers' Association) is setting up a similar scheme for schools and colleges in the UK.

If European and US publishers were disturbed by the trend on their own doorstep, they had even more cause to be concerned by the situation in the Third World, where a flood of piracy was overwhelming their business. The pattern was exactly the same, with educational publishers the main target, but the circumstances were completely different. The hunger for education in the streets of Hong Kong and Karachi was intense, the poverty appalling, and the pirates were fulfilling a desperate social need. In fact, they had a captive market.

Print piracy

Although there are borderline cases, the piracy of printed material usually falls into one or another of these categories:

Counterfeit editions. The reproduction of books by offset lithography to simulate the original and sold as such for profit. The jacket design, publisher's imprint, etc. are accurately copied, but the books are sometimes reduced in size.

Pirate editions. Cheap reproductions of books by photocopying or offset lithography, with low-quality paper and binding. These are not intended to be passed off as the original and are sold at reduced prices.

'Pavement' editions. Forgeries of books using the names of best-selling authors but written by others, usually in the form of cheap paperback thrillers.

Organized seepage. The photocopying of books, magazines, and papers for use in institutions such as schools, colleges, clubs, and offices. Limited print runs are usually carried out 'in-house' and distributed at cost, or commissioned from commercial photocopying centres.

Seepage. The photocopying of printed material by individuals for their own use, similar to the home taping of records and video cassettes.

The phrases 'seepage' and 'organized seepage' were coined to describe the piracy of computer software, but they can be applied to any media where the established distribution system is bypassed (or 'leaks'). This is particularly appropriate in the case of photocopiers.

5

The book pirates

Steal This Book.

(Book title by Jerry Rubin)

New publishing centres are springing up like islands of technology in the sea of Third World poverty. They are strung out along the Equator, from West Africa through Cairo, Beirut, Riyadh, Karachi, Bombay, Delhi, and Singapore to Hong Kong and Taiwan, north to Seoul, and west to Manila. The names run like a litany through this book. They mark out the trade routes of modern piracy, which lie across Asia between the Tropics, from the old pirate stronghold of the Barbary Coast to the South China Sea.

These cities are the centre for all kinds of piracy, from the mass production of tape cassettes to the forging of computer chips. But they also represent the centres of book piracy that western publishers became aware of in the late 1970s and seriously concerned about in the early 1980s. With losses around the world amounting to £500 million a year, something had to be done, and in 1982 British publishers struck back with a campaign to sue the pirates in their own countries.[1]

Collins and Pitman took offenders to court in Malaysia; cases were started in Nigeria; Longman and Butterworth tested Indian law in Calcutta;[2] and Macmillan threatened a trade boycott of South Korea unless it stopped pirating their *Grove's Musical Dictionary*.

The Kukje Publishing Co. had been selling copies of this massive, twenty-volume work, which took twelve years to develop and normally cost £850, at £70 a set. Another pirate edition had appeared in Taiwan. But what made the Korean one exceptional was a twist in the law, by which the pirate edition could be registered, and therefore legalized. This meant that Macmillan's version could be declared 'illegal' and actually banned from being imported![3] Macmillan couldn't sue, but they were determined to make a stand and threatened to cancel their annual order of £500,000 worth of paper and print from Korea unless the government reversed the situation – which it did.[4]

The scale of the problem in Korea could be judged by the fact that the pirates had even formed their own trade association, the Foreign Publications Reprinting Association (FPRA), with over a hundred members, one of whom boasted of having 2,500 titles in production.[5]

Textbooks, especially on medicine and engineering, were the most popular targets, but reference works like *Grove's Dictionary* were also very profitable. The Chinese version of the *Oxford English Dictionary*, and the Taiwanese and Korean editions of the *Encyclopaedia Britannica*, were all outselling their legitimate rivals in the Far East markets. This was hardly surprising when a bound and photocopied version of *Britannica* could be bought in Seoul or Taipei for half the list price of £1,200.

In their efforts to get the legal screws on pirates, the publishers discovered how few countries have effective copyright laws and turned up some interesting anomalies. In Jordan, for instance, they disinterred a 1911 Ottoman law, still not repealed, under which a publisher could go to Constantinople and register his copyright for one Ottoman dollar. Unfortunately, royalties had to be collected in the same coin.[6]

They also discovered, to their dismay, the full scale of the piracy operation, and the movement of books that was taking place. One of the main trade routes ran from east to west, with container loads of pirated textbooks from Taiwan being shipped through Hong Kong and Singapore under the guise of 'picture books' or 'religious works' to the huge markets of India and West Africa.[7]

The Taiwan pirates now send regular trade delegations to Africa to take the orders that once went to British and United States publishing houses. Ironically, their main competition comes, not from the west, but from home-grown pirates, because the photocopiers are just as busy in Accra and Delhi as they are in Taipei.

'I could name fifteen of our titles that have been pirated in Eastern Nigeria,' said Philip Attenborough of Hodder & Stoughton,

> books that are not available elsewhere. One is a collection of plays for schools by an Eastern Nigerian author which would normally sell 100,000 copies a year. The pirates wait until a book is established and they know there will be orders for it next year, then they get stuck in.[8]

They found that nearly all the English language textbooks in Pakistan were pirated, and the same story was repeated in country after country. 'There is not much doubt', said Clive Bradley of the Publishers' Association in an interview, 'that this is the result of what is virtually an international gangster conspiracy.'

The conspiracy, moreover, is insidiously woven into the legitimate trade. Ian Taylor of the Campaign Against Book Piracy reported, returning from a delegation of British publishers to Indonesia:

We were assured by local publishers that foreign books were not being pirated, only local books. We didn't find much in Jakarta at first, but outside the main centres in Java, the local publishers gave us the address of a printer in Bandung who supplies booksellers throughout Indonesia – and the whole thing came out.

I went to his retail outlet, which specializes in construction engineering textbooks, and the manager proudly showed me an order from one of the main bookseller-publishers in Jakarta ordering pirated books from him. That was one of the main importers from UK firms and had only a few days before been standing up at a meeting telling us how much they condemned piracy. It shows a certain double standard.

(from a personal interview)

It was not only textbooks. The mainstream publishing of popular titles was also affected. The novels of Jeffrey Archer were being counterfeited from Amman to Jakarta,[9] and on the stalls outside the Regal Cinema in Delhi one could buy pirate paperbacks of any best-selling author – even books they hadn't written.[10] Fake Alaistair Macleans and forged Harold Robbinses which the authors had never set eyes on, these 'pavement editions' which borrow an author's name and copy their style must be the pirates' ultimate accolade.[11]

Some authors took it philosophically. When Professor Milton Friedman, the right-wing economist, was told that his book *Free to Choose* had been pirated in China, he was not upset. 'That's all right,' he said, 'because I have serious doubts about the principle of royalty payments anyway.' The advocate of market forces added that there were four other pirate editions, one English and three Chinese, and he wasn't getting any royalties from them either.

Others were not so complacent. Salman Rushdie's prize-winning novel *Midnight's Children* was pirated in Pakistan almost as soon as it was published, and when it came out in paperback a new half-price version appeared in India. Rushdie was so incensed that he began a personal campaign to protect his rights. When a pirate edition of his next book, *Shame*, appeared, he pressured the authorities into raiding bookshops in Karachi and Lahore.

'Contrary to their protests,' he wrote,

the authorities in countries like India and Pakistan can move swiftly and effectively if it suits them to do so. The sadness is it doesn't often suit them. Where the state itself acts as a pirate, it is hardly surprising that small entrepreneurs follow suit.[12]

Author Paul Theroux is equally bitter: 'The thing I really hate is that a lot of the customers in eastern countries are British and American tourists, not downtrodden Third Worlders.'[13]

A few authors had enough clout to settle matters directly. Henry

Kissinger was able to pull strings at the highest level to get illegal copies of his *Memoirs* removed from sale.[14] And when ex-President Richard Nixon heard that a pirate edition of his book *Leaders* had appeared in Pakistan, he telephoned General Zia al-Huq personally to complain. The General was so embarrassed he invoked the Federal Investigation Act and ordered the police to arrest the pirates immediately.[15]

In the main, however, western authors and publishers are forced to stand helplessly by while their royalties evaporate and their businesses are hijacked. The Indian Minister of Education, Mrs Sheila Kaul, estimates that 500 titles a year are copied in her country. Another £22 million's worth are exported from Taiwan, which is regarded as the leading centre of book piracy.

In fact, book piracy is now a billion-dollar-a-year world-wide business, and it shows every sign of expanding. More than a quarter of all the books on sale in Jordan, Saudi Arabia, and the Gulf states are pirated; and the practice is just as common in South American countries like Peru and Chile, where 30 per cent of the book trade is in illegal copies.

In Singapore, where British publishers are losing an estimated £16 million a year, one can go into any one of six photocopying centres in the Katang shopping centre and have a 320-page book copied and bound in minutes for less than £4. The pirates even exhibit their wares alongside legitimate publishers at the Singapore Book Fair. The publishing industry estimates that there are £15 million's worth of pirate books circulating in Singapore, Malaysia, Thailand, and Hong Kong at any given time.

Book piracy now costs British publishers alone £4.5 million a year in Egypt, £6 million in Nigeria, and £11 million in Korea – not to mention the fortune lost from photocopying in commercial and academic institutions back home.[16]

In spite of their legal actions and diplomatic pressures, and a growing international awareness of the problem, western publishers are pessimistic about the future. 'If book piracy continues at this rate', warns Tom Rix of Longman, 'it could lead to the breakdown of the structure of international publishing'.

Novelist Maureen Duffy points out that writers suffer a double indemnity. She says:

> Piracy affects two authors at once: the author who has written the work, and the author who might have written the work it is replacing, like a cuckoo's egg. The writer whose work is pirated is not just hit in the pocket. There is a unique relationship between the artist and the work, which is close to that between parent and child; and piracy induces a reaction of bereavement and anger.[17]

Another writer, Brigid Brophy, puts the threat of piracy in more apocalyptic terms. 'The great advantage of abolishing copyright', she says, 'is that it will quickly abolish the need for copyright. Deprive writers of their livelihood and English literature, followed by the English language, will die.'

Drastic as this sounds, there are some who would not regard it as a disaster – people who, on the contrary, regard the growing dominance of the English language as the main threat to their own culture. They might point out, for instance, that it is almost impossible to qualify as a doctor or engineer in the Third World today without being fluent in the language; and one of the strongest arguments against the pirates is that they are *reinforcing* this trend by reprinting nothing but English language textbooks.

We return to this issue later, but for the moment it shows how easily the arguments about piracy can be turned inside out or reversed, according to your point of view, and how cautious one should be about expressions of moral outrage. To give another example, the arguments for book piracy (and there are some, just as there are for black markets and other unofficial forms of wealth distribution) are largely ignored by the western media. Yet even Salman Rushdie admits that there are circumstances

> in which I find it possible to forgive, even to support, the unauthorized publication of books. Where a book cannot be published legitimately, because of the repressive character of the country's regime, covert publication loses the stigma of robbery and becomes, in fact, an important public service.

It is one of the paradoxes of copyright that the countries to which Rushdie refers are the Soviet Union and the Eastern European states, where the state controls what is and is not published, where private citizens are banned from owning photocopiers, and even typewriters are licensed. In these countries, moreover, the finest flowering of post-war literature occurred without copyright, royalties, or publishers of any kind, in the form of illegal samizdat papers.

In other words, one person's piracy can be another person's freedom of speech. Like the distinction between 'freedom-fighter' and 'terrorist', it largely depends on which side you're on.

6

The tape-recorders

Today's technology means that one copy of a book, a tape or a computer disk is sufficient raw material to found an industry.
(CICI Anti-Piracy Group report, 1985)

Unlike the photocopier, the tape-recorder was given away for nothing. Twice during its development, the copyright and patents were lifted and the designs let loose to live a life of their own. It was a most unusual story, and one which led to the founding of the largest international pirate industry in the world.

The first magnetic sound recorder was built in 1899 by a Danish engineer called Valdemar Poulsen. It didn't actually use tape, but his patent, with remarkable foresight, proposed 'a strip of some insulating material such as paper covered with a magnetized metallic dust'.

The use of paper proved impractical, and the idea languished until the 1930s, when the invention of plastics provided an alternative. Experiments by the German firm BASF showed that ferrous-oxide particles bonded easily to the plastic strip, and they set up a plant to manufacture it.

In 1935 the first modern recording tape was demonstrated to Hitler and Goebbels at the Berlin Radio Fair. Two years later AEG/ Telefunken produced the first commercial tape-recorder, the Magnetophone. The machine was regarded as something of a curiosity. As the clouds of the Second World War closed in, the German scientists were left to develop it in isolation.

The Nazis gave the media high priority. During the war German radio stations and recording studios were equipped with more sophisticated machines than anything the Allies possessed. When the United States forces liberated Radio Luxembourg in 1944, they disovered these new German tape-decks and were amazed at their quality. Compared with the clumsy wire recorders used by the Americans, or the heavy, disc-cutting machines dragged around by BBC reporters, they represented a new generation of sound technology.

There was no question of copyright. Like the V2 rocket research, it was regarded as the spoils of war. The Americans helped themselves. The Telefunken recorders and their blueprints were sent back home, and within five years the first mass-production reel-to-reel recorders, using 3M plastic tape, were on sale in the USA. The machines, including the new Grundig models from Germany, were primarily intended for home taping and were marketed as 'sound cameras'. It took time for the music industry to realize their potential, and it was not until May 1958 that RCA/ Victor introduced the first pre-recorded tape cartridge.

The technology soon caught on, however, and the host of other 'magazine' and 'cartridge' systems were introduced, including, in 1963, a miniature 'cassette' recorder from Philips in Holland. Its sound quality was poor, and the skinny 3.8 mm tape used to break and tangle, but it was the first truly portable machine. Philips clinched its success by literally giving the designs away; instead of hanging on to their patents, they issued royalty-free licences to anyone who wanted to manufacture them, provided they stuck to the basic design.[1]

It was an unprecedented step but it paid off. By the end of the decade the cassette had become the industry standard. Not that anyone minded; the 1960s music boom was under way, and the market was expanding so rapidly that there was room for everyone, whatever their standard, legal or illegal. Including the pirates.

Tape-recording was a gift to them. No other medium was as easy to duplicate. Copies could be made anywhere by anyone with the minimum experience. Instead of the presses needed to counterfeit records, a single person could copy a hundred tapes simultaneously on synchronized machines; and the cassettes themselves, with their cheap plastic mouldings, were easy to manufacture.

It was the ideal specification for a Third World industry, and the tape factories in Taiwan were soon turning out cassettes by the thousand for high-spending American teenagers. From the early 1960s onwards, they were shipped in bulk to the West Coast and distributed throughout the USA, establishing the first link in what was to become a vast international network.

In those days, taped music meant hi-fi on wheels. It was the sound of Elvis and the Beatles played on the eight-track Motorola of their parents' Oldsmobiles and Chevys at a million coast-to-coast burger-stands and drive-in movies. It was as American as apple pie, and the pirates virtually owned it.

The counterfeiters and bootleggers also made fortunes. Organized crime was said to be involved, and there was more than a flavour of Prohibition days. It got to such a state that, at one point, illegal recordings were outselling the legitimate product by two to one. By the early 1970s it was calculated that 60 per cent of the records and tapes on sale in New York were pirate issues. In 1971 a bootleg recording of Jimi Hendrix made it to the top half of the LP charts.[2]

It couldn't go on for ever, and the party came to an abrupt end in the USA in 1972 when a new, tougher Copyright Act was passed. The pirates suddenly found themselves stuck with thousands of unsaleable records and tapes. With production still running, it was imperative that they find an alternative market that was English-speaking and, if possible, unsuspecting. So it came to pass, in a classic roll-over operation, that £90 million's worth of pirate material was suddenly dumped on the United Kingdom.

'They were everywhere,' said a British Phonographic Institute spokesman:

> Scotland, the North and the South of England – everywhere – being sold at all sorts of prices. Some more expensive than the original, many much cheaper. They were popping up in odd outlets, camera shops, small supermarkets and garage forecourt racks. For two years or more we had a terrible time.

The success of the operation showed how easy it was to bypass the traditional distribution system and exploit new markets. There was no going back now. The virus had escaped from its host and within a decade it was to infect the world.

For the next few years, the US pirates enjoyed a bonanza and switched much of their production to Europe, but they didn't have it all their own way, because the European pirates were busy establishing their own pattern of trade. Each country was different in laws and custom. As the tide of piracy rose, it adapted to this cultural geography like water finding its own level.

Holland, for instance, became a major manufacturing centre which exported nearly all its pirate product, while Denmark imported all its illegal recordings. Greece, on the other hand, was self-sufficient in making and consuming its own.

American pirates continued to export to the UK. But their main emphasis shifted to West Germany, where pirate material was channelled through the huge US Army bases, and then to Italy, which is still the main point of entry where nearly all the records are high-quality US counterfeits.

The type of music which attracted the pirates also varied. In Northern Europe the market was swamped by rock and pop music, but further south it was dominated by the 'national and ethnic' repertoire – or folk music – which reflected the tradition of Mediterranean countries. In Greece pop music represented only 15 per cent of the pirate trade, and in France the pirates discovered rich pickings in Arab music. In fact, this proved so successful that they ended up exporting more than half their output to Africa and the Middle East.[3]

These countries were all members of an 'economic community', but piracy reflected more realistic frontiers and was quite prepared to exploit local needs. Immigrant groups such as the Turks in West Germany and the Pakistani and Indian communities in Britain set up brisk trade links with their home countries. And there were many smaller examples, such as the export of German language tapes to Switzerland and Austria. About the only common denominator was the market for classical music, which accounted for 5 to 10 per cent of the pirate trade in most countries.[4]

One of the overall trends was the widening gap between records and tapes. The counterfeit albums were nearly all imported from the USA and the Far East and sold through record shops at a high unit cost. Tapes, on the other hand, were a cheap, disposable, essentially *local* product, often selling for a half or even a quarter of the original price. They were outselling records by roughly five to one, in bars and supermarkets, newsagents, and service stations, from the back of vans, or out of suitcases in flea markets.

It was the biggest rip-off the music business had ever faced, but it was not until 1978, when the losses began to surface in their annual balance sheets, that the music companies realized the full scale of the operation and the damage it was doing.

Audio piracy

There are four kinds of pirate records and cassettes:

The *Counterfeit* is an exact replica of the original, including the packaging and labels, which is sold as the real thing.

A *Pirate* copy makes no such pretence. The packaging is cheap, the label photocopied or typed, the sound quality variable, and the price reduced accordingly.

The *Bootleg* is the unauthorized release of an artist's work, such as recordings of their concerts or music which has not been published.

The *Home-Tape* or back-to-back copy is usually a cassette made by an individual of a record they have bought, for use in their car or as a favour for their friends.

From time to time, hybrid forms appear such as the collections of disco music prepared by DJs which are illegally copied and marketed. Pirate albums are sometimes disguised as bootlegs so that they can be sold as collector's items. In the past, additional instrumental tracks have been added, or applause dubbed on the beginning and end to make it sound like a live recording. Decca once discovered a pirate copy of a

Little Richard album which had been slowed by 1 rpm in the hope of avoiding recognition.

Home taping (which is discussed later) is probably the most extensive form, though the industry can do little about it. Counterfeiting is a highly organized criminal activity targeted by police and enforcement agencies. Bootleggers are seldom prosecuted because of the difficulty of proving copyright, and there is less pressure on them because there is no direct loss to the industry. However, because there is no legitimate version to compare it with, the poor quality of the recording (or performance) can damage the artist's reputation.

Ironically, bootlegs can also help artists' careers. For instance, Bob Dylan originally decided not to release *The Basement Tapes* because he was unhappy with the recording quality. But the bootleg versions were so successful that his record company remixed the original, did what they could to improve the scrappy sound balance, and issued it as an official album.

7

The sixth transnational

The music business is dominated by six giant transnationals – CBS, EMI, Polygram, RCA, WEA and the pirates.

(Karry Knops, 'The information wars', 1985)

Nineteen seventy-eight was a good year for the music business. Polygram became the first billion-dollar record company. Sales in the UK were at an all-time high of $3.6 million, and trade was expanding at 11 per cent a year. But 1978 was also the moment of truth, when the full scale of piracy became apparent. The industry took stock of the damage it was doing and began to fight back. The writing was on the wall, and the recording companies were only just in time.

In March, EMI announced that its pre-tax profits had been slashed by 47p in the pound to £19.4 million, which may seem a healthy sum to the uninitiated, but was £3 million less than even pessimists expected. 'Cassette Pirates Raid EMI' ran the headlines. Pirate treasure, pirate gold, pirate cassettes: the words were almost synonymous, and the statistics backed them up.

Organized piracy in Britain now amounted to £20 million a year. In the United States, where 1 in 5 cassettes was illegal, it was worth $200 to $300 million.[1] On a world-wide basis the pirates had managed to take over 15 per cent of the entire market. What was worse, these figures represented only organized activity, for a new insidious form of piracy was becoming apparent. It was so widespread, so innocent, it had not been recognized before, though its effects were incalculable. It was the problem of *hometaping*.

It was particularly easy with the new music centres. You put the record on, and the tape in, you pushed a button, and you had a copy. You did it to avoid overplaying your records, or to use in your car, or to give to a friend. Anyone could do it. Everyone did it, and every copy was (potentially) a lost sale.

On average an album might be copied two or three times over. No money changed hands, there was no criminal intent, but the results were devastating. While organized piracy in the UK was worth £20 million, the industry now estimated it was losing £75 to £100 million a year from home taping.

'Ten years ago the problem was negligible,' said Richard Robinson, chairman of the BPI, 'but at the present rate of increase, in another ten it could destroy the industry.'

'It's the most significant factor in the business,' declared Leslie Hull of EMI.

Not everyone agreed with this gloomy diagnosis. The Tape Manufacturer's Federation pointed out that there had been no noticeable rise in the 60 million blank tapes sold each year. In fact, while the music industry claimed that 44 per cent of the population were illegally taping records, the tape industry estimated that only 20 per cent of the population bought blank tapes for *any* purpose.

The matter was settled by a market research survey commissioned by the BPI the following year, which showed that 226 million LPs a year were illegally taped at home. When the respondents were asked if they would have bought their last taped LP if easy recording facilities were not available, 41 per cent said yes. By this calculation the loss to the industry was a staggering £228 million. If one added the home copying of pirate tapes, and the copies of copies, the figures spiralled into absurdity. Whatever the exact extent of it, home taping was now added to the counterfeiters, bootleggers, and cassette pirates as a threat to the legitimate industry. It couldn't have come at a worse time, because in 1979 the music business hit its worst slump in twenty years.

Sales dropped by 28 million units in Britain and 65 million units in the USA. Over the next three years legitimate sales in the UK dropped by $600,000, the annual rate of expansion slowed to 1 per cent, and the increase in royalties fell from 22 to 3.9 per cent. It was the same throughout Europe. In France the number of new releases a year fell from 6,975 to 6,154, and in West Germany from 3,654 to 3,030. The golden days of the 1960s and 1970s were over; the charts were dominated by independent record labels, and half the teenage buying public were unemployed. The recession bit deep.

In 1980 the UK exported 2 million LPs. In 1984 a third of all LPs and half the cassettes sold were imported. Four record factories had closed, and 3,000 jobs had been lost.

The pirates were not the only cause, but at least they represented a visible target, something the industry could fight back against. The media coverage was intensified, new enforcement agencies were set up (see Chapter 17, 'The enforcers'), and prosecutions became more frequent – and for a while they seemed to be successful. In Italy, one of the centres of European piracy, sixty-six counterfeiting plants were raided between 1978 and 1981, and 1.6 million tapes and records were seized. By 1982 pirate sales in that country had dropped by 21 per cent. They were reduced by 25 per cent in West Germany and as much as 50 per cent in France.

It is difficult to know how much of this was due to policing tactics, because the pirates were also hit by the recession. Like any parasite, they were dependent on the health of their host. The effects varied in different parts of Europe. In the UK, for intance, the sale of counterfeit LPs was reduced, but the sale of the much cheaper pirate cassettes increased substantially.

If the music companies could claim some success on their own doorstep, in the world outside there was no doubt about who was winning. In 1978 the total sum of world music piracy amounted to $880 million. In 1980 it reached $1,000 million for the first time, although the pirates' share of the market dipped the following year to $990 million. But it soon recovered and by 1985 was approaching $1,500 million. It was a sobering thought that the pirates were now equivalent to the second largest international conglomerate in the business.

The reason for their astonishing success lay outside Europe and America, in the pirate centres of South-East Asia. Following the routes established by the print pirates, their trading empire now stretched from the Middle East to Korea. The small-scale business which started by supplying tapes to American counterfeiters had virtually taken over the Third World markets.

EMI was forced to close down its record factory and tape-duplicating plant in Singapore, which was now a major exporter in its own right, shipping out £50 million worth of pirate cassettes a year. They were produced by six syndicates, with investments of £1 million each,[2] which issued catalogues of 400 titles at a time and had their own logos, such as 'GMR' or the sign of an open hand. Most of their product went to Africa or India, or to the Middle East for distribution through the United Arab Emirates to Jordan and Saudi Arabia. Saudi Arabia was now a pirates' supermarket, with 1,700 licensed audio-cassette shops and 650 video rental firms where hardly anything on offer was genuine.[3]

The other main manufacturing centre was Indonesia, which exported £19.35 million of tapes a year and where the pirates had completely taken over. It is said that not one legitimate cassette or record of western music was bought in Indonesia in 1985; of the 8.75 million copies of UK recordings sold in the country, 8.75 million were pirated.

The pirates supplied 85 per cent of the cassettes sold in Malaysia, 90 per cent in Korea, and 95 per cent in Pakistan. While in Europe pirates struggled to maintain 10 to 15 per cent of the market, in Asia they had a stranglehold on it, and the enforcement agencies faced an impossible task.

In 1984 IFPI initiated 450 criminal and civil actions in South-East

Asia and seized more than 1.5 million cassettes, but in their own words 'it was a small percentage of the total, and the problem remains'. Mike Edwards of IFPI was typically blunt about it: 'A criminal can become a cassette pirate for the same cost as obtaining a sawn-off shotgun for a robbery – with no risk and a higher return' (IFPI handout).

In October 1984 IFPI swapped the stick for a carrot. In an attempt to get retailers in Singapore to stock 'the real thing' – legitimate tapes in preference to pirated ones – they got all the major western recording companies to agree to drastically lower their prices and thereby undermine the attraction of the cheaper illegal tapes. The genuine tapes normally cost $12.50, and even at half-price were more expensive than pirated copies, which sold for under $5; but the pirates recognized the threat and decided to fight back.

IFPI set a deadline of 1 November for retailers to dump all their pirated stock and hang up the sign outside their shop declaring that they had joined the clean-up scheme. When the fated day arrived, not only were there no signs, but most of the shops had closed in a 'day of protest'. The Singapore Soundtape Retailers' Association even met to organize a 'war chest' aimed at replacing tapes confiscated in the anticipated police raids, and to pay the fines and legal costs of its members.

The shop owners complained that they were still selling 'locally produced tapes' because they had no guidance on what was right or wrong. 'If it is illegal,' said one,

> the government should say so. If I have to buy originals I might as well close shop. Who wants to pay $12.50 to hear maybe one or two nice songs? With pirated tapes, the stock can be returned and in exchange we get the latest. No money is involved. We get new ones for old, for exactly the same price. With originals you can't do that.

Within a month the IFPI scheme had collapsed. Even with government backing, could it have worked? Singapore student Anthony Sua had the last word. Asked if he would pay more for original tapes, he replied, 'If we do not have enough money we will share. Tape it and share'.

It seemed that nothing could stop the inexorable rise of the Asian pirates, and only one event in the early 1980s so much as slowed them down. This was the case of the Live Aid tapes. The pirates finally overreached themselves with the Live Aid album. The original Band Aid record, 'Don't They Know It's Christmas' had been widely pirated, and there were at least thirty illegal editions of USA for Africa's 'We Are the World' (including Turkish and Portugese versions), but Live Aid was different. The concert had been a triumph in global communications, watched by a third of the human race, and most of them felt they had a stake in it.

To the pirates, though, it was just another record, and within six months a million copies had been distributed from the tape factories of Singapore and Jakarta. The counterfeits were of a high quality, with the Band Aid logos and 'For African famine relief' accurately reproduced; but the £2 million proceeds were not destined for Africa. This, more than anything, caused the outcry.

'There is no question that these are being sold in such a way as to encourage people to believe the money is going to famine relief,' said Dave Laing of IFPI. 'It's big business. The people who manufacture these tapes have large factories and their own relationship with the auhorities.'4

'They're stealing food from the starving,' said Bob Geldof furiously, directly accusing the Singapore and Indonesian governments and threatening to organize a boycott of their tourist trade unless they took action.

The same sense of outrage was expressed in country after country. For the first time world-wide publicity was focused on a single example of piracy, with irrefutable evidence to back it up, and the authorities blinked uneasily in the spotlight. Press conferences were held, and government officials made statements.

The Foreign Minister of Indonesia, Mochtar Kusunaatnadja, promised to arrange for payments of the proceeds from the pirate cassettes, though he was reticent about how they would be collected.5 The Singapore government were so embarrassed by the scandal that they agreed to introduce tougher copyright legislation based on (some said pirated from) Australian law. What was left of the Live Aid stocks were seized, and the pirates, while not exactly going out of business, kept a low profile for a few weeks.

Unfortunately one battle doesn't win a war, and things were soon back to normal. Of the 144 raids carried out in Singapore in 1985, only eight cases came to court, and only six of these resulted in convictions. Six months later IFPI had to abandon an experimental anti-piracy scheme because of a 'poor response from record companies and retailers'.

In 1985 it was estimated that 540 million pirate tapes were in circulation. Stanley M. Gortikov, president of the RIAA, admitted grimly, 'Around the world sales of counterfeit and pirate recordings have displaced some £1 billion in sales'.6

For the first time, the pirate distribution network was actually *larger* than any of the transnationals, and the figures were still rising. There is every sign that they still are.

8

Home movies

Piracy engulfed the film industry like a wave, before people could apreciate its impact. Especially home video. The industry just didn't think about it.

(Elizabeth Greenspan, consultant to the MPEAA, personal interview)

In many ways, television was born before its time, an embryo technology trying to run before it could walk. The transmitters were underpowered, everything ran on valves (the transistor had not yet been invented), and, above all, there was no way of capturing the images. Programmes had to be broadcast as they happened or they were lost for ever.

Experiments in the 1930s using aluminium discs were unsatisfactory, so they turned instead to film as a means of storing and editing pictures. To begin with, this was an uneasy compromise, but film cameras could go anywhere and proved so reliable that they became an intrinsic part of the medium. In fact, in the 1960s and 1970s, BBC Television used to shoot more film footage a year than the whole of Hollywood.

It was not until twenty-seven years after the discovery of magnetic tape that the first documentaries were made with portable video cameras. Looking back, it seems extraordinary that it took so long to develop an *electronic* recording system, but the step up from sound recording to capturing pictures was immensely difficult, because the tape had to carry so much more information. Each line of a television picture represented the equivalent of a hi-fi audio signal, and 3,500 of them had to be presented on the screen each second to produce an image – quite apart from the controlling signals which held the picture steady and the sound which accompanied it. So, in theory, the tape had to be much wider and run at very high speed to obtain a passable result.

The US firm Ampex, which inherited the results of German wartime research, was the first into the lead and in 1952 produced what was described as 'an almost recognizable picture'. The following year the RCA laboratories made the first crude recording of a television programme, while in Britain a team of BBC scientists, under Dr Peter Adams, began work on the Vision Electronic Recording Apparatus (VERA).

It was Ampex who made the important breakthrough. The secret which lifted them from relative obscurity to a $250 million corporation was to *reverse* the audio tape process. By using *spinning* heads rather than fixed ones, and running the tape relatively slowly past them, Ampex achieved the four million cycles a second necessary to produce an acceptable picture.

In 1956 Ampex produced the first viable recording system, called Quadruplex. The BBC broadcast the first demonstration of VERA (which still relied on fast tape) on a *Panorama* programme two years later. These huge, floor-to-ceiling machines, using tape the size of 35 mm film, on vast spools, could still record only ten to fifteen minutes at a time; but the advantages over film – especially in terms of instant playback – were obvious.

The BBC eventually abandoned VERA in favour of Quadruplex, and as the length of recording time increased and the quality improved, it became the broadcast standard throughout the world. The nature of television, which up till then had been a live medium, began to change as more programmes were recorded off the studio floor, and the word 'repeat' began to creep into the schedules.

The pressure was now on to shrink the size of the recording devices so that they could be taken out of the studios, on location. But this proved extremely difficult. In order to become a practical substitute for film cameras, the tape had to be drastically reduced in size. But the thinner the tape, the more rapidly it would have to be run through the machine, and the problem then was how to scan it fast enough without ripping the magnetic surface.

It was obvious that the basic concept would have to be reinvented from scratch. While Ampex was refining its existing systems for broadcast television, this new challenge was taken up by the Japanese and European manufacturers, and it became a race between them as to who could produce the first practical, miniaturized video system.

The Japanese were well ahead in the technology. In 1953 Toshiba had developed the first helical-scan with spinning heads; and in 1959 Professor Shiro Okamura patented the tilted-azimuth system which allowed the revolving scanners to track diagonally across the tape, substantially increasing the amount of signals they received. Sony combined these developments with their experience in transistor electronics, and in 1965 they produced the first high-quality portable video system, using half-inch recording tape: the CV2000.

They were bulky machines by today's standards. The CV2000 was like a very heavy suitcase, and it required considerable stamina even to stand upright under the combined weight of a Portapak recorder, battery belt, and camera. But they could be taken anywhere, in the back of a van or slung over the shoulder, and anyone could use them. They were 'people's television', and by the end of the 1960s there was hardly a community group or arts workshop that didn't have one. They became a feature of the hectic street life of the times and could be seen at every pop festival and demonstration.

Sony followed up with the even more professional U-Matic system (with ¾-inch tape), but although the picture quality was improving by leaps and bounds, their machines were far too complex and expensive to be sold as a domestic product.

In the end it was the Europeans, not the Japanese who took the next step forward, when Philips introduced the world's first video cassette recorder in 1971. Like their sound recorders, it was a revolutionary machine that was half the size and cost of its competitors. The paraphernalia of cables and batteries was dispensed with, and the elaborate process of lacing up the tape was replaced by the simple spring-loaded cassette. In the hope of repeating their earlier success, Philips once again licensed their designs to manufacturers all over the world. This time, however, they made a serious miscalculation.

Although their VCR contained many modern features, such as a built-in tuner and time-switch and its own rf remodulator, they lacked the sophisticated electronics and scanning systems of the Japanese, and the picture quality was poor. On the other hand, it was just what the Japanese were looking for. By combining their know-how with Philips' basic design, they managed to leap-frog the opposition and regain the lead.

In 1975 Sony introduced their Betamax system, followed a year later by JVC with their VHS (Video Home System) recorder – and the rest, as they say, is history. Between them they launched a new industry and ensured that Japanese machines were to dominate the world markets for a decade.

Unlike the street videos of the 1960s, these were mass-produced domestic products, primarily intended for recording programmes off television. At the time, there was nothing else they *could* be used for. The idea of releasing films on video cassette, let alone *hiring* them from corner shops, was no more than a dream in the corporate minds at Sony and JVC. Whey they approached the Hollywood studios about it, they were turned down flat.

As far as the film industry was concerned, television – in any shape or form – was anathema. It was television that was responsible for the decline in cinema audiences. Year by year, the cinema chains were shrinking, while great studios, like Twentieth Century Fox, were now reduced to churning out weekly soap operas. Television was killing their business, and they had no intention of co-operating in their own demise. It was several years before they realized that *this* form of television was on their side and that video cassettes offered a new, and highly profitable, form of distribution.

Two factors were responsible for changing their minds. The first was the extraordinary success of the Japanese in opening up their new markets. The sales were slow at first; but once they had managed to persuade the public that VCRs were reliable and as easy to handle as a washing machine, the demand began to exceed supplies, and their factories had to work overtime to meet it.

The second factor was that in 1979, just three years after the VCR was introduced, the world's first pirate cassette appeared. It was a recording of the film *Soldier Blue*, which had never officially been released on video. It was a straw in the wind, little more than a novelty, but the implications were enough to give them pause.

It was obvious that the owners of video recorders soon tired of recording television programmes and were demanding more pre-recorded cassettes – especially films – to play on their expensive machines. The market was there, growing every day. If the film companies didn't satisfy it, there were others who would. The studio executives could no longer ignore the fact that, if sales continued to rise, video would soon present a greater challenge to the industry than television ever had.

The industry had faced challenges before, of course. In the 1940s and 1950s it withstood scrutiny under anti-trust legislation of its exhibition monopoly, with the famous *Paramount* decision requiring the studios to divest themselves of control of cinema circuits. Later it learned to live with, and gradually incorporate, the spread of broadcast television. But piracy was something new.

Prior to home video technology, film piracy consisted largely of unlicensed exhibitions and broadcasts of 16 mm and 35 mm prints. The reproduction of celluloid prints was expensive, and only a restricted market for illegal copies existed. But the threat posed by electronic technology, in making it so difficult to identify where, when, and by whom the illegal use of copyright material is occurring, was of a different order entirely.

Astonishingly, the major studios continued to prevaricate for another three years as cassette recorders became increasingly popular, the pirates prospered, and the industry suffered what Jack Valenti, president of the Motion Picture Association of America, called 'the savage rape and ravages of this machine'.[1] It was not until 1982 that Warners, RCA, MGM, and Columbia, in what amounted to a fit of panic, released a large backlog of their films on video cassettes. If they had acted earlier they might have controlled the situation, but by then it was too late. The sudden appearance of so many titles was like pouring fuel on the flames, and the pirates had a field-day.

The main base for video piracy was in Britain, where the established pattern of television rental services, the absence of cable television, and the quality of British programmes all contributed to this country leading the world in home video ownership. In 1979 there were 250,000 recorders in just 1.2 per cent of British households. By 1982 there were 3.5 million machines in use, in over 20 per cent of households, and the figure is now 8 million, exceeding 40 per cent of homes.[2]

The video boom of the early 1980s seemed perfectly in keeping with the Thatcher government's 'on your bike' enterprise philosophy of the time. Video rental was the model 'small business', requiring the minimum of start-up capital. By 1983 there were 16,000 shops dotted across the country, especially in areas of high unemployment – the North-East, Scotland, and Wales. For most of them, the considerations of copyright were academic.

When the Hollywood studios began issuing sixty to seventy films a month, at £30 to £40 a cassette, the high-street dealers could not hope to buy them all. So they formed combines, each buying titles from different distributors and copying each other's to stock up their shelves.

David Rozalla, chairman of the British Videogram Association and boss of Warner Home Video, described this period as the 'Klondyke phase'.[3]

Or, as one retailer said about the efforts of the anti-piracy agencies, 'We spend £1 million a year trying to stop the effects of our own stupidity'.[4]

Britain's lead world-wide in a total market of 135 million recorders in 1986 is surpassed only by Japan (14 million machines in domestic use) and, proportionally to the number of households with television sets, by Bahrain, Singapore, and the United Arab Emirates. The United States, due to the early development of cable and satellite television, has consistently lagged behind in the video revolution, with just 14 per cent of households (11 million machines) plugged in.

The rise in the pre-recorded cassette market in Britain was equally staggering. By 1983, the boom year, it had become a £92-million-a-year industry, falling back slightly in following years as the novelty (and stock of new blockbuster films) declined.[5]

In 1980, 70 per cent of VCR owners rented at least one film on video every week. By 1985 it was down to just 26 per cent. But the market has started to pick up again, with the new marketing strategies of video dealers. Big high-street chain stores like Woolworth, W. H. Smith, and British Home Stores have been persuaded to use their economies of scale to offer classic movies at knock-down prices, from £6.95 upwards. Barely more than the price of a blank tape, this is a move to copy the paperback book market, leaving the specialist dealers, and casual outlets like newsagents, off-licences, and Chinese take-aways, numbering about 20,000 in all, to operate diverse video libraries on rental.[6]

The chain stores were predicting 3 million cassette sales in 1986. The total video software market now tops £100 million a year.[7] More importantly, it has opened up yet another twist in the ever-extending chain of film distribution. As David Rozalla put it, 'It's shown the Hollywood majors that there's life after rental exploitation'.

From the executive suite on Wilshire Boulevard, Los Angeles, that chain (in chronological order) now looks something like this: first-run cinema release; roll-out theatrical; airlines; military bases; hotels – pay per view; public performance video in discothèques, video bars, etc.; home video rentals; home video sales; pay per view cable; hotels – free to guests; network television; subscription pay TV; off-network pay TV; domestic TV syndication; pay TV basic cable; return syndication; and now the 'bargain basement' sale.[8]

Depending on local circumstances, the pattern is repeated in every territory in the world. From its West End première to Woolworth, the life-span of a feature film is about fifteen years. Small wonder, then, that reactions border on apoplexy when, in defiance of that rich vista of potential revenue, international piracy operations step in at the very top, before the chain even begins to roll, before the first cinema audience sees a single frame.

William Nix of the MPAA describes it as 'a fast spreading cancer which threatens the vitality of the entire film industry'.[9]

Such world-wide distribution requires a massive billion-dollar investment in marketing and pre-publicity. From the very beginning, the temptation has proved irresistible for the pirates, to capture a film print before its release, hurdle the entire distribution cycle, and offer it at basement prices to an already expectant public – video short-circuited the entire ball-game.

Peter Duffy of the Federation Against Copyright Theft (FACT) has no illusions about what he is up against: 'It's like a licence to print £20 notes' (personal interview).

Video piracy

Like audio piracy, there are four types of video piracy:
  The pure *Pirate* is a copy of a motion picture that has not been released in video cassette format and for which, therefore,

there is no legitimate packaging (sleeve, labels, etc.). It is the favourite product of organized criminal gangs.

The *Counterfeit* is a copy of a legitimate video tape, dressed up in illicit packaging (sleeve, labels, artwork) in order to pass it off as a genuine cassette. Because of the expense, this too is confined to organized commercial pirates operating within the established black market.

The *Back-to-Back* is a copy of a legitimate video tape where no attempt is made to pass it off as a genuine cassette, there is no packaging, and the title of the film is either handwritten or typed on a plain label on the cassette. The name of the video dealer may appear on the label of the cassette.

The *Home-Tape* is a copy of a legitimate videotape or a recording of a film or television programme recorded from broadcast transmissions without the permission of the copyright owner. It may be made at home or work to 'timeshift' the viewing of a programme from the time it is broadcast to a more convenient time, to store a particular programme in a collection, or swap recordings between colleagues and friends.

9

The video game

It's a tough profession, The pimps, black-market arms dealers, and counterfeiters all play along.

(Bruno Alexander, video pirate)[1]

Company fraudster, international conman, and bearer of a dozen aliases, South-African-born Bruno Alexander (needless to say, not his real name) might have added 'double agent' to the list of players in the piracy game. It is something he knows a lot about. Operating a world-wide illicit film and video distribution business from Dusseldorf in West Germany, Alexander seems a character out of *film noir*, encapsulating every amoral and parasitic trait of the unacceptable face of capitalism.

A screenplay might go something like this: *Outwardly the very model of a serious, conventional business man, a milliner manufacturing hats in the well-heeled district of Dusseldorf, – he is in fact a leading dealer on the video black market. The millions made from pirated cassettes are reinvested in the drugs trade. To those who know about his dealings, he supplies drugs or sends professional assassins after them. The police cannot see through the veil . . . .*

Such a scenario was convincing enough for film makers Rolf Gebel and Michael Luettenberg, of Atlas Films, to start production in West Germany in 1985 of *The Video Pirate* with a modest budget of 600,000 marks. A powerful US video dealer immediately acquired the cassette rights. The producer and author of the original screenplay were none other than Alexander himself.

Alexander's talents, however, lay not in creating fiction but in counterfeiting it. And his real career, culminating in the biggest crackdown on video piracy ever seen in Europe, was more dramatic than anything he was likely to write. Thirty-seven-year-old Alexander started dealing in pirate videos in 1980.

'At first everything ran very simply,' he explained. 'We paid off the projectionist with 200 to 500 marks, made pirated copies at night from their films, and sold the stuff to videothèques and collectors. We made quite a bit of money.'

The level of piracy in West Germany was eating up 75 per cent of the entire video market, and losses of up to £90 million were being claimed by legitimate dealers. Fierce competition, meanwhile, was pushing down prices on the black market.

In order to sell large quantities, Alexander set about giving piracy a legitimate cover. With a partner who invested capital, he formed companies in Holland and West Germany:

> We had empty cassettes sent to us from Holland, which were officially declared as having recordings on them. For example, 200 of the Western *Make a Cross and Go to Hell* were declared. We sold 3,000 pirated copies of this film in Germany. If a videothèque owner asked about the origin we showed the invoice from Holland and added that the licence rights were there. No one ever checked.

By 1984 he had established companies in Dusseldorf, New York, Panama, and Bangkok. They had impressive names like International Media Communications, telex numbers, conservative letterheads, and registered titles. Dubious agreements go a long way in the black-market film business. Even legitimate distributors have difficulty establishing who has film rights in the international market.

Through their network of companies, they issued forged film licences to themselves – mostly for low-budget 'B' movies. Then they rented independent small cinemas and posed as exhibitors to get first-run films which they transferred to video. Only much later did it dawn on the distributors that these cinemas were making bids for films which it was impossible to recoup from the sale of cinema tickets alone in their tiny auditoriums.

'If trouble arose with the real licensees, we showed Panamanian contracts as proof of licence fees we had paid to Panama. In effect it was to ourselves, but nobody knew that.'

Alexander's audacity knew no bounds. When the Munich company VCL discovered that the pirate had sold them the film *Truck Driver* illegally under the name *Chicago Poker*, they insisted on exclusive rights, but to no avail. Alexander took VCL to court, and on the basis of fake contracts obtained an injunction against them. 'The judges could no longer make head or tail of the situation, which is what we banked on.'

Nor was there much evidence of honour between thieves. Alexander persuaded a novice in the video business to part with 90,000 marks for a Franco Nero film, which of course did not belong to him. 'The guy did not sue us,' laughs Alexander. 'He himself had a crooked deal in mind. Yes, it was often like the TV series *Crooks against Crooks*.'

Never more so, perhaps, than Alexander's decision in 1984 to become an informer for the police and the West German anti-piracy federation, the GVU. This was a dangerous decision, motivated less by a desire to go straight than by the handsome profits he anticipated once his competitors had been eliminated. Manfred Goeller, head of the GVU, was thankful for all the help he could get. It seemed wise, at first, not to ask too many questions.

Alexander's tip-offs netted the first big catch for the GVU in February 1985, when an Italian gang, reputed to have Mafia connections, was raided. The police seized 4,450 cassettes and nineteen recorders.[2] In another raid, counterfeit copies of *Supergirl* and *The Chorus Boys* were discovered, out on illegal videos before they had been released to West German cinemas. They were thought to have originated from US film prints and been dubbed and copied by West German pirates in Holland, Luxembourg, and Switzerland.

Alexander took to carrying a gun. In the closed world of the pirates the threats and suspicions between dealers became as intense as the surveillance of the authorities. Alexander finally decided to turn himself in, for his own protection, agreeing to become the chief witness for the police in return for immunity from prosecution.

On 10 April 1985, forty-five simultaneous raids in twenty West German cities smashed five major duplicating rings. Police seized fifteen truckloads of illegal material, including a staggering 1,500 pirated 35 mm film prints, stock of over 30,000 illegal cassettes, and six duplicating factories. It had been a £15-million-a-year business.[3] After the trial, Alexander was released. He now lives in South-West Africa. The film *The Video Pirate* has still to appear, legitimately or otherwise.

In Britain similar gangs to Alexander's had been operating with impunity since 1978. London and Amsterdam became the piracy capitals of the world: London because of its connection with the US film industry, and Amsterdam as the European gateway to the international black market.[4]

By 1983 piracy was said to be running at 60 per cent of the £200-million-a-year UK video retail market. In the first year of its operation, the film industry's private investigation agency, the Federation Against Copyright Theft (FACT), uncovered 30,000 illegal tapes and started sixteen prosecutions for criminal conspiracy. Within three years, due to its own activities and the introduction of a tough Copyright Amendment Act in 1983, which increased criminal penalties from a derisory £25 fine to a maximum of two years' imprisonment and unlimited fines, FACT were claiming that the scale of piracy in Britain had been reduced from 70 per cent to under 20 per cent of the market.

The picture was not so rosy world-wide, however. The Motion Picture Association of America (MPAA) estimated that international piracy in 1986 accounted for $1 billion in losses to the film industry, representing *one-quarter* of the industry's total $4 billion annual revenue. This was all the more alarming in that 1986 was the first year when the revenue from video distribution outstripped the receipts from cinema screenings.

Video piracy is currently running at 65 per cent in West Germany, 50 per cent in Italy, and over 40 per cent in the Netherlands and Spain. The trade routes have reversed. London and Amsterdam are no longer the world's exporting capitals of illegal tapes. The Middle East, Singapore, Malaysia, and the Philippines have taken over. 'Releasing videos to the Arab peninsula and East Asia is like granting licences to steal,' according to the president of CIC, video distributors of MCA and Paramount.[5]

In those countries where anti-piracy enforcement and copyright law is rudimentary, 'control is only possible if a government has another interest to protect, such as censorship control', claims MPAA's president, William Nix. He had Singapore, Malaysia, and Brazil in mind. As for the continents where the video recorder has only just arrived, like most of Latin America, 'attempting to control piracy in these countries is like attempting to enforce Prohibition'.[6]

The evidence in Britain suggests that the trend is upward again. Perfect copies of *Rocky IV* and *Back to the Future* have been found, imported from the United States, or the Far and Middle East. Copies of *Rambo* were in Britain several months before it opened at the cinema. The only odd feature was the subtitles in French and Arabic. It wasn't hard to trace the tape's origins. The credits at the end ran the name and address of the facility house in Beirut where the subtitling (and illegal copying) had been done. Meanwhile cases against piracy rings operating from US Army bases in Europe and within major industries, such as the Trident submarine shipyards at Barrow-in-Furness, are pending.[7]

Unlike print and audio piracy, where *any* copy of a book or record can be used as the master to make unlimited duplicates, the most lucrative form of video piracy has been to acquire and copy a legitimate print of the film just before its cinema release. The quality of the video recording is thus assured; and more importantly, a healthy demand for the pirated copy will have been generated by the extensive publicity and hype that now precedes the release of every potential 'blockbuster' film.

Those on the inside of anti-piracy enforcement have little doubt that senior executives within the major US studios have taken 'handbacks' for arranging pre-release film prints to go astray. Piracy expert Philip Demonti puts it this way:

There's a *pyramid*, with people at the very top who, should they become known, would have to change their job. If you observe the life-styles of some of those executives, they would need three other jobs to support it.

The pyramid follows the same route as the drugs trade, only in reverse:

A courier in Hollywood is tipped off by the executive, and a 'lab print' is 'borrowed' from a facility house to make a video master copy, suitable for Europe. The courier brings it over in his personal luggage and delivers it to his contact in London. He keeps that one and sells, say, ten sub-master copies to agents in Europe, Beirut, Singapore, and Bangkok, sending them by car or parcel post. It's not one organization, but organizations, in different territories. The London contact makes 500 per cent profit and has done his deal. He's not interested in what happens on the street. The next tier down then make VHS and Beta copies at the local twenty-machine duplicating plant and distribute them in pubs, clubs, and factories. Like the drugs trade, the quality gets worse the further down the line you go.

(personal interview)

Such was the paranoia of twentieth Century Fox before the release of their £20 million property *Return of the Jedi* that only one print was brought into the UK, under a different title, for the première in June 1983. Yet despite elaborate precautions even they were taken by surprise on the weekend before its general release when pirates smashed their way into the locked projection booth of the Classic Cinema, Hastings, and made off with the precious three-foot-wide silver can. Within days the pirate version was being sold in pubs for £30. It was a departure from the usual practice of simply bribing the cinema manager with back-handers worth up to £4,000 for a major box-office hit.

The master-mind behind one such gang was alleged to be a former solicitor, Stephen Sharman of Muswell Hill, London. When the case came up for trial at the Knightsbridge Crown Court he had jumped bail, and an international warrant for his arrest was issued. Together with Michael Tepper, Sharman was charged with organizing an international pirate ring that distributed video master copies of films like *Superman III*, *Never Say Never Again*, and *Airplane II* across a network reaching to Thailand, Hong Kong, and South Africa. They were said to have bribed the managers and projectionists of the Ace Cinema, Stoke Newington, and the ABC Golders Green, running off copies overnight on their £50,000 Rank Cintel copying machine. Their turnover was estimated at more than £1 million a year.[8]

The more down-market version of video piracy, and far more

difficult to eradicate, has been the widespread practice of 'back-to-back' copying from one video cassette to another. Just like copying from one audio tape to another it requires no more initial investment than two recorders with a lead between them.

In the early days of the video rental business, when many new titles were being released simultaneously, the more disreputable high-street shop owners clubbed together and swapped 'back-to-backs' in order to keep up their stocks of the latest material. It still continues of course, at the lower end of the market among the non-specialist outlets like corner shops, Chinese take-aways, and garages, and provides the livelihood for the maverick operators dealing from council flats and mobile 'libraries' on industrial sites and outside factories.

Twenty-three-year-old Kevin Perry was the first pirate in Britain to be sentenced to imprisonment for illegal possession of video cassettes. When police raided his Peckham council flat in May 1983 they uncovered five recorders linked together for copying, and a library with over 1,000 pirated cassettes from floor to ceiling, worth £70,000 on the open market. Two photocopying machines for duplicating covers were also found. Perry was the unfortunate victim of his own security system. Worried by a possible police raid, he had installed a closed-circuit video camera over his front door. In the event, it served only to arouse the suspicions of the local constabulary.[9] But perhaps he was not as unlucky as Darlington brothers Caleb and William Lowther, who proved to be a little too enterprising for their own good. Being unemployed they thought they had the makings of a legitimate small business. They rented films from the local video shop, copied them, and started a rental business of their own. They were caught after going to a government enterprise agency to ask for advice on how to expand their business. They received two-month gaol sentences.[10]

Personal 'back-to-back' copying, along with recording films and programmes off television (still technically illegal), is just another form of home taping, practised by film buffs, pornography enthusiasts, specialist collectors, immigrant communities who swap films in their own language, and families generally, motivated by the desire to send loved ones living abroad their favourite programmes. But increasingly, as with other forms of piracy, the phenomenon has permeated into the working environment, with sly corporate executives making copies of hired training videos, teachers making copies of television programmes to help them in their classes, and international companies sending regular tapes of television shows to their staff overseas, on North Sea oil rigs or Saudi Arabian construction sites.[11]

Video technology has extended the grasp of the pirates far beyond the film industry. The 'wave' that engulfed the movie business has swept across all the audio-visual media, and is set to exploit the new outlets of satellite and cable television with a vengeance. Unauthorized decoding of satellite signals, and recording movies off the premium film channels before their legitimate release on video, presents the pirates with fresh opportunities. And the performance in public places of illegal recordings, from pop videos to Hollywood classics, gathers pace across the globe, in cafés, discothèques, and bars in every city.

In September 1985 the *Chinese People's Daily* reported that police in Canton had smashed a pornographic video smuggling ring inside the Shenzhen Tourist Co. and seized 25,000 illegal tapes. Shenzhen, the pioneering special zone for foreign investment near Canton, was easily accessible from Hong Kong, and the scandal was used to highlight the dangers of China opening up too far to western influences and the market economy. The *People's Daily* complained, 'The video recorder is a propaganda and educational tool which must be used to teach officials and workers about patriotism, socialism, and communism'.[12]

White-collar pirates

Extraordinary as it may seem, the Bank of Ireland has twice been sued for video piracy and, by settling out of court, it has tacitly admitted its guilt in both cases. Banks and insurance companies make unlikely villains; in fact, they are usually at the receiving end of frauds, but there is one area of the video business where the most respectable institutions succumb to temptation: the training film.

These useful and often amusing illustrations of management techniques now form a £10 million slice of the UK video market. But they are expensive items. A thirty-minute video cassette or film, which can cost £100,000 to make, is normally sold for £500 to £700, or hired out at £100 a time. It is a lucrative business for the producers, and reason enough for their customers to run off a few 'spare' copies.[13]

The Dorset branch of the National Mutual Life Association of Australasia certainly thought so. Having rented a 16 mm sales training film from Rank Aldis, they took it to a facility house to have a video copy made of it, and later made several duplicate cassettes on home video recorders. Unfortunately, not all their staff were in on the secret, and one of the copies was conscientiously returned to Rank Aldis, who promptly took them to court.[14]

It is a feature of such cases that corporate pirates tend inadvertently to turn themselves in. The accountancy firm of Arthur Young recently returned two tapes to Video Arts, complaining about the quality of the pictures. The company immediately demanded that they return their other pirated copies, and Young's eventually paid out £6,500 in damages. Video Arts, founded by the comedian John Cleese, are a leading producer of video tapes on selling and finance, and a pioneer of copyright litigation. They recently obtained the first Australian High Court 'Anton Pillar' search-and-seize order (explained in Chapter 17) against a firm called Ingham Enterprises; and when the company's solicitor halted the search, they sought to have him committed for contempt of court.[15]

It was Video Arts' cassettes which were pirated by the Bank of Ireland. Once again, the defendants unintentionally blew the whistle on themselves by complaining about the quality.

The extent of this kind of piracy is difficult to determine, but it is certainly widespread. The legitimacy of an organization is no guarantee that its employees (or the management itself) are not pirating videos or illegally copying computer software.

10

The chip forgers

The Ten Commandments shouldn't be any less protected because they were engraved on stone.

(Jack E. Brown, Apple legal adviser)[1]

On its own, a computer is a useless machine. If you plug it in it won't actually do anything. It doesn't even know what the signals from the keyboard mean, let alone what to do with them. It becomes a computer only when it is programmed, and the instructions it gets will decide whether it is a machine for playing Space Invaders, imitating violins, or double-entry book-keeping.

The basic instructions, such as how to store and retrieve information and display it on the screen, are fed to the machine in an incomprehensible string of mathematics called 'machine code'. To make things easier for the user, this is translated into a computer language like Basic or Cobol which turns letters into numbers and allows groups of keys to control each function. The keyboard is wired accordingly, and the computer is ready to load your game program.

These basic programs have names like BIOS and MSDOS and are known as 'operating systems'. In the early days of computers they had to be fed in on punched tape every time they were used. Nowadays, they are etched on to a silicon chip and built into the machine itself, so that a personal computer or micro will work as soon as it is turned on.

The microscopic layers of circuits and switches on these ROM (Read Only Memory) chips are among the best-kept trade secrets in the world. They take years to develop, and the designs are jealously guarded. The quality and versatility of the machine depend on them, not to mention the sales. So they became an obvious target for pirates.

It began in the Far East, in the late 1970s, when the forgers of Taiwan turned their attention from Rolex watches and designer sportswear to the ROM chip of the Apple II computer. Once they had cracked this key element, the other components were relatively easy to manufacture. Using chips from Taiwan, computers were assembled in their thousands in the backstreets of Hong Kong and Singapore – and Taiwan itself – and a flood of rotten Apples appeared throughout South-East Asia.

A makeshift factory down a dusty lane on the outskirts of Taipei was able to turn out 150 computers a month, and by the spring of 1983 there were more than fifty such factories. The fashionable arcades which once sold fake antiques and perfume became a cut-price electronic wonderland where the tourists could buy an Apple II for $250 and could have any software they required run off, there and then, for $30 or less.

Apple did what they could to stem the tide, but in February 1983 a Taipei court rejected their suit on the grounds that the company was not registered in Taiwan. Back in California, the directors ground their corporate teeth in frustration. Worse was to come, because American distributors now began importing and selling these replicas in the United States under such look-alike names as Pineapple[2] and Orange. Sales of the original article slumped, and the sunshine image darkened. The orchard was being poisoned with bitter fruit.[3]

The development of a semi-conductor microchip can cost $100 million before arriving at the final 'mask' or plan of the circuit. On the other hand, though it is difficult to break the chip apart and duplicate the mask, the pirate copy is unlikely to cost more than $50,000.[4] From the pirates' point of view, computers were an excellent business proposition. Like a Cartier watch, they were an expensive one-off product, for which they were not required to provide any after-sales service. There were no overheads from research and development, the matter of quality control could be largely ignored, and they discovered to their delight that the chips were not even copyright.

The reason for this, in legal terms, was that these complicated little blocks of silicon occupied a no man's land between hardware and software. They were neither machinery (which was protected by cumbersome patent laws), nor writing (which was automatically copyright). It was a form of 'solid' information that lay half-way between a gear stick and the instructions for using it. When the US corporation lawyers turned to their reference books they could find no parallel. Computer chips fell outside all the usual definitions, and it would be up to the courts to decide whether or not they were 'literary works'. A major new field of litigation was opening up.

'It even raises the question', said Dr Ralph S Brown, Professor of Law at Yale University, 'of whether we need a whole new system just to deal with computer chips.'[5]

While the lawyers argued, the Japanese moved into the game, and the stakes were raised dramatically. Pirates were one thing, but the sophisticated electronics industry of Japan was a different matter. For years they had been trying to get into the competitive market for logic chips. They were only too glad to copy, and if necessary improve, US designs; and the look-alike computer would give them a strong advantage in the electronic trade war that was developing between their countries. For the Americans, it was a serious and very worrying development.

In 1983 Itel accused a large Japanese company of stealing one of their microprocessor designs, but the case was settled out of court, and the influx of clones continued. The price of an Apple II was reduced to $1,300 to compete with the foreign imports, which were now selling for $800 to $1,000.[6]

The threat from the Japanese encouraged the US Appeal Court to settle the copyright issue. After a bitterly fought case, Apple Inc. were awarded $2.5 million damages against the Franklin Computer Corporation for copying fourteen of their operating systems in an almost identical product. It was a landmark decision which established for the first time that programs were copyright even if indistinguishable from hardware. The court decided, in its own words, that the medium was not the message.

The US Trade Commission ruled that Apple designs had been infringed by 'nearly two dozen manufacturers in Asia' and banned the import of their computers into the country.[7]

Then the giant IBM Corporation, market leaders in personal computers, weighed in by filing suit againt Corona Data Systems and Eagle Computer Inc., which had been copying their BIOS (Basic Input – Output System) chip, and the Handwell Corporation, which had been importing look-alike personal computers from Taiwan. All three agreed to stop copyright infringement of IBM systems.[8]

In the space of a month, in which computers had rarely been out of the US headlines, the industry had finally struck back. In October 1983 Congress ratified the situation by approving a Bill which extended copyright protection to semi-conductor chips for ten years after their design, with fines of up to $250,000 for pirating a single mask.[9] This was signed into law by President Reagan a year later. A traditional protectionism asserted itself, and the USA tried to seal itself off from the mutant offspring of its own technology.

Although the US markets were now denied to them, the pirates continued to flourish in the world outside. But their days were numbered, because the whole industry was about to be overtaken by a new and quite extraordinary phenomenon. Though IBM and the other computer manufacturers finally had a means of suppressing the blatant imitations, they had no defence against a new form of piracy: the near copy, the *almost* identical replica which came as close as possible to the original without actually infringing copyright. The most astonishing example of these were the IBM clones.

The clones

> It's compatible with you know who, at a price that only we know how.
>
> (Amstrad advertisement for the PC 1512)

IBM were slow to enter the market for personal computers, and the company-within-the-company that was commissioned to produce the designs thought carefully about the kind of machine they wanted. It was decided to make it as simple as possible, and the designers opted for a set of modular units consisting of a 'mother board' with its chips, a couple of disk drives, a keyboard, and a monitor, together with a couple of boards for graphics and the plug-sockets (or ports).

When the computer was finally launched, at the end of 1981, it was an immediate success. The simplicity of the assembly was one reason why they were able to turn out over a million machines. But it made it just as easy for anyone else to produce them. IBM indirectly encouraged this by their 'open-door' policy of making the technical specification available to outside companies to encourage the development of software and peripherals for the machine.[10]

This helped to establish their market position, but it meant that the IBM PC became the most imitated computer in history. Its popularity was itself an invitation to piracy because there was no need for IBM to update it or bring out 'improved' models. Pirates are conservative by nature and, like most parasites, prefer to concentrate on an established product with a long shelf life.

On every count, the IBM PC was a prime target.

The computer was built around the Intel 8088 processor chip, using Microsoft's operating system, but the heart of the machine – the uniquely copyright element – was the BIOS ROM input-output chip which co-ordinated its functions. Without the BIOS ROM, it was not an IBM PC.

However, US manufacturers were soon producing BIOS chips which imitated most of its functions, and IBM's competitors, including Compaq (and later Tandy and Epsom), brought out the first IBM clones. Although these were designed to undercut IBM, they were quality products which often included additional features. And they were, of course, perfectly legal.

These imitation chips, the most popular of which was called the Phoenix, were also the basis of 'emulators', a new form of computer product. The emulators (or IBMulators, as they came to be called) used the computer's screen, keyboard, and so on, but bypassed its operating system and substituted one which made it *behave* like an IBM.

When the US Semi-Conductor Chip Protection Act was finally passed at the end of 1984, and the pirates began to suffer from the success of cut-price clones, the Taiwanese government commissioned their own Electronic Research Standards Organization to come up with a look-alike BIOS which did not infringe IBM's copyright. The result was ERSO, the cheapest and most successful substitute chip yet produced. ERSO meant that the pirates could come in from the cold. For the first time it was possible to manufacture really cheap copies of the IBM PC, that could be openly sold throughout the world, *including* the United States. The message soon got around, European manufacturers began producing their own clones, and Taiwan discovered a highly profitable new export market for its chips.

The UK became the centre of the trade, with numerous businesses, often without proper financial backing or experience, setting up to produce a single product. The electronics were brought in from the Far East and the machines assembled on the spot; with no necessity to provide a back-up service, it could be a short cut to fast money. Companies with less than ten employees and a turnover of £1 million a year or more were common. But the turnover of companies was just as rapid, and bankruptcies were frequent.

IBM watched these developments with a wary eye, but it was only when there was an obvious infringement of copyright, or a company started acquiring too big a share of the market, that 'Big Blue' took action. It seldom went as far as a court case; when a $56 billion corporation wants a quiet word with you, you tend to listen. For instance, two British firms, Walters and PC Compatibles, which were recently leaned on in this way, discretely changed the design of their casing and began ordering their chips from a different manufacturer.

The success of the clones was hardly surprising, since they offered much the same facilities for £400 to £500 as the IBM PC offered for £4,000. At the beginning of 1983 there were twenty clones on the market; two years later the programs originally designed for IBM were being pirated wholesale and adapted to run on other machines, and it was almost impossible to sell a middle-range personal computer without the magic label 'IBM compatible.'

From IBM's point of view, it was both a blessing and a curse. On one hand, their markets were flooded with low-cost replicas, which limited their sales to 'Rolls-Royce' customers who could afford the 'real thing'. On the other hand, it put a brake on the development of genuine competition, because manufacturers were reluctant to bring out original alternatives. The real losers were the customers themselves, because the introduction of industry standards, which were so useful in terms of video hardware and tape-recorders, was disastrous when applied to software. It was one thing to make machines compatible; but if the operating systems, or 'thought processes', were standardized it was impossible to introduce new ideas or uses.

All that was required was to make the clones faster and easier to operate, and this was the direction the manufacturers took. The process reached its peak in the UK when Tandy, Spectrum, and Olivetti all brought out personal computers which were superior to the IBM, and they were capped, in September 1986, with the launch of the Amstrad 1512, which was not only *ten times cheaper* than the original, but *three times faster*.

The wheel had come full circle. The IBM PC was an expensive museum piece. The original pirates had been put out of business, and even the 'cowboy' clones had been undercut. It was the copy-of-a-copy-of-a-copy which became the industry standard.

11

The softlifters

If you could photocopy cars, we'd all have Ferraris.
(David Potter of Psion, the company which sold half a million
Flight Simulator games to Sinclair users)[1]

The piracy of computer hardware ran its course over a ten-year period, and was eventually brought under control by a combination of legal action and the success of the 'legitimate' clones. It could be argued that computers themselves are not copyright material in the first place, but follow the pattern of other machines, like tape-recorders or cars, where patent follows patent and one generation of hardware succeeds another. But the information processed by them – the programs themselves – are another matter.

The theft of computer software is as ruthless, widespread, profitable, and unstoppable as any form of piracy. And for the most part, the victims are helpless to do anything about it. Big corporations, like IBM, can look after themselves; but a small software firm, with nothing but bright ideas and a couple of programs to sell, can be bankrupted overnight by piracy.

The law has offered them little protection in the past. In the early 1970s the US Supreme Court ruled in three separate cases that software was specifically *excluded* from copyright protection. The revisions to the Copyright Act which were introduced in 1976, and became law in 1978, still left it in a legal limbo. The Copyright Office in Washington accepted computer programs in coded form but warned the applicants that it could not certify them as a 'work of original authorship' because the code was not readable. A judge in the federal district court in Philadelphia ruled that they were 'an essential element of the machine' and not designed to 'explain or communicate information', which is the traditional test of whether something can be copyrighted.

Companies were, in any case, reluctant to reveal their secrets on a public register. Texas Instruments Inc. registered their programs in both coded and uncoded versions, but deleted what they called 'proprietary information', which upset a lot of people.

'It is an abominable notion,' said Professor Brown of the Yale Law School. 'The companies are trying to have it both ways: to deposit something in the Copyright Office and to keep it inaccessible.'

It made little difference anyway, because the computer itself is a copying machine. The first lesson that a user learns is to make a 'back-up copy' of their programs, a duplicate copy for safety, just in case the original gets lost or spoiled. It says so in the manual and becomes second nature. It is easy, and it happens every day on every computer in the world. Every time someone lends a back-up copy to a friend or lets them photocopy a page of the manual, it is software theft – the insidious, unstoppable 'home taping' which is known in the computer business as 'softlifting'.

There are two main kinds of 'softlifters', two age groups which form a family pattern, like parent and child. What separates the grown-ups from the kids is the cost of the software. The most expensive packages of software are the word-processing and accountancy programs such as Wordstar, Visicalc, Supercalc, and the Lotus 123 spread sheet; these are known in the industry as 'standards'. They are primarily business programs that cost around £200, come equipped with expensively bound manuals, and attract a particular form of white-collar piracy.

It usually begins when a company buys a word processor, or a program for filing a lot of complicated information, such as Ashton Tate's dBaseII. Once it is installed and working (and they recognize its advantages), they decide they need more: one for the accounts department, a couple for the branch offices, another for the chairman's secretary, and so on.

They are happy to pay for additional terminals and VDUs, but when it comes to the software . . . well, who is to know if they run off a few copies? One common excuse is the need to transfer the programs from floppy disk (the form in which most are sold) on to the hard disk drives of bigger machines, which not only are faster but can store up to fifty times more information.

One way or another, if they think they can get away with it, the boardroom pirates are no more scrupulous than any other. Studies carried out by the US software industry indicate the astonishing fact that *one-half of all business programs in use in the United States are illegal copies*.

Organized 'in-house' piracy is not limited to businesses. It is just as common in schools, where teachers, starved of resources and overspent on their budget, are forced to copy program tapes for their classes.

'Teachers are the worst offenders,' according to Ronald Robertson of the Federation Against Software Theft. 'Piracy in the educational field is one of the main reasons for the lack of good educational software.'[2]

The effects of this organized seepage can be seen in a firm like

Micropro, who market the best-selling Wordstar program. Their managing director, Robin Oliver, recently estimated that there were 60,000 illegal copies of Wordstar in the UK alone, with as many as 100,000 unauthorized users. By this calculation, there may be as many as 250,000 pirated copies world-wide, with a value of over £57 million in lost sales.

To recoup some of this staggering loss, the company recently offered an amnesty to pirates if they registered their programs for a nominal sum of £40. In the first week the offer was taken up by just twenty people. When Brikat offered a similar deal for their Pegasus accounting program, only fifty pirates owned up in the first three months, and the 'fines' barely covered the paperwork.

The software companies are now resorting to the courts whenever the pirate is big enough, and rich enough, to make it worthwhile. Ashton Tate recently tracked down six corporate softlifters of their database programs, though in each case they settled out of court. It is difficult to discover how much is recovered in this way. As with any form of computer crime, there is a reluctance to publicize the details, but the figures sometimes show up in the annual accounts.

In 1983, for instance, the UK firm Systime made a substantial payment of £3.5 million to the Digital Equipment Co. for what was described in their accounts as 'licence fees, interest, and copyright infringement'. Digital, with a £400 million annual turnover, estimate that they lose £10 million a year from UK pirates, and Roger Tuckett, their senior commercial lawyer, believes that the deterrent effect of court actions is considerable. To give some idea of the scale of this operation, Donald McLean of FAST estimated that there were £9 million of settlements in 1984 in the UK alone.[3]

This represents only the top end of the market, because computer piracy knows no age limit. When the average softlifter gets home from the office, he may well find his children playing with 'borrowed' software on their games computer. Games programs are valuable, and vulnerable, software. They are usually supplied on tape cassettes, which makes them easy to copy, and the main users are children and teenagers.

It is difficult to estimate the extent of under-age softlifting, but a recent MORI poll discovered that nearly half the children using machines had copied programs. The implications of this go further than questions of profit and loss. It is no exaggeration to say that a whole generation is growing up who see nothing wrong with piracy.

'Many of the youngsters who do home copying will be looking for employment in the industry,' warns Nick Alexander of Virgin Games:

When they start ringing round the software houses for jobs as programmers they will find there is only a fraction of the jobs there used to be. A year ago there were 300 software houses (in the UK); today there are around a hundred, and piracy is the major factor contributing to this situation.

However, the junior softlifters are unrepentant.

'I've never bought a piece of software in my life,' said David, a typical 18-year-old games player. 'I have an expensive hi-fi deck which lets me do an excellent back-to-back copy. If I want disks copied I use a disk-copying utility sold by a reputable company. Practically everyone I know pirates stuff.'[4]

Another 18-year-old, quoted in a computer magazine, put it down to teenage finances. 'By the time you've forked out money for disk drives and the micro itself, there's no cash left. If a game costs over £1.99, I might as well copy it. It's not done to own a micro and not pirate.'[5]

The only moral judgement they exercise concerns the quality of the games. On the whole, if they are good enough they tend to buy them, almost out of respect for the designers. If not, they copy them. And they are critical of an industry that sees them as passive consumers.

'They think we're just dumb kids,' said Mike, aged 16. 'Most of the stuff on sale is junk, games copied from other games. It's a rip-off; and if they pirate each other's ideas like that, how can they blame us?'

David agrees: 'They will break into the code for a routine they find useful for their own programs. They will deny it, but it's an absolute fact' (personal interview).

It is true that programmers 'borrow' each other's ideas, indeed the whole computer industry was founded on the practice, but it is taken to extremes in this competitve market. Nick Tilsen of the UK games firm Quicksilva makes an interesting comparison. He estimated that, for every one of his games bought, seven copies were being made by users for their friends. But at the same time, he knew of twenty-three different firms that were copying Quicksilva games. It was difficult to say which was costing them the most.[6]

Well-known games like Space Invaders and PacMan have a hundred imitations. The Bally Manufacturing Corporation, which owns the rights to these classics, was in and out of the courts no less than sixty-five times between 1981 and 1983.[5] In most instances it won the case because the pirates hadn't bothered to change the design of the little figures on the screen. The courts might argue about software theft, but it was accepted that the design and sound effects of games were copyright.

A cynical dog-eat-dog attitude has lead to widespread piracy of the sort known as *disguised counterfeiting*. Provided you changed the title, altered the graphics, and rewrote the machine code to fit another computer, you could steal the idea with impunity. The British firm Acornsoft, which supplies programs for the best-selling Acorn BBC micro, published a PacMan look-alike called Snapper and a mirror image of the Williams Co.'s Defender called Planetoids. Another Acorn BBC supplier, Micropower, marketed a version of the popular Atari game Donkey King called Gorilla King, which joined a proliferation by other firms including Kongo Kong, Wally Kong, Killer Kong, Dinkey Kong, Krazy Kong, and Donkey King. The game's original designer, Nintendo, watched helplessly as their royalties evaporated.[7]

Games piracy is so lucrative and easy, it now accounts for about two-thirds of all software theft. Computer software firms in the UK are losing £100 million a year on games, out of a total loss of £150 million through software piracy; and the figure in the USA is close to £450 million.[8]

But we must be careful here, for there is a warning that applies to all forms of piracy. The industry's estimates of its own losses cannot always be taken at face value. This is not to say they are falsified, but the industries have an axe to grind. The figures are seldom backed up with firm evidence and they vary wildly from one source to another. Software piracy is a classic example of this.

The only rigorous academic study of the problem in the UK was the Staines Report, published in October 1984. Anne and Ian Staines of Newcastle Polytechnic carried out an in-depth survey of 467 businesses, including all the main software houses. The results were carefully analysed, and they concluded that the total loss from piracy ammounted to £25 million a year.[9]

Four months later, in February 1985, the Conservative MP William Powell announced to the House of Commons that the figure was £150 million.[10] He was speaking on behalf of a Private Member's Bill to extend copyright laws and, like the industry spokesmen, he had a point to make; but a discrepancy of 600 per cent is surprising.

It may be unfair to quote the cliché about lies, damned lies, and statistics, but it seems to be a law of economics that any sum over eight figures contains an element of propaganda. Not that there is anything wrong with propaganda. It may, in the long run, turn out to be the most effective weapon of all in the fight against piracy.

Software piracy

There are four main forms of software piracy, which are defined as follows:

Counterfeiting – the production or sale of exact copies.

Disguised counterfeiting – the theft of an idea which is then altered, or incorporated in another program.

Seepage – the one-off copying by home or business users.

Organized seepage – copying within clubs, schools, or other organizations.

The UK software firms surveyed in the Staines Report (1984) reported that their main losses were from seepage (40 per cent) and disguised counterfeiting (31 per cent), followed by counterfeiting (17 per cent). It is interesting that most firms saw seepage (i.e. the home user) as a greater threat than counterfeiting (i.e. organised crime). It is we who are the pirates; the only question is whether our activities are a crime, or a right.

12

Stealing the system

It's hard to say why they do it, but once they get involved it becomes an obsession to see what they can do next. The biggest problem is that they are hooked up to a phone line. If the kid is at home with a computer there's no problem. Once they hook it up to a phone line they have access to the world.

(Detective investigating the New Jersey hackers)[1]

It was the computer story of the decade, whiz-kids beat the system, the movie *War Game* come to life, and the newspapers loved it. But the authorities were less amused when the local New Jersey police arrested seven teenagers from the respectable suburb of South Plain Fork on 17 July 1985 and launched a scandal that involved the FBI, AT&T Corporate Security, the US Defense Department, and the Secret Service.

Their hardware consisted of little more than cheap micro-computers that kids play games on; but these were hackers, and their game was the system itself. By adding a 'modem' (the device which transmits computer signals by telephone), they were able to talk to each other and dial up any other computer in the country. They then set up an electronic 'bulletin board', so they could pool their information, and set about exploring the nation's telecommunications system.

At first the only sign of their activity was an increase in their parents' telephone bills. In one household they were surprised to receive a bill for five times the normal amount. They were even more surprised a month later to receive no bill at all – because by then their son had penetrated the telephone company's computer and 'adjusted' their account.

They cracked the international telephone system and made long-distance calls to Spain and England. By experimenting with pass-words and log-on procedures, they gained access to medical and financial data banks, altering their own accounts and shopping by phone with other people's credit-card numbers. They read the classified files of TRW Incorporated, a US Defense Department contractor. They obtained the telephone numbers of private work-lines of US Army generals. They even broke the secret Pentagon codes and, through them, were able to alter the position of military communications satellites in space.

With patience and ingenuity, they literally stole the system, and no one was aware that it was happening. It was only when a mass of unclaimed goods began piling up at the local post office that the police became suspicious. Police Officer Michael Grunier, himself a computer buff, eventually got through to the teenagers' bulletin board and obtained enough evidence for a search warrant, and the boys' notebook and logs revealed the whole story.

'Most of the parents were surprised to find what was going on,' said Detective George Green with disarming understatement. 'They just thought it was great that their son was upstairs playing with a computer' (radio interview).

At first it was thought they could be dealt with under New Jersey state law, which allows for up to five years' imprisonment for 'breaking and entering a computer', but no one was going to send them to gaol. They were media heroes. Besides, it soon became apparent they were only the tip of the iceberg. Their bulletin board had been accessed by other networks, involving hundreds of people across the country, all of whom were now busily trying to cover their tracks.[2]

Detectives Green and Grunier were hopelessly out of their depth. The whole system had obviously been leaking like a sieve, and responsibility for dealing with it lay at the highest levels. For the hackers themselves it had been a joke, for the press a good story, but for those who depended on the security of the system – including almost every state institution and business organization in the western world – it was a desperately serious matter.

Buckminster Fuller once described the telephone system as 'the biggest machine in the world'. In the last few decades it has increased tenfold with the addition of radio and mircowave links and satellite relays. This immense network, which has been described as an 'information environment', is not only the largest, but the most complex structure ever created; for the surprising fact is that it is literally one single entity. In theory, any piece of information, the telemetry of a spacecraft, the details of a bank statement, or the harmless gossip of a phone call, can move through the entire system. And, in theory, given the connections, it can be accessed at any other point.

This vulnerability has given rise to a new kind of piracy which takes many forms but can be summed up as the theft or misuse of information. Its origins can be traced back, in almost legendary fashion, to a particular time – in the late 1960s, before there were hackers (or the multiple access to mainframes that makes it possible) – and a single individual, an 8-year-old American boy called Joe Egressia.

Joe happened to be blind, and the main interest in his life was the telephone and the access it gave him to recorded tapes and messages. He would spend hours dialling these public services throughout the USA and one day, while waiting to be connected to a number, he began whistling to himself. To his surprise the recording started and then abruptly cut off. He rang the engineers to ask why and was told that he had accidentally produced the tone signal used to switch long-distance circuits.

He tried again and found that, with a little patience, he could whistle his way out from his local exchange to almost anywhere he chose, without the call being registered. It opened up exciting new possibilities, and the hobby became an obsession as he set about exploring the international telephone network.

In 1971 *Esquire* magazine ran a feature on him. Joe – or Blind Joe as he soon became known – found himself a celebrity. Kids and college students across the country began experimenting with his techniques, and the subculture of the 'phone phreaks' was born.[3] Over the years, the telephone companies tightened up their security to make free dialling more difficult, and the network pirates turned their attention to bigger game. But two elements remained the same: the remarkable youth of most hackers and their casual familiarity with the telephone system.

As the electronic networks began to take shape in the 1970s, there were frequent examples of people gaining illegal access to data banks, eavesdropping on commercial transactions, breaking into the electronic mail systems, and penetrating the highest levels of government security. The ease with which the network could be exploited created the possibility of near-perfect crimes. The scope for electronic fraud, alone, is enormous.

The financial world has long been aware of this. Ever since Stanley Rifkind (the first person to be prosecuted for computer crime) persuaded Pacific Securities main frame to transfer $5 million from the Bank of California to his personal account on the East Coast, financial institutions have known how vulnerable they were.[4]

At the time of the New Jersey case, the banking world was discussing an even more audacious exploit of a UK systems analyst who had broken the codes of a major clearing bank and transferred £4 million to a secret account in Switzerland. The person concerned had made sure he was out of the country at the time, and had since disappeared, so the bank was rather surprised to hear from him a few months later. He explained that by careful speculation on the currency markets he had increased the sum to £6 million and was now prepared to give back the original £4 million, provided the bank made no further attempt to track him down. It was an offer they could hardly refuse. Faced with the choice between embarrassing disclosures or retrieving their money and keeping their mouths shut, the bank agreed. With the consent of his victims, he had successfully stolen £2 million.

Most of these crimes are committed by insiders with a working knowledge of the system, and their techniques are highly sophisticated. For instance, there is the 'Trojan Horse', or unauthorized instructions buried within the system which are timed to start operating weeks or months ahead. Once they have performed their task – moving money to a private account or transmitting data to a remote terminal – they can wipe themselves out and remove all trace of their existence from the computer's memory.[5]

Then there is the 'Logic Bomb', a sinister development of the Trojan Horse which is designed for sabotage or blackmail. The illegal program is planted in the same way, but instead of stealing information it is designed to damage or 'crash' the system by altering its operating programs. For instance, it could refuse to recognize passwords, change people's identity numbers, or simply wipe out the memory.

Logic Bombs can bring the whole system to a halt and cost the company vast sums of money, so they are the ideal weapon for extortion or revenge by disgruntled employees.

The classic example of this was the IBM programmer who decided to wreck the company's latest model by planting an instruction in its operating system, which caused the internal clock to malfunction and shut it down. Every machine that came off the assembly line contained this Logic Bomb, though IBM, of course, knew nothing about it until 7.30 a.m. on 11 April 1980, when all their 4,341 computers simultaneously stopped working.

The use of satellite links, and the speed with which money is moved around the world, makes computer crime easier every day. As Donn Parker of the Stanford Research Institute points out, 'The criminal no longer has to be at the scene of the crime. Theoretically, if he has access to a telephone in Outer Mongolia he can instantaneously commit a computer crime in Toronto.'

It is not only money which can be stolen through the computer network, but information itself, which in some cases can be even more valuable. Specialized computer chips are increasingly designed by customers on their own computer terminals, linked around the world, which puts in peril of piracy not just specific ideas but whole electronic libraries of designs. The lack of reciprocal legislation in other countries means that UK firms like Inmos and Plessey now risk having their designs pirated by foreign competitors via the United States! And like other forms of electronic theft, it can be carried out in seconds from a computer terminal the other side of the world.

The commercial data banks are another tempting target. These vast stores of information, which first came on line in the early 1970s, are emerging as one of the main functions of the network. One of the earliest data banks was established by two of the largest US news-gathering organizations, Dow Jones and the *New York Times*. By 1982 the Dow Jones system alone had more than 40,000 subscribers. They have now been joined by hundreds of others, including the *Reader's Digest* database (ominously called The Source) and Compuserve, to which the *Los Angeles Times* transfers 70 per cent of its daily output. There are databases which deal with every kind of specialized interest, including legal, medical, and commercial information, which can be consulted for a call-in fee or on a regular basis, by subscription, in the same way that one can buy a magazine or newspaper. Most of the information is reference material of the sort one could find in any library. Indeed, many people see them as the libraries of the future that will eventually replace the printed word. But their ability to cross-reference and process information goes well beyond this. In some cases they are becoming as powerful (and profitable) as any media conglomerate.

Take, for instance, the International Reporting Information System (IRIS), described by Ian Reinecke in his book *Electronic Illusions* (1984):

> Through its London-based computers, IRIS analyses massive amounts of information on the activities of governments and the political, social and economic status of countries. The international advisory panel for the organization includes a former British prime minister, an ex-president of the World Bank, and others with privileged access to information. IRIS's computers monitor information published and broadcast from all sources in building its pictures of the state of national economies. The level of information collected in IRIS's computers is of a higher order than it is possible for individuals ever to acquire. And entry to that information storehouse is denied unless the subscriber pays a $25,000-a-year admission fee. Subscribers are, not surprisingly, corporate entities – institutions in commercial and banking fields, large industrial companies and financial and insurance groups, as well as central banks and government agencies. The point about organizations like IRIS is that not only do they have a formidable capacity to acquire knowledge about technology and many other matters, but they use computers to turn that information to the advantage of their subscribers.

The implications of this are discussed later, but there is no doubt that the product which the information bankers buy and sell is as valuable as currency, and just as vulnerable to electronic piracy and theft. And theft doesn't even need a computer, because – in addition to hacking, sabotage, and computer fraud – a more traditional form of piracy has emerged, known as 'signals theft', which involves stealing information direct from the airwaves. And all this requires is a television aerial.

Signals theft

> Signals injected into space half a world away can be captured on anybody's rooftop and exploited in a new kind of spider's web – that of cable television.
>
> (Michael Freegard, UK Performing Right Society)

Stealing information off the airwaves, while it is being broadcast, is a new form of piracy which involves commercial organizations and even governments. A common example of this is the theft of another country's television programmes. For instance, Ian Reinecke gives a telling account of how one famous cable-television network got started:

> One of the pioneers, Ted Rogers, head of the cable-television conglomerate in North America that bears his name, began business by erecting a simple television antenna just across the border in Canada from the then-new television stations in the United States. The antenna received the programmes from those stations, and Rogers went around his neighbours and offered, for a price, to run a cable from his antenna to their television sets. The American operators were impotent to prevent money being made from their broadcasts, without any profits flowing back to them. That background of piracy and *laissez-faire* has characterized the later history of cable systems.[6]

It was certainly the case in Europe, when the first cable networks began to establish themselves in the early 1970s. They were so hungry for material that it became common practice for companies in Belgium, Ireland, and Holland to pirate British television broadcasts from across the Channel or Irish Sea, and relay them to their subscribers.[7] It became possible, for example, for the respectable citizens of Antwerp to pirate three Dutch television stations, two French ones, BBC-2, the ITV programmes from Anglia or Southern Television, and ZDF from West Germany – at the touch of a button.

In such cases, the question of fees or royalties is ignored, the advertisers on the commercial channels are delighted to reach a wider audience, and there is very little the broadcast companies can do about it. Under UK copyright law they could take legal action only in the country concerned, and when the Performing Right Society brought a test case against the cable pirates in Dublin in 1975 they found that British television was not protected in the Irish Republic.

The British barrister Geoffrey Robertson has described satellite broadcasting as 'the greatest invention for the legal profession since legal aid':

> When Air Canada advertised recently on Russian television, the signals from the Soviet satellite, Gorizant, were picked up in Holland and relayed through its cable system. Dutch viewers saw advertisements for a Canadian airline on a Russian television network. In cases of libel or breach of copyright who do you sue? How do you sue?[8]

The situation is compounded right on down the line, because the cable television networks, in turn, are also having their programs stolen. For instance, the New Jersey seven (see the start of this chapter) were not the only pirates in their particular neighbourhood. A survey carried out in 1984 showed that just under 5 per cent of people living along the cable routes in New Jersey were illegally plugged into the system; and a similar survey carried out in Texas the previous year showed almost identical figures.[9] David Schreff of Showtime Entertainments estimates that the cable industry is losing $392 million a year from signals theft, and the figure is bound to grow as the networks spread.

Like the computer networks, cable television is open to malicious attacks. In 1984 the French pay-television channel, Canal Plus, was nearly bankrupted by a teenager in Provence, who opened up their signal decoder, worked out the circuit, and published the blueprint in a national newspaper. As a result, the company was forced to issue every subscriber with a new, more expensive device and recorded devastating losses in its first six months of operation.

The advent of DBS (Direct Broadcast by Satellite) has confused the situation still further, because there is no control of who receives the programs. Anyone with a dish aerial can pick up the transmission, virtually anywhere. In one of the most bizarre cases so far, the government of Indonesia has recently begun stealing commercial data from a US space satellite.

Landsat IV was the latest in a series of earth resources satellites, originally launched in 1972. Their surveys of rock formations, mineral deposits, and agricultural patterns have proved invaluable, especially to developing countries, and many Third World governments buy the data from the operating company, Eosat. But in 1984 the Indonesians refused to pay the annual fee of $600,000 (£414,000), though they continued to download the data from satellite dishes on the rooftops of Jakarta. The transmissions were switched off while the satellite was in orbit over the country, but they had to be turned on again over Bangkok (for the Thai government) and Darwin (for the Australians). The technicians of the Indonesian Institute of Aeronautics and Space, who were originally trained by Eosat, found they could pick up the signals quite easily from both directions.[10]

Once again, there was little the Americans could do. They did not want to end their close scientific co-operation – NASA had already launched three Indonesian satellites – so they let the matter go. From the Indonesian point of view, the argument was simple. The Americans might claim to have copyright on the satellite pictures, but it was their country they were photographing.

'Tiger teams' and secret crime

> There are just too many people with access to secret information. When you can get the whole Library of Congress on a machine smaller than a dining-room table, and it's full of classified information, it becomes a tempting target.
> (Donald C. Latham, US Deputy Under-Secretary of Defense)

It is difficult to grasp the scale of network piracy because of the openly acknowledged conspiracy by the authorities to suppress the facts. For instance, it is not considered 'in the public interest' to reveal the extent of computer fraud, the criminals are almost never prosecuted, and banks and government departments deny it even happens.

'Foul play on computers is all too often swept under the carpet,' according to the UK magazine *Which Computer?*. 'The fear of bad publicity from revelations in court and a media campaign about how the fraud was allowed to happen at all usually overshadows a criminal prosecution.'

In 1984, according to the UK Audit Commission, 943 companies notified seventy-seven cases of computer fraud, resulting in a loss of £1 million. Independent authorities, on the other hand, put the figure in excess of £2.5 million. But this represents only the cases which, for some reason or other, were too public to deny. A more realistic figure can be deduced from the fact that in 1985 the four major UK clearing banks allocated £85 million to compensate for losses from computer fraud. And that represents only one sector of the financial system in one country. Some experts estimate the world-wide losses for 1985 at around $730 million, and they are rising rapidly.

The US government has passed a law making it illegal not to report such crimes, but unless the victims are willing to provide the evidence it is impossible to enforce, and the maximum fine is only $5,000. So it is reasonable to assume that the same situation applies there.

If one adds in the loss of royalties by signals theft, the damage done by computer hackers, and the frauds committed on insurance houses, the stock market, government departments, and the thousands of public and private companies in business and industry throughout the western world, the total must be staggering. It is not surprising that journalists have called it 'the crime of the 1980s'. There are two aspects to this assault on the electronic network: the enthusiastic amateurs, like the New Jersey seven, testing and probing the system from the outside; and the sophisticated professional attacks from within, by the technicians and computer programmers themselves.

The UK security expert Dr Ken Wong estimates that 63 per cent of computer fraud involves bank employees taking money out of accounts, speculating with fund money on the foreign exchange market, creating overdrafts for imaginary customers, paying off their own credit-card debts, or illegally transferring money from one fund to another.

'The problem', says Adrian Norman of the British Computer Society,

> is that now there are employees with low levels of seniority who have access to information which previously was in the hands of only the financial director and very senior executives. The situation has democratized white-collar crime.[11]

None of them are 'criminals' in the traditional sense; they defy the usual economic and social assumptions. They are the élite, predominantly white, privileged, middle-class schoolchildren and executives. Like the crimes they commit, they are a new social phenomenon, a product of the network itself.

But there is another enemy, capable of more damage than all the others combined and of deep concern to the highest levels of government. To put it bluntly, if the New Jersey seven could get into the Pentagon files, so could a Soviet agent. If schoolboys could guess the passwords, then a computer in the basement of a Communist embassy or trade mission could number-crunch its way through every possible combination. It is believed that in 1981 Soviet scientists working in Eastern Europe twice managed to break into major western computer networks, and it has probably happened many times before and since.

'I'm sure there have been many attempts,' admitted Donald C.

Latham, the Pentagon's chief security expert. 'It is not surprising, as there has been an incredible growth of classified information stored in computers – and there's just too many people with access to secret information.'[12] It is the kind of thought that keeps the head of the CIA awake at nights.

The US government has been well aware of the risks since the early 1970s, when it set up covert groups of experts, code-named 'Tiger teams', who were instructed to test the security of Defense Department computers. The system then in use, called Multic, was designed to check an individual's password before deciding what level of access they were allowed. But it was neatly outsmarted by one of the 'Tigers', a USAF major called Roger Schell, who wrote a special program which he fed into the system.

It looked just like a part of the operating system, so that anyone phoning in assumed they were speaking to the computer and politely gave it their password. The program then pretended something had gone wrong and handed them over to the real computer, which went through the same routine again. The user shrugged it off as a minor glitch, and Major Schell had another password to add to his collection.

He tried them out, one at a time, and within a week he had worked his way into the inner sanctum and was reading the most sensitive information in the nation's archives.[13] Needless to say, the system was changed, and has been regularly checked and tightened since.

Like the publishers and record companies, the video industry and software manufacturers, the networks have fought back in every way they could to make the system more secure. It was obvious that information in transit was as vulnerable as information stored on vinyl or paper; and the telephone, originally designed as the first truly open means of communication, needed to be protected by its own internal 'gates' and 'barriers' – and, if necessary, sealed off entirely from all but the privileged few. With so much at stake and public money available, electronic security became a boom industry.

By 1985, according to the New York research company Frost & Sullivan, the market for devices to prevent hacking, the illegal use of telephones, and the theft of software was worth $741.13 million and was expected to rise to $1.5 billion by 1990. Of this enormous sum, it is estimated that 95 per cent is spent on the security of computer networks.

Part three
The counter-attack

13

The battle of the machines

Manufacturers who find that new technology is making their products unwanted often think the best solution is to get it banned or taxed out of existence.

(Adrian Berry, in *Daily Telegraph*)

The first and most obvious response to piracy was a direct frontal attack – to ban the machines which made it possible, disarm the brigands, and restore the status quo. The problem was so serious it was even suggested that the use of the new technology should be restricted by law, or cautiously licensed, like firearms and drugs. But like many of the 'solutions' to piracy, this was to prove more difficult to implement than at first appeared.

In the case of photocopiers and computers it was impossible to ban the machine outright, because they had a perfectly legitimate function. It would have been like trying to ban cameras or carbon paper. But video and tape-recorders were different. They were designed as recording machines and had to be *adapted* to perform a copying function, if only by being plugged into each other. They were intended for home use, as an extension of cameras and microphones, or for playing pre-recorded material, like a gramophone – not *specifically* for duplication.

Yet this was exactly what they were being used for, and every new development introduced by the manufacturers was designed to make it easier. Their advertisements were actually encouraging people to become pirates, as if they were a party to the conspiracy. At the very least they were accessories to the fact. The line had to be drawn somewhere; and if anything was to be done to stem the flood of piracy, it was here, in the industry's own backyard, that the battle had to begin. But the legal system was as baffled by the new phenomenon as everyone else. The laws did not take into account the possibility of students printing their own textbooks or a $20 million Hollywood movie being simultaneously duplicated in 20 million homes. There were no precedents for such things. It was not even certain whether they were crimes.

Piracy was undermining not only social and economic concepts, but the law itself. It even called in question the definition of words like 'ownership' and 'theft'. If the legal system was to have any relevance, it had to absorb the implications of electronic technology, rethink its assumptions, and redefine its role for the future. So the test cases which followed were to have far-reaching effects.

In the United States the attempt to halt the advance of technology began in 1981, with the Betamax case, which decided, for the first time, what the video recorder could or could not be used for.

The Betamax case

Only 4 per cent of US homes had video recorders at the time, but it was already clear that their most popular use was for recording films off television. This outflanked the whole movie distribution system, and the Betamax case was brought by Universal City Studios (who objected to their films being taped) against the Sony Corporation of America (who provided most of the equipment for doing it).

The first round went to Sony when a California district court ruled that home taping was a 'fair use' of the equipment, and there was therefore no case to answer.

Universal then took the case to the Ninth Circuit Court of Appeals, which flatly reversed the decision. The court decided that it was not 'fair use', but the outright theft of copyright material. Furthermore, Sony were guilty of encouraging the practice by the sale of their machines. This produced a storm of protest from the retail industry.

'In my opinion,' said George Atkinson, president of Video Station, a chain of 335 video stores around Los Angeles, 'I think the judges paid one too many visits to Disneyland.'[1]

Sony then appealed to the Supreme Court, which again reversed the decision. Under US law, it was finally decided, this form of non-commercial copying was *not* an infringement of copyright. It was a narrow decision, of just five votes to four, but it established two clear facts: that home taping and all other domestic uses of the new technology were legitimate and – perhaps more importantly – that Sony were not guilty of condoning any infringement simply by selling the equipment.

'There is no precedent in the law of copyright', said Judge Stevens, 'for the imposition of vicarious liability.'

The manufacturer of tape-recorders was not responsible for what was recorded, any more than the gunsmith was responsible for an armed hold-up. To paraphrase the famous argument of the US gun lobby, 'It's not recorders that pirate material, it's people.'

But the Betamax case was not all it seemed, and the background is revealing. In fact, the legal battle masked a fierce marketing battle between two rival technologies: videotape and the video disc.

Since 1976 the film industry, with Universal and Disney Studios in the lead, had been selling a system based on permanently pressed discs and the proprietary equipment to play it on. But they were losing the battle, and the public clearly preferred the reusable tape cassette, produced by Sony. Universal were all in favour of video recorders. They were well aware of their potential and had as much to gain as Sony. It was just that, like many before them, they had backed the wrong standard; and the case fits comfortably on the shelves of law libraries alongside Edison's frustrated attempts to suppress the phonographic disc, Marconi's failure to monopolize wireless, and AT&T's effort to throttle the early US radio networks.

The film industry has played an ambiguous role since then, and has often been suspected of working both sides of the video street. The legal challenge was taken up by the music business.

The Toshiba case

The 'vicarious liability' ruling of the US Supreme Court made it difficult to attack the manufacturers in the United States. But in Europe, and especially the UK, it was still very much an open question. The opening shots in the battle had been fired the year before, in the summer of 1980, when the BPI (British Phonographic Industry) took the Japanese firm Toshiba to court.

Toshiba had just introduced a £190 portable cassette recorder, the RT 85605, which was advertised as having two microphones, 'so it records in stereo from the FM waveband, turntable, or live music.'

According to Koji Hase, marketing manager for Toshiba (UK), the advertisement was simply a means of 'explaining the recorder's function'. According to the counsel for BPI, it was an incitement to commit an illegal act – an act, moreover, that was responsible for the current slump in the record industry.

The BPI was to repeat this rather ambiguous claim in later cases, but there was no doubting the facts. If there were no tape-recorders there would be no home taping. The judge found for the plaintiff, and Toshiba were forced to alter the offending words.[2] In other words, it was all right for the gunsmith to sell guns, provided he wasn't too specific about how to use them.

The industry had won its point in law, but this brought little comfort, because recorders of all kinds continued to flood the market. The advertising material was carefully vetted, and there were no invitations to pirate records or radio programmes. But everybody did it; it was what recorders were for.

The BPI needed to attack a specific machine – an instrument that was unambiguously designed for piracy – and get it banned on the grounds that *the mechanism itself* was illegal. The next development in recorder design seemed to provide the perfect opportunity, because both sides were well aware of what that would be – a commercial version of the pirate's own machine, the tape-to-tape cassette copier.

The Amstrad case

Amstrad must have known they were sailing close to the wind when they launched their new high-speed twin-deck cassette recorder on the UK market, because on each machine they fixed a discreet notice that read, 'The recording and playback of certain material may only be possible by permission. Please refer to the Copyright Act 1956 and the Performers Protection Acts 1958 and 1972.' It could hardly be called an incitement to piracy, but the BPI were determined to get Amstrad to court, so they wrote to eleven leading electrical retailers warning them that the machines might be illegal, and selling them could be an offence.

This left Amstrad with no alternative but to sue. So, ironically, it was BPI who found themselves the defendants in High Court action before Mr Justice Whitford in June 1985. Stranger still, it was the defendants who opened the case because, as Mr Sydney Kentridge QC explained, it was up to Amstrad Consumer Electronics to prove they had acted within the law, before they could obtain a declaration.

Kentridge argued that the printed warnings were totally inadequate. The decks were sold without a microphone and could be intended for *no other purpose* than to copy copyright tapes. In other words, the machines, by their very existence, were an incitement to piracy.

Anthony Grabiner, for the defending plaintiffs, begged to differ. There was nothing illegal in providing people with a system that recorded from one cassette to another at twice the normal speed. He pointed out that the BPI had already tried to block Amstrad's advertising by complaining to the IBA and the Advertising Standards Authority, and that both had turned them down. Amstrad had already sold 25,000 decks, and he claimed that they were fully entitled to go on doing so.

But the judge found against Amstrad, declaring that the marketing of such a product amounted to 'authorization of copyright infringement', which placed Amstrad in 'a position of joint wrongdoing' with any hometaper. So the 'vicarious liability' argument, which had been dismissed in the USA, was now acceptable in the UK. However, the judge, stopped short of criminalizing the machine itself. It was the marketing, the way it was sold – in other words, the *words* – which were once again at fault.

The BPI put a brave face on it. 'It might be difficult to sell unaltered machines to a wider public,' said Patrick Isherwood, the BPI's legal adviser. 'Each machine will now have to be accompanied by adequate warning notices – notices so explicit that they are likely to make the machines unattractive to retailers.'[3]

The gunsmith could sell guns, but only with strict instructions to his customers not to use them. It was a wholly unrealistic proposition. As everyone knows, twin-cassette decks proved as attractive to retailers as they did to the public. Dozens of makes and designs appeared on the market, and whatever the label said, every one of them was used to copy tapes.

If the law was ineffective in such an obvious case, it seemed unlikely to halt, or even slow down, the growth of this technology. If the courts in Britain and the USA came to such different conclusions, what hope was there for international sanctions? And how could one possibly control the sale of copiers and recorders in the Third World?

It seemed that the law should concentrate on what it did best, in defining the crimes of piracy, prosecuting the more blatant wrong-doers, and licensing the righteous. The battle would have to be carried into the enemy camp by other means. For instance, if the machines could not be banned, could they be defeated on their own terms? If piracy was a technological problem, was there a technological solution? Was it beyond the ingenuity of scientists to produce records that couldn't be taped, and tapes that couldn't be duplicated?

This is a question as old as counterfeiting itself. Every generation has had to develop methods of detecting or preventing forgery, and we are better equipped to do it than our predecessors. With all the resources at our disposal, surely we could *invent* our way out of the situation? It was a natural enough question, but electronic piracy has unique characteristics, and the search for countermeasures was to take some unusual twists and turns.

14

The spoilers

Manufacturers should take care to protect their music, video, and software. If they don't, they shouldn't go to court to complain.
(Andrew True, Legal Technology Group)

The oldest form of counterfeiting – the forging of money – has been regarded as serious a crime as treason and murder, and still carries the death penalty in many countries. To prevent it, coins were designed to an exact weight with intricate patterns and milled edges that were difficult to copy; and when banknotes appeared, a battery of new devices, from watermarks and metal strips to special inks, were used to make them almost impossible to imitate. In the same way, efforts have been made to frustrate the modern pirates by making the product as difficult as possible to counterfeit.

The music industry was the first to make use of this 'banknote defence'. From the 1960s onwards, records have been produced with elaborate packaging and give-away booklets and posters, or pressed from coloured vinyl incorporating patterns or photographs. The technique is reasonably effective, and it is rare to find counterfeit versions of these 'one-off' specials – though it is still possible to buy cheap pirate tapes of them, without the trimmings and special effects.

In 1981 the first 'watermark' for records was produced by the Californian firm Pik Discs, in collaboration with A&M Records, consisting of an image etched on the surface of the LP by a laser. It does not affect the tracks, which are 50 to 70 microns (millionths of a metre) deep, because the pattern is cut to a depth of only 2 microns, producing a shimmering interference pattern, similar to the surface of a compact disc. This technique was first used on an album by the New Zealand rock group Split Enz and one by Styx, but it has proved too expensive to be adopted generally. Although it has since been used on other records, they are likely to become collector's items.[1]

Other forms of media have found it difficult to adopt the 'banknote defence', because their products – audio tapes, video cassettes, and computer discs – are sold as *blanks*, as well as in pre-recorded form. Unlike records, these are turned out in vast quantities by independent manufacturers, and, apart from the label, pre-recorded music cassettes are identical to the blanks a pirate could buy in any shop.

However, the technique was eventually tried out on video cassettes in August 1984, when Steven Bernard of RCA/Columbia announced that the film *Tootsie* would be released in a distinctive, bright red box with the company logos etched on the window over the tape. This made the genuine product easy to identify, provided you knew what it was supposed to look like in the first place. Without that vital bit of information, the customers were likely to buy any form of packaging that was well enough produced, in mistake for the real thing.

If $10 notes came in a variety of different designs, it would be impossible to tell the real from the fake. Anything designed to prevent counterfeiting must, like banknotes, be universally recognized. What was needed was a label of some kind that was easy to spot, cheap to produce, and impossible to copy. The most promising device came, as one might have expected, from the people who make dollar bills. In the early 1980s the American Banknote Co., which provides paper currency for half the countries in the world, decided to develop an unforgeable label that would prevent products – any products – from being counterfeited. It took the form of a hologram.

The traditional hologram captures the pattern of light waves from an object on a glass photographic plate, so that when a laser is shone through it from behind the light waves resume their course and the object 'reappears' in space. These are very expensive to make, but it is now possible to produce a cheaper and more robust version by embossing the pattern on metal foil. The cloudy swirls of the original plate are reproduced as fine ridges on 0.003 mm foil, which is then sealed in plastic for protection. The three-dimensional effect is not as dramatic, but they work under normal light conditions, and without the original hologram they are impossible to forge.

The system had first been developed by engineers at Hologonics and Holotron, two West Coast firms which had pioneered holography in the early 1970s and had since gone out of business. The American Banknote Co. bought up their patents. They also bought up Eidetic Images of California to obtain the services of Dr Ken Haynes, one of the world's leading experts in optics, and a firm in Virginia called Dominion Foils, which manufactured the necessary ultra-thin aluminium sheets – and in 1982 they went into business.

The idea was an immediate success. Among their first customers were MasterCard and Visa. Shimmering little images no bigger than postage stamps began appearing on plastic money and security badges around the world, and others began to realize their potential.

The Sultanate of Brunei became the first country in the world to have a hologram (showing a brightly coloured mosque) on its passports. And the US publishing company Zebra placed an order for 2 million a year to incorporate in the covers of their books, though curiously enough this was not designed to prevent piracy. The hologram they chose was a hearts-and-flowers design of a couple kissing, intended to make their range of romantic novels, with titles like *Stolen Ecstasy* and *Rapture's Tempest*, more attractive to readers.

By 1985 the American Banknote Co. and their subsidiaries had sold over 300 million of them. Firms using slightly different techniques had begun manufacturing embossed holograms in Europe. It may be some time before we see the trade mark of major manufacturers in holographic form on all their products, but the option is now there. A simple device is now available, for a few pence each, which can be welded to the surface of a video cassette or floppy disk so that it cannot be tampered with or counterfeited.

Or so it would seem. But plastic can be dissolved, moulds can be made, patterns can be duplicated. Who is to say that some day a pirate consortium might not decide to invest in a £200,000 Holo-copier machine, and go into business for themselves?

That chapter in the story has yet to be written. But in the meantime even more unusual forms of labelling are being developed, including one that was recently launched by the Cardiff-based firm BioTechnica, which depends on *genetic coding*. This involves putting a smear of animal tissue, including its unique strands of DNA, on each product. A marker of this sort would be impossible to counterfeit, and it is estimated that the chances of a pirate even identifying which organism it came from, let alone which part of the DNA chain was used, would be about '1 × 10 to the power of 60 against'.

'The beauty of the system', said Dr Peter McDougall, 'is that we can mark things overtly – on a tag, say – or covertly, with a small bio-dot hidden somewhere on the product.'

There is no doubt that it is now possible to distinguish the original from a copy in such a way that makes the counterfeiter's job extremely difficult, and provides unambiguous proof when cases come to court. But separating true from false is only the beginning of the story, because the more exotic the technology, the less likely the customers are to recognize it. It is easy enough to hold a banknote up to the light to check the watermark, it is but somewhat optimistic to expect people to identify a genetic code. Always assuming that the customers actually care – for the truth is that most of them are well aware (from the price if nothing else) of what they are buying, and have no scruples about it. Most pirate copies of tapes and books make no pretence to being legitimate; their smudged print and labels typed on cheap coloured card advertise their origins.

If anti-counterfeiting devices are an essential step in protecting copyright, they are still only a skirmish in the overall war against piracy. The main battle was, and is, to prevent the mass production of cheap, substandard copies.

High-pitched whistles and invisible ink

The first line of defence against this form of piracy must be at the point where the copy is made. Some way had to be found to sabotage the copying process itself. So, for the last couple of decades, the hunt has been on for the elusive 'spoiler', a system or device which would make magnetic tape, records, or paper impossible to copy, or produce such a distorted version of the original that it was useless. A device of this sort, if it was generally accepted and widely enough used, would save the industry concerned millions and earn the inventor a fortune.

If this proved impossible, it was necessary to make the copy somehow *traceable*, so that the pirates could be tracked down. In other words, the original products – each individual film print or document – needed to be coded in some way so that the source of any leaks could be established. And if possible (though this was an optimistic hope) each individual copying machine should leave a distinguishing mark, so that it too could be identified later.

These were the objectives that the recording and information industries set themselves in the early 1970s, and the pursuit of them has taken some curious twists and turns. Each medium in turn – audio, video, print, and computer software – has exploited its own particular technology, and the search for the 'perfect spoiler' has attracted a host of private inventors. The strategy was simple enough, and the rewards were obvious; but not all the problems had answers, and some answers produced even more problems.

The invention of pirate-proof paper was a case in point. A good photocopy depends on the contrast between the lettering and the background of the original, and the obvious way to sabotage the process is to use very dark paper or very pale ink. Anyone who has tried to copy coloured paper knows what a mess it makes. But the text is usually still legible, and to be completely copy-proof the original would need to be virtually black.

The answer eventually turned up, like so many inventions, as the result of an accident. Two Canadians, Norman Gardiner, a Toronto advertising executive, and Michael Voticky, a Montreal furrier, had spent five years experimenting with different treatments of paper. 'We tried everything,' said Gardiner, 'in an effort to keep the fine line between making the original legible and preventing the machines reading it.'

Then one day in 1985 they accidentally spilled some red dyes on a sheet of paper, and found they had discovered the answer. Like most photographic processes, copiers are more sensitive to the red end of the spectrum than the blue, and this particular colour so excited the machine that it obliterated the page with carbon dust, blacking out everything that was written or drawn on it. Gardiner and Voticky patented the discovery and now produce a range of copy-proof papers, from a shade of pink, that obscures normal typing, to burgundy, which wipes out anything.[2]

They found what they were looking for, and copy-proof paper is now available, but does it really solve the problem? It is certainly of interest to security officers as a way of preventing the leaks of confidential documents and state secrets. But these sorts of document are already numbered and coded in such a way that they are easily traceable. The recent leaks of Cabinet documents in the UK, for instance, were rapidly identified in this way.

The effects on piracy in general are problematical. It is unlikely that publishers will start printing burgundy books, and a world full of pink paper, though it has its attractions, is rather improbable. The problem of finding a technical solution to piracy is one of scale. It is easy to control the distribution of a few papers, or the master copy of a film or recording, but piracy feeds off mass media. It is a form of mass communication, and any effective spoiler system has to be mass produced to work on everyday equipment, automatically everywhere.

In audio piracy the search has concentrated on the legendary 'high-pitched whistle'. The idea has been discovered, tested, and discarded so many times it has achieved an almost mythical status. Like the fuelless car or the perpetual motion machine, every generation has an urge to to reinvent it for itself.

One of the earliest examples was a system developed and patented by an engineer of the Beatles' firm, Apple Records, in 1969. His simple and apparently foolproof idea was to include an inaudibly high-frequency signal, behind the music, which could not be heard when the record was played, but became painfully obvious when it was recorded. The whistle would have to be above the 20 Hz to 20,000 Hz range of audible sound and was intended to 'beat' against the inaudibly high-pitched bias signal used on all tape-recorders – producing a loud audible whistle.

The first problem they came up against was that such high frequencies required very fine grooves, which were difficult to print on the surface during manufacture and easily damaged. In fact, the average low-fi stylus simply gouged them out. On the other hand, if the equipment was sensitive enough, and the pick-up light enough to track it, the ultrasound would probably burn out the speaker coils and drive the neighbourhood dogs crazy.

Even if it worked, and the record was impossible to re-record, there would be a storm of protest from people like radio producers and disc-jockeys, who tape their programmes beforehand. Indeed, there has been just such an outcry, with DJs threatening not to give records airtime, every time the idea has been raised. Quite apart from this, electronics manufacturers have frequently announced that appropriate filtering devices were easy to design, and would be put on the market as soon as a spoiler was introduced.

But the problem was too tempting to leave alone, and in 1978 the BPI commissioned the Wolfson Unit at Southampton University to reinvestigate the possibilities. After £10,000 of research they were told, yet again, that it would not work. Or, as the researchers' report put it more diplomatically, 'It is possible to introduce a tone on to a tape or cassette, but the process does slightly impair the quality of the product'.[3]

However, it is unwise to predict that anything is impossible, and the search goes on. The latest investigations involve two ingenious developments. The first is a spoiler system that fluctuates randomly, so it *cannot* be filtered out;[4] the other does away with high frequencies altogether and all the problems associated with them.

Research carried out by the UK firm Design Electronics shows that it might be possible to introduce a spoiler signal at 16kHz, well within audible range and easy to print on an LP. Unfortunately the signal cannot be added to tape cassettes; and when challenged on this, managing director Gerry Bron had a simple solution – the record companies should stop producing them. As for the DJs, they could have special records made for them![5]

The record companies were not impressed. In fact, it is difficult to find anyone in the music business who still believes in a technological solution to piracy. It has generally, if reluctantly, been agreed that spoilers have inherent contradictions, and an electronic 'arms race' would be self-defeating. Besides, music companies have found a more effective means of fighting piracy through the use of legal and political sanctions and the kind of covert operations we describe in later chapters.

The perfect spoiler

> Compare it to the motor industry – they don't allow people to bring
> out cars which don't need petrol. They'll give them twenty million
> to go and sit on a desert island instead.
>
> (Philip Demonti, security consultant)

While the idea of an audio spoiler seems like whistling in the wind,
the video spoiler has fared much better. The reason for this is that
the 'carrier' signals on a video are more complex, and therefore easier
to sabotage. The word 'video' actually refers to this background
information, which includes instructions on how to assemble the
pictures and line them up on the screen.

The most vulnerable of these signals is the automatic gain control,
which keeps the picture steady and prevents it fading. This is
broadcast, along with all the other information, and arrives as a
series of weak negative pulses which your television set locks on to.
However, in order to record on to videotape these signals have to be
converted into strong, positive pulses. This is done by a kind of
amplifier, called a wave shaper, which is built into all video
recorders. Without them, the machines could not record television
programmes.

Pre-recorded cassettes, of course, carry the same negative pulses.
But if, in addition to these, you add a series of strong, positive
pulses, it has an interesting effect. The television set ignores them,
and plays the video in the normal way. But if the signals were fed
into another tape-recorder, the positive pulses would be boosted still
further, and the gain control would be fooled into reducing the
signal strength. The picture would fade away, and the copy would
be useless.

A system like this was developed in the early 1970s, and it worked
perfectly. The signal was easy to apply, was difficult to filter out, and
made it impossible to copy a video cassette from one recorder to
another. To all intents and purposes, it was the perfect spoiler,
which could have saved the industry millions.

Yet it never went into production and was never used – and for an
interesting reason. In 1976, with uncanny foresight, Sony had
bought up all the rights and patents to the invention.[6] People
wondered at the time what a manufacturer of television sets wanted
with a system that made them unworkable, but the answer was
simple. They didn't want anyone else to use it, and have sat on the
idea ever since. The film and video trade may be frustrated, but
then Sony don't make films.

Ralph Waldo Emerson said that if you build a better mousetrap
the world will beat a path to your door. Sometimes it will.

Sometimes they just come and take it away. Many variations of the idea were tried, but the more they departed from the Sony patent the less effective they proved.

In July 1984 the Swiss company Haute Sécurité (HSV) announced a new anti-piracy system based on coding the recorded signal.[7] IFPI and FACT took an interest at the time, but like all such systems it required an expensive decoder on the television sets, which made it economically unattractive.

A few months later the Hampshire firm of Supavision unveiled another encoding system, this time intended to identify the source of the piracy. TVS (Tape Verification System) did not interfere with the audio or visual signals, but carried the day, date, and batch number of every cassette.[8] By using Supavision's equipment, pirate tapes could be immediately identified when produced as evidence at a trial. Up till then, the courts had relied on expert analysis of the 'degradation' of the tape signal, which was often refuted by the defence. TVS left no doubt about it and was just as useful in other circumstances as a means of telling whether police tapes had been edited or tampered with.

But the development of a spoiler was as far away as ever. The most promising was a close cousin of the Sony spoiler, which attacked another part of the 'carrier' wave, called the synch pulse. The synch pulse is a timing device which ensures that you receive exactly twenty-five pictures a second and reverses the scan at the top and bottom of the screen. In video recorders they turn the spinning helical scanners on and off to prevent them oscillating.

The effect is to produce two black bars across the picture, which are normally out of sight at the top and bottom of the screen. But if you delay the signal between two video recorders, and the pulses arrive out of synch, two more bars appear on the screen, then four, then eight (depending on how many times it is copied) until the picture is obliterated.

Spoilers like these, with names like Copyguard and Macrovision, began to appear on the US market. Unfortunately Copyguard was designed for United States television and failed to work on the PAL (Phase Alternated Line) system used in most other countries. To add insult to injury, alongside the advertisements for Copyguard-protected products in the trade magazines, there were advertisements for debugging kits to unscramble the system.

Macrovision initially fared little better. The system was first applied, in 1985, to the film *Cotton Club*, when it was released on VHS cassettes by Embassy Pictures. It meant that the video could not be copied on another VHS recorder, but, as the pirates soon discovered, if you copied it on a Betamax machine and then back on to VHS, you got a perfect copy, with its carrier wave and synch pulses intact. Within weeks of its release, illegal cassettes of *Cotton Club* were in circulation, and shortly afterwards a decoding device known as Macrobuster was on sale for £150.

However, the corporate executives decided that even partial protection was better than none. It might not prevent the professional pirates who are prepared to invest in decoding equipment, but it dramatically reduced the losses from amateur back-to-back copying. So a number of companies, including CBS, decided to incorporate protection on their videos. Between 1985 and 1987 about 25 million US video cassettes were protected by Macrovision. Although pirate copies continued to appear, Stewart Till, managing director of CBS/ Fox, estimated that it was responsible for a 15 per cent increase in legitimate sales.[9]

The uncopiable, pirate-proof form of recording seems as far away as ever, though one intriguing possibility still exists. The perfect spoiler system may already have been invented without anyone knowing about it, because, behind the technical confusion and conflict of interests in the industry, there is another, more powerful group of people who monitor this kind of technology and are quite prepared to suppress it if it suits them – the state security organizations. This may sound overdramatic, but departments like the CIA and MI6 have little regard for the laws of copyright, and if you build a better mousetrap the spooks are fully entitled to confiscate it.

The case of the Lamont spoiler showed just how easily, and casually, it happens. Jim Lamont, a Yorkshire television engineer, developed a magnetic spoiler system which he believed could stop the piracy of tapes, videos, and computer data, and even prevent the interception of radio signals. But in January 1984, when he applied for a patent, he received notice under Section 22 of the Patents Act that it was 'information which could be prejudicial to the nation's defences' and must be handed over to the Ministry of Defence.

There was no appeal or argument. Lamont's device was seized, and he was told that even the application must remain secret until the ministry decided what to do with it.[10] Lamont was too furious to keep quiet. 'I just couldn't believe it,' he said. 'I had spent two and a half years designing the system, and it was ready to go into production.'

For once someone was prepared to buck the system, and when the newspapers took up the story, the whole operation was dragged into the light of day. It was admitted that more than 800 of the 40,000 patent applications a year are confiscated like this. Most of them are handed back, but if the Intelligence Services are already using them (or would like to) the inventor is made an offer he cannot refuse, which begins with signing the Official Secrets Act. About one in seven, or roughly 100, of these key inventions are censored every year, to disappear from history like something in Orwell's *Nineteen Eighty-Four*.[11]

Embarrassed by all the publicity, the Ministry of Defence eventually returned the spoiler, with the comment that it was not sensitive enough to interest them. This effectively sabotaged any attempt to market it, though a modified version was later developed for computers. The Lamont case was unusual in that it was handled so clumsily, but it is far from unique. Government's use of copyright to censor information is a widespread phenomenon with disturbing implications, some of which we touch on later. For the present it is worth pointing out that there is more than one form of piracy; and in the confusing world of copyright it can sometimes be difficult to tell the cops from the robbers.

15

The dongles

Anything a scientist can invent, another scientist can uninvent.
(Peter Duffy, FACT, interview)

The records and tape cassettes used on computers are remarkably similar to those used for music and video, but there is one significant difference. They interact with the machine they are played on and actually *control* what it does. A computer disk contains not only 'passive' information, like music or text, but orders to the machine and instructions to report on what it is doing. It can ask questions and decide on different courses of action. It can sense when it is being copied and physically intervene to stop this happening. If an LP could talk to record-players in this way there would be no need for spoilers, and it gives the software manufacturers a head start in devising countermeasures to computer piracy.

The floppy disk has other useful advantages. For instance, the programs are recorded on invisible magnetic tracks, which are divided into sections like the partitions of a filing-cabinet. This allows the designers a number of ways to 'conceal' the information. Instructions can be divided between several sections; the code which signals the beginning and end of each track can be changed; the position of tracks can be shifted, or they can be programmed to wipe themselves out if they are tampered with.

In one form or another, these auto-destruct programs are the most common means of protecting software. The most popular method is to bury secret instructions in the program, which are activated only by the copying process and turn the instructions into gibberish if the user tries to read them on the screen. A more sophisticated version allows the customer to make one back-up copy for their own use, before wiping out key sections of the original. They are then left with two copies, neither of which can be copied without being destroyed.

It seemed like a perfect anti-piracy system; the industry controlled the software, and the software controlled the machines. But as Peter Duffy gloomily remarked, anything a scientist can invent, another scientist can uninvent; and in the early 1980s a range of software appeared on the market whose sole function was to bypass the system.

The program, called a bit map copier, instructed the computer to scan a floppy disk track by track, without activating any instructions, until it had worked out the entire layout. It was then possible to avoid the booby traps and reproduce the original in pristine condition without triggering the security systems. Under trade names such as Locksmith and Copywrite, the bit map copiers enabled computer buffs to duplicate programs at will.[1] For instance, Copy Plus, a £50 copier produced by Apple Software of Milton Keynes, was designed to map a floppy disk in just thirty-five seconds. Anyone could do it.

Other software manufacturers were outraged by this development. Ashley Ward of Intelligence (UK) said that they would lose 70 per cent of their sales without software protection and that the copiers were 'only produced for criminal purposes'. But John Chesney, managing director of Apple Software, was unrepentant. 'I'm against piracy,' he said, 'but the responsibility for this is collective and cannot be laid at my door.'

The idea of collective responsibility in the electronics industry was optimistic, to put it mildly, and the copying devices proliferated.

Bob Hitchcock of Micro Centre, which produced a combined tape and microdrive copier called Interface-3, was blunt about their attitude, saying in 1985:

> Piracy is a load of rubbish. It doesn't affect sales in any way. We've been selling products of this kind for two years and, if anything, it's increased sales. Interface-3 doesn't encourage piracy. After all, when people hear a record, they go out and buy it. Hearing encourages people to buy.[2]

In the face of the evidence, this was a blatant example of special pleading, but the same scepticism was expressed in the United States by Jim Stockford, a contributor to the *Whole Earth Software Catalogue*. 'These software people are not missing much,' he said. 'I do not believe any company is really being ripped off by the use of pirated computer programs.'

To avoid the wrath of their competitors (and possible legal action), some manufacturers produced a curious hybrid, a copier that was itself copy-proof. The Microdriver, produced by the UK firm Mirage, was designed to copy games and other relatively simple programs used on microcomputers. But the programs were recorded in code and could be played back only through another Microdriver.

'If someone bought our device for piracy,' said Mirage director Gerry Bassingthwaite, 'he is wasting his time. He could make as many copies as he wanted, but if the people he sold them to don't have our device, they can't use the programs.'

Since the main threat to this kind of down-market software was from back-to-back copying, this was also a little naïve. Or put another way, anyone who wanted to 'borrow' software or copy their friend's games had only to buy a Microdriver. Every pirate should have one.

As it became obvious that software could not be protected by its own anti-copying instructions, attention turned to other forms of security, from turbo-loaders to colour charts. High-speed loading had been introduced on certain computers, and it was hoped that this would discourage copying because the programs were loaded so fast the signals were scrambled. But it was more of an inconvenience than a protection and, anyway, it did not apply to floppy disks.

Other games manufacturers experimented with codes on their packaging. To prevent people copying their game Jet Set Willy, the Liverpool firm Software Projects sold it with a special colour chart. When the program was loaded, the user was required to type in the colours in the correct sequence to begin the game. In theory it was impossible to run the program without the original packaging to refer to. In practice, of course, it could easily be written down and passed on by hand. Within weeks of the game's release, advertisements appeared in computer magazines offering a means of bypassing the chart to make the copying easier.

Another version was Hewson Consultant's game, Avalon, which contained a security sheet in fugitive ink, invisible to photocopiers. But once again there was nothing to prevent people typing it out in triplicate. Distinctive forms of packaging, include the use of holographic labels, have been tried, but in the DIY world of back-to-back piracy no one is concerned about packaging. It is the contents, the program itself, that they are after.

The most effective new security system was a device called a 'dongle', which made its first appearance in 1982.[3] The dongle was a small card containing a microchip which was plugged into the computer. They were sold with each software program and contained a serial number associated with the particular customer. While the program was running, the computer was instructed to check periodically whether the dongle was in position, and stop if it was not.

Their great advantage was that programs could be tied to a single dongle by giving them code numbers (which the customers knew nothing about) that had to match each other before the program would work. This meant that, however many copies were made, they would work only on one machine. Unlike the spoilers, they provided an individual lock-and-key system for each piece of software, which turned out to be remarkably effective against piracy. Advertisements for dongles with name like Padlock and Copylock began appearing in the trade magazines, and the software houses took a keen interest.

The only drawback was that they cost money. The cheapest version could be turned out for about £1.50, but this was a substantial addition to a micro-computer game that sold for £10 or £15. On the other hand, it was a small proportion of a £200 to £400 word-processing program, and the up-market version of the dongle could include sophisticated cipher keys (like a random number that had to be subtracted from the program to make it work) that enabled the manufacturer to 'license' how many computers could use the software, and even identify a particular user.

For the first time the scientists were ahead of the pirates, with an effective anti-copying device, but it was almost too late. The industry was feeling the backlash from a public who felt that the obsession with security was getting out of hand. There were frequent complaints that copy-protected software was difficult to use. Systems using a 'key' disk, for instance, were often impossible to run on a local network. Above all, customers resented having to pay for these additional security devices, and firms that introduced them tended to suffer a loss in sales.

The leading software manufacturers began to have second thoughts about whole subject. At the Softcom '85 exhibition in Atlanta, Georgia, Seymour Rubenstein of Micropro announced they were dropping protective systems from their new Wordstar 2000 package; and Will Zachman of IDC described them as 'negative features'. 'The users don't want them,' he warned, 'and any company laying plans on the basis of copy protection is heading for disaster.'[4]

It was an astonishing admission – a complete about-face by an industry which, up till then, had fought the pirates every inch of the way and now had the means to defeat them. But, one by one, other firms began to follow suit.

In 1986 the US Software Publishing Corporation removed copy protection from their programs, and Microsoft dropped it from their MSDOS software in the USA on the grounds that their customers 'now understood what is legal and what is illegal copying' (though they retained it for sales in the UK, where presumably the customers were regarded as less responsible!).

Even those firms who stuck to their guns, like the giants Ashton Tate and the Lotus Development Corporation, had their doubts. Adine Deford, a spokesman for Lotus, recently admitted that they were 'worried about the nuisance factor in copy protection'.[5] Yet it was obvious that sooner or later security would reach a point of diminishing returns. Inevitably, at some point a balance had to be struck between the protection of copyright and an

escalating 'technology race' which, like the arms race, would bankrupt everyone.

It was a mass market; the software firms were in business to sell
their programs, and if that involved a certain level of piracy, so be it.
Ironically, it barely interrupted the development of electronic
security, because the industry had discovered a new and vastly more
profitable market.

16

Sealing the system

All communications will be encrypted in a few years. It's a natural
development of the use of computers.
(Fred Weingarten, US National Science Foundation)

Scramblers and ciphers

In previous chapters we have described the attempts to protect
information which is stored on tapes and disks, or as printed text.
But this still leaves the information stored on main-frame computers
or actually *in transit* over the electronic network or airwaves.

In some ways this is the most valuable information of all, because
data banks really are *banks*, and the contents of their vaults are every
bit as valuable as money. But the crucial difference is that in this case
every customer has an electronic key, and they can be entered by
hundreds of people at a time, many thousands of times a day. The
contents are then transmitted over great distances by telephone and
satellite links.

As we described in Chapter 12, this makes them particularly
vulnerable to theft, piracy, eavesdropping, and general misuse.
Since the clients include government and military agencies, financial
institutions, and every kind of business organization − and the
information is not only copyright, but highly classified − it is not
surprising that more effort has gone into protecting this system than
any other form of anti-pirate technology.

In fact, the demand has been so great that it has generated a whole
new service industry of security consultants, who have, in turn,
developed a range of high-tech methods to seal off the system from
intruders. The problem they face is different from other forms of
piracy in that the focus is not on the *reproduction* of material, but on
access to it. Many of the solutions are too complex to describe in
detail, but they all come down to the same basic essentials.

There are two problems in protecting a network. The first is to
ensure that the users are who they say they are. The second is to
disguise the information, whether it is a television broadcast, a
telephone conversation, or the blips of computer data, in such a way
that it cannot be understood by anyone else. In their simplest form,
the solutions to these problems are the password and the scrambler.

There is a wide variety of 'scramblers' now available, mostly in the form of sealed, black-box devices which are connected to either end of a telephone line. They are relatively expensive but, unlike the dongles and devices used to protect commercial products, they are an optional extra. It is up to the individual or company to decide whether their communications are worth protecting.

Some allow you to select your own private code and change it as often as you like. Inmac's Data Scrambler, for instance, offers the user a choice of code formats and passwords from more than 6 million combinations.[1] Others, like the Crypton scrambler, by Black Box, are 'hard wired'. A different code is built into each pair of machines, which are claimed to be impenetrable even by those who know the system's password.[2]

However, words like 'scrambler' and 'code' are confusing, because these devices are actually cipher machines, and there is a significant difference between them.

Scramblers, which have been in use for more than fifty years, were designed to distort the human voice on a telephone line or radio transmission, by altering frequencies and introducing jamming signals or echos that are filtered out at the other end. This works well enough with a continuous, analogue signal like the human voice, but is less effective with information transmitted in the form of pulses. If you listen to short-wave radio, for instance, it is surprising how easily Morse code can cut through the heaviest static. These 'discrete' digital signals (like the letters of a word or the binary numbers used by computers) are easier to disguise as a code or cipher.

Simple codes, such as Morse or the 'secret' messages in children's games, depend on substituting a different letter or symbol for those in the original. Because the substitutions are regular and the text remains intact under its 'disguise', it is relatively easy to break a code. One of the simplest methods makes use of letter frequency – the fact that E is the most commonly used letter in the English language, followed by T, A, O, I, and N. Once you know this, you have only to count the frequency with which the substitutes appear to guess which letters they stand for.

Ciphers, on the other hand, are much more complex. The code can be changed for each letter, sequences can be altered, and the text can be juggled around in a variety of ways according to a mathematical formula known as an algorithm. But that is not all. The way an algorithm works will depend on the key, or password, which the user inserts into the cipher machine along with the message. The recipient, who has the same key, then reverses the process on an identical machine.

The first automated ciphers of this kind were the 'Ultra' machines used by the Germans in the Second World War, and it is ironic that the first computer was invented specifically in order to break them. It seemed an impossible task at the time because the key (and therefore the cipher) was changed every day; but as soon as it was worked out, the radio traffic of the entire Nazi war machine, including the most secret messages from Hitler himself, were easily translated. The story has been told in detail many times, but it is notable that it was electronic piracy – no more, no less – which won the war and launched the computer age in which we live.

The clicking dials and electric relays of the Ultra machines seem primitive by today's standards when the key to a cipher can be changed every few minutes and the algorithms are immensely more complex. But the principle remains the same, and so does its most vulnerable point: the key itself. In order to change it, the new one must be transmitted as part of the message or stored at the receiving end, and if it is discovered it can be used to unlock the whole system.

In 1984 the US National Bureau of Standards announced a new invention which overcame this problem by separating the coding and decoding processes. It was based on a device invented by Dr Whitfield Diffie and Dr Martine Hellman of Stanford University, which used two sets of keys, one to transmit the message and the other to decipher it. They are completely different, and the sender and recipient have no idea what the other's key is.

This means that, if a disgruntled employee of a defence contractor or bank stole the cipher key from their headquarters, they couldn't get back into the system or do any damage. In fact, the company could publish it in the national press and still maintain complete secrecy – which is why it is called the Public Key Cryptosystem (or PKC).[3]

Step by step – in the United States, at least – the networks are being secured. By 1988 all electronic banking in the USA will have to conform to the Data Encryption Standard (DES), a complicated equation devised by IBM, based on a cipher key that is fifty-six digits long, which makes the odds against guessing the key for a particular transaction about 72 billion billion to one! It's impossible even to remember such a figure (deliberately so, because the system is intended to be automatic), so the electronic keys are embedded in microchips; and their role in US business and industry is so sensitive that it is forbidden to export them from the USA, under the US Export Administration Act 1979.

To illustrate how seriously the authorities take these developments, consider what has happened at FORSCOM, the US Army Readiness Command, whose computer is broken into in the film

War Game by a group of teenagers who nearly start the Third World War. To improve the level of security. FORSCOM drew up a specification for the ideal, or 'trusted', computer. Their require- ments for this were so stringent that so far only one machine has been awarded the 'Category A1' status: the Honeywell SCOMP (Secure Communications Processor).

The FORSCOM SCOMP is a masterpiece of paranoia, with eight levels of security classification (from 'mildly secret' to 'not-even-the- President-can-know'), with thirty-four entirely separate categories of information (nuclear, financial, etc.) at each level. It is impossible to gain access to the operating system, so no one can plant a 'Logic Bomb', and the central data bank is entirely sealed off. This electronic Fort Knox is itself surrounded by outer defences which screen any approach to it. The most effective of these is a deeply suspicious modem called Horatius, designed by Steenbeck Systems.[4]

If you wish to contact SCOMP, you can do so only from a licensed terminal which has the correct cipher built into it, and your call is first intercepted by Horatius, which accepts your password and then rings off. It then informs SCOMP that you are calling, so that your security clearance can be checked and Horatius can verify your location and phone number. It then rings you back and only when it is satisfied that you are calling from an authorized terminal will it let you through to carry out your business, in cipher of course, which the computer changes every few seconds.

Sealing the airwaves

Alarm bells have also been ringing in other areas of the electronic net. This was forcibly brought home to the US public when the cable television companies recently began to encode their programmes.

This form of television first became established in 1977 and gradually spread through the country via hundreds of small, local stations. Few had any equipment, let alone production facilities, and they mostly relied on programmes picked up from satellites. But Americans were used to free television and many preferred to buy the dish aerials for themselves rather than pay an expensive subscrip- tion for a landline. By 1985 satellite dishes were selling at a rate of 2,000 a month, and about 1.5 million Americans were bypassing the cable networks and receiving programmes direct from space.

However, the video hackers received an abrupt shock in January 1986, when one of the most popular cable companies, Home Box Office (HBO), began to scramble its signals. Viewers were now forced to buy a $400 decoder to receive them – not to mention the payment of an additional $12.95 a month 'copyright fee'. The Showtime/Movie channel and Ted Turner's news channel both followed suit. The era of free television came to an abrupt halt, and the sale of satellite dishes slumped as people began to think twice about acquiring such an expensive, and apparently useless, status symbol.

Three months later a disgruntled dish salesman struck back by beaming a signal of his own up to the HBO satellite. Because of its comparative strength, it swamped the official transmission (a broadcast of the film *The Snowman and the Falcon*), and viewers from coast to coast saw a pattern of coloured lines and the message: 'Good evening HBO from Captain Midnight. $12.95 a month? No way. (Showtime/Movie Channel beware!).'

The public reacted with a mixture of irritation and amusement, but the broadcast companies took Captain Midnight's warning to heart. One can reasonably predict that future satellites will have their own signals encrypted so that they receive only *authorized* transmissions. However, the scrambler system was a success, and most viewers seemed prepared to pay the toll. Even the sale of satellite dishes began to recover, and the market has been growing steadily ever since.

The system used by HBO and the others is called Video Cipher II, a device which alters the synch pulse in much the same way as a video 'spoiler'. The result is that without a decoder the picture rolls up the screen or slides off sideways, making it intolerable to watch. The system has two additional factors that make it especially effective; the synch pulse is altered in a continuously changing pattern, and the video signal contains instructions to the receiver on how to correct the distortion from moment to moment.

In addition to this, each receiver is identified by a unique number so that the broadcaster can switch an individual set on or off. If the individual has not paid their subscription, a warning can be flashed on the screen, and the service can be reduced to nothing but trailers (to show them what they are missing) and eventually withdrawn until they pay their bills. The system is very difficult to crack. Although there are rumours that a decoder has been developed, none have so far appeared on the market.

Several European companies are now using similar forms of protection for their broadcasts. Filmnet, a channel specializing in feature films, uses a scrambler developed by Matsushita in Japan. Rupert Murdoch's Sky Channel, which is widely pirated by Italian cable companies, uses another US synch scrambler developed by Oak Orion. Filmnet also applies an ingenious bit of psychology, by scrambling the end of each feature, so that pirate viewers never find out what happens! Neither of these methods prevent piracy, and there is a large market in illicit decoders, but the system has increased the companies' revenue by 10 to 15 per cent, which more than justifies their use.

The satellite cable nets were slower to develop in Europe. By mid-1987 only 20,000 satellite dishes had been sold, so video hacking has been less of a problem. This is partly because the overlapping pattern of broadcasting already provides a rich diet of broadcasting, partly because the dishes cost £2,000 or more, and partly because everyone has been holding their breath for the long-awaited DBS, or Direct Broadcast Satellite.

The DBS is intended as a major addition to the global network, using a satellite transmitting at about twenty times the strength of existing ones, which is powerful enough to be picked up by individual households using a receiver no larger than a conventional aerial. Broadcasting on sixteen channels simultaneously to an audience of 150 million, DBS is designed as an alternative to cable television, rather than part of a combined system, and may eventually take over as the main source of public television. It is also intended to have the most sophisticated form of protection against pirates yet devised.

At the time of writing, the first new DBS satellite, ASTRA, is designed to operate by a new transmission system known as MAC, or Multiple Analogue Components, which is easier to encode than the systems now in use – PAL (Phase Alternation Line) in Western Europe, and SECAM (Sequential Couleur à Mémoire) in France and the eastern bloc.

One of the possibilities that MAC opens up is a system that many engineers regard as the ultimate protection against pirates: the full encryption of the video signal itself, rather than simply scrambling the synch pulse. Because MAC transmits the components of each picture separately, it will be possible to cut up each line on the screen and rearrange them to form a meaningless jumble, a method known as 'cut and rotate'. Because MAC transmits in digital sound (another technological first), the instructions to the receiver on how to reassemble the picture would be buried as digital 'words' in the soundtrack – and this, in turn, is easier to do because MAC receivers already incorporate memory circuits to combine their images.

The system represents a new generation of broadcast technology incorporating many of the features appearing elsewhere in the electronic net: the change from analogue to digital forms of information, the breaking of this down into parallels flows (which allows for high-speed multiplexing and multi-tasking activities), and the use of increasingly complex codes and ciphers to protect it.[5]

Yet there is still one enormous loophole that allows the pirates to bypass and defeat the purpose of the exercise. A chain is only as strong as its weakest link; and the weakest link in any form of communication is at the very end of the chain, where the message or television programme is received. To put it bluntly, if pirates with sufficient skill can get inside a decoder and discover its identity number, they can produce hundreds of copies, each of which will receive the signals. And once the signals are broadcast, a satellite has no way of detecting how many counterfeit 'viewers' are watching.

The only way to counter this is for broadcast companies to issue tokens or plastic 'keys' like credit cards to each subscriber, which alone can turn on their set. Unfortunately, this kind of validation is expensive to operate and may, in the long run, be self-defeating. After all, if it is possible to copy a decoder, or the identity of a television set, why not the 'key' that turns them on? In other words, how can you be sure that the listener or viewer is who they say they are?

It is a problem that affects every area of the network, and some ingenious research is now going into solving it.[6]

Who goes there?

> Computers have no doubts, they either believe you or disbelieve you. They don't know how to be suspicious.
> (Larry Bienek, 'The philosophy of machines', 1978)

The Achilles' heel of any network is the point of access, the interface between human beings and the machine. For no matter how complicated you make the ciphers and security systems, there is no way of *guaranteeing* that the person sitting at a terminal is the one entitled to use it. Provided they know the right procedures, and sound convincing enough, anyone will be taken at face value and admitted to the system.

The traditional method of checking an intruder's identity is the password, but hackers have discovered that passwords are subject to very human limitations. In theory, it would take a hacker 12,500 years to go through every combination of a random six-letter password; in fact, they are relatively easy to guess. To make them easy to remember a husband will use his wife's name, and employees will chose their company's initials, the military prefer words like 'valiant' or 'chieftain', and it is astonishing how many people still use 'secret' or 'sesame'. And they nearly all spell them backwards in the optimistic belief that this makes them more secure.

When they are not easy to guess they are easy to find, because people who choose longer or more difficult passwords nearly always write them down, usually on the back of a credit card or a scrap of paper in their wallet.

There again, the system itself can sometimes give the game away. As an experienced hacker remarked in a recent magazine interview, 'If you write a program that asks for a password, the program must know that password. So if you look at the program carefully, you'll find it.'

A more sophisticated version is the numerical password or PIN (Personal Identity Number) which is commonly incorporated on security badges or credit cards in the form of a magnetic strip. Anyone who uses the electronic networks regularly will acquire (and have to remember) a different mathematical identity of this sort for each data bank or bulletin board they wish to enter.[7]

PINs have three major advantages: they have no literary or personal connotations, so they are impossible to guess; they can be much longer, so each individual's is different, and they are easy to code electronically. Like cipher keys, they can be stored on a microchip, so that the user does not have to remember them, or even know what they are. The similar characteristics of dongles, ciphers, and identity codes has led to one of the most significant developments in electronic security: the 'smart card'.

The idea for the 'smart card' was developed in 1974 by a French journalist, Roland Moreno, and was originally designed for cashless shopping in a country whose telephone system was not, at that time, sufficiently reliable for the on-line transfer of money. It was intended to carry a record of your credit limit, which was progressively cancelled out by each purchase, in the same way that telephone credit cards work today. But recent developments in micro-electronics have made it possible to turn them into miniature computers capable of a whole variety of functions.

Microscopic circuits embedded in the plastic can transform a credit card into an electronic cheque-book which carries an 'audit trail' of all the transactions it is used for, adding and subtracting from the owner's account as it goes along. It can contain all your personal details including a whole directory of identity numbers, and for extra security it can be programmed to change them each time they are used. By plugging it into a computer, it can give the machine an equally distinctive set of characteristics, unlock the most complex ciphers, and even be used to change the typeface on programmable typewriters. Its effect on piracy could be dramatic.

'The smart card will virtually eliminate the mass illegal copying that has troubled our industry for so many years,' claims Mike Hall of Electric Software, Cambridge.

From cash dispensing to the protection of software, smart cards were such an obvious solution to the problems of electronic security that large sums were spent on their development. By 1985 a variety of designs were being marketed by Philips and Bull in Europe, Copra in the USA, and Casio in Japan. The first generation carries a 32K microchip, but these will soon be upgraded to a substantial 128K memory; and there is already a rival system, developed by the US firm Drexler Technology, which has no processing power but an astonishing 16-million-bit memory, etched on the surface by laser.

But for all their sophistication the cards still have no means of telling who is using them, any more than a car knows who is driving it. They can be lost or damaged or stolen, and the more information they contain the more valuable they are to a potential thief.

So the advent of smart cards has given new impetus to the search for a foolproof identity check, the final link in the security chain that bridges the gap between deceitful, or forgetful, human beings and the stubborn neutrality of machines. And for the first time an answer seems to be emerging from the study of 'biometrics', the recording and measurement of physical characteristics, such as fingerprints, which are unique to any individual.

Persuading machines to recognize these characteristics is more difficult than one would expect, because the patterns are so complex. For instance, years of research have gone into developing computers that 'understand' human speech, and though voice-activated processors are now a reality, they still cannot distinguish, with any degree of accuracy, between one individual and another. People's voices change from day to day, the pitch and rhythm vary according to their mood, they are affected by such things as colds – and computers are easily fooled by impersonations. But other kinds of measurement are more reliable, and in the last few years a number of biometric devices have been developed.

The US firm Stellar Systems have produced a device which recognizes palm prints to within 97 per cent accuracy. Fingermatrix of New York claim to have achieved 98 per cent accuracy in identifying fingerprints. IBM have come up with the bank manager's dream – a machine that can spot 99 out of 100 forged signatures, by identifying variations in the pressure and speed at which they are written.

It is never wise to make predictions about state-of-the-art technology, but the most likely of these devices to go into mass production is a machine produced by EyeDentify of Oregon, which recognizes the pattern of blood vessels on the retina of a person's eye. The manufacturers of cash dispensers, known in the business as ATMs (Automated Teller Machines), have already expressed interest in the device, which contains a binocular eyepiece, like traditional 'what-the-butler-saw' machines. Users see nothing when they look into it, but peering into the darkness their eyes are scanned by a beam of invisible infra-red light which analyses the pattern and checks it against one stored in the machine or recorded on their smart card.

Retinal scanners are markedly more efficient than other systems, with a failure rate of less than 0.0001 per cent, because the pattern is 'sealed' in. Fingerprints are confused by cuts and abrasions, signatures can vary under emotional stress, and not even a palmist can read dirty hands; but (except for rare medical conditions) your retina remains in pristine condition all your life.

In the long run, however, a more practical (and portable) solution may be the system designed by the UK inventor Joe Rice currently being developed by the British Technology Group. This identifies the pattern of veins on people's wrists or the back of their hands.

The problem with biometrics is that the present machines are large and very expensive. The simplest 'readers' cost about $5,000, and the cheapest version of the EyeDentifier will set you back $7,000. So, for the immediate future, their use will probably be limited to high-security environments or ATM networks. The first smart cards to carry biometric information will probably be produced by the 1990s, but the dream of a computer which recognizes its owner's voice or identifies their fingerprints on the keyboard is still a long way off.

Even so, Joe Rice has no doubts about the future of biometrics. He foresees a time when the reader is small enough to be incorporated in the cards – 'So you will only have to draw it across the back of your hand, and it will know that it's you.'[8]

Rice has already designed a transporter which can be strapped to your wrist and transmits your biometric signature to any security system. It could, for instance, be linked to the ignition system of a car to prevent anyone but the owner driving it away. It could even be used to license firearms.

'We could put vein-pattern readers on rifles which would say "you're one of the people authorized to fire me". In short,' he adds, 'I'm trying to reinvent the key, except that the key will recognize you and no one else.'

If a rifle or car could be protected in this way, so could any other machine. Telephones could be customized so that only certain individuals could dial out or receive incoming calls, and anyone else would be automatically disconnected. Photocopiers could only be turned on by 'authorized' users; and computers, like pet animals, would fail to respond to anyone but their owners. Passwords, PINs, and the whole paraphernalia of electronic security could be replaced by a single biological signature that was impossible to steal, lose, change, forget, counterfeit. It is ironic, after all the ingenuity devoted to finding a technical solution, that the answer should lie in flesh and blood – that the ultimate link in the chain, the key to the electronic network, will be human beings themselves.

17

The enforcers

> At the end of the nineteenth century, the London music publishers,
> led by Chappel and Co., employed retired police sergeants and other
> tough characters to raid the premises of pirates, and cases are
> reported of pitched battles with buckle belts and even pokers.
> (Denis Thomas, *Copyright and the Creative Artist*, 1978)

If a technical solution to piracy was proving elusive, the producers,
publishers, and software manufacturers facing the explosion of
piracy at the beginning of the decade had to look elsewhere for an
answer. The only weapon at their disposal was a copyright law
drafted for an earlier age, that of mechanical reproduction, the
printing press, record manufacture, the photographic process (extended to motion pictures), and terrestrial broadcasting.

After their failure to get legal backing to ban the culprit machines
– audio and video recorders – the media industries had to redefine
their objectives. It was now necessary to distinguish between the
unstoppable and the deterable. They had to draw a line between the
public and the profiteers, and adopt different tactics to contain the
home tapers, on one hand, and the commercial pirates, on the other.

Against the profiteers it was time to unleash the bloodhounds.
Private detective and enforcement agencies were set up, supported
not by individual companies but by new industry-wide associations,
acting together against a common foe. Like sheriffs in the Wild
West, their task was to ensure that the newly prospected 'territories'
of electronic media remained lawful and that the legitimate supplies
of film prints, books, records, and tapes 'got through' without being
ambushed along the way. Indeed, the early days of the video rental
business, peopled by high-street 'cowboys' anticipating bonanza
profits, became known in the trade as the 'Klondyke phase'. The
Western analogy was not always fanciful.

Swapping tented wagons for custom-built caravans, the flat fields
of southern Holland offered a safe haven for affluent gypsy
communities – 'campers' – into which professional criminals had
married. They lived an outlaw existence in huge sites with up to
3,000 inhabitants outside the major cities. Beyond the reach of the
authorities, the police regarded the sites as no-go areas. And in
recent years, their traditional trade of selling knives on doorsteps had

diversified somewhat to include drugs and piracy. It was a life perfectly suited to cross-border counterfeit trading and the delivery of untraceable pirated stock to city-centre shops.

In October 1984 the law officers of Stemra-Buma, the Dutch copyright enforcement agency, had mounted a military-style operation to catch the pirates red-handed. Two mobile units of twenty-five policemen had converged on a street of video shops in Utrecht. Informed that the dealers were not only armed but trigger-happy, they had come prepared with plastic shields and bullet-proof vests.

Surprise was crucial. Their objective was to make a hit-and-run raid, seize the tapes as evidence, and withdraw before the dealers could make contact with the campers squatting outside the city. But they hadn't counted on the twentieth-century version of smoke signals. The dealers had set up a pyramid telephone network, through which one alarm call instantly triggered twenty more, on and on, until the narrow street was crammed with campers in less than an hour. Threatened with a shoot-out, the police had to withdraw empty-handed.

Six months later in the Stemra-Buma offices Gert Mannheim had already planned his revenge. The show-down this time was to be in The Hague, and only he and the chief of police knew the plan. To avoid leaks, even his scouts, the local investigators on whom he depended for tip-offs, had been kept in the dark. An armed convoy of 100 police was to set off from Amsterdam over the quiet Easter weekend. The operation's cover was to be the eviction of illegal squatters. Only on the Saturday morning the chief of police in The Hague was visited by a delegation of campers, informing him that they knew about the planned raid and had already taken the necessary precautions – encircling the street of shops with old caravans that were primed with petrol and ready to be set alight. Half-way down the autobahn, the massive police convoy was halted and turned round.

Mannheim never got his 'High Noon', and Stemra-Buma returned to its former, and in the long run more effective, practice of low-key discreet investigations and 'softly, softly' raids. The campers remained at large.

Until the true scale of electronic piracy became clear, problems of copyright infringement – plagiarism by authors, counterfeit book publishing, stealing film prints for cinemas abroad, importing cheap record albums to avoid EEC controls – had all been dealt with in the civil courts. The culprits were few in number and traceable. The physical stocks of illicit material were easily located, and the remedies sought were civil damages and an injunction to get it stopped. It was one of the accepted irritants of the business. Apart from the bigger firms, which were prepared to mount lengthy, complex, and above all expensive copyright suits, it was written off as a predictable business loss.

As for copyright infringement being a *criminal* offence, there was indeed an offence tucked away deep in the 1956 Copyright Act setting the maximum fine at £50. There hadn't been a criminal prosecution for copyright infringement in twenty years.

Towards the end of the 1970s, warnings by copyright owners were still failing to arouse public concern, or the interest of the authorities. But as the threat became more international, the reality of inadequate legal protection became alarmingly apparent. As the potential profits soared, the pirates ceased to be backstreet con-men and more and more became organized criminals operating undercover.[1]

As James Bouras of the Motion Picture Association of America (MPAA) put it, 'This is no longer a "gentleman's game" between old-fashioned publishers and the literary establishment. It's big bucks, with sophisticated professional crooks and thieves'.[2]

This was a power struggle against unfair market competition. The goals had become deterrence and punishment. Commercial piracy had to be criminalized; and the weapons were muscle and propaganda.

In October 1982 Jack Valenti, president of the MPAA, flew into London for a meeting with the Home Secretary, William Whitelaw, and the Under-Secretary at the Department of Trade, Ian Sproat. Valenti wasted little time in declaring his purpose.[3] The previous year the UK government had itself published a Green Paper recommending increased criminal penalties for piracy – but had then sat on it. It was time, said Valenti, for them to come off the fence and start taking action:

> Britain is at the centre of a world-wide piracy racket financed by organized crime. Gangsters are attracted to Britain like thieves to a honey-pot, and unless they are brought quickly under control the film and television business in the UK is a terminal case.[4]

The lack of hard evidence to support such claims was less important than the strategic element of cleaning up London, the primary foothold in Europe for the United States majors.

Valenti was in London to attend the launch of the Federation Against Copyright Theft (FACT), the private investigative body of all the major US and British film producers and distributors. Its chairman was Admiral Sir Derek Empson, former Second Sea Lord and head of Thorn/EMI Entertainments. He had spearheaded a campaign by the British Videogram Association six months earlier, described as 'a battle which has been planned like a military exercise.

We are planning to go for the centre of the problem, destroy it, and have the whole situation under control within twelve months'.[5]

FACT had been modelled on Valenti's own security organization in the USA, set up in 1975 to ferret out the film print pirates and co-operate with the police and federal agencies. It was manned by four former FBI agents and an ex-police inspector. In 1981 the MPAA had been successful in persuading the Reagan administration to pass the heaviest criminal penalties against piracy in the world. Possession of infringing materials for the purpose of trade attracted maximum gaol sentences of five years and fines up to $250,000.

Producers in the USA were already getting much better co-operation from the FBI. In Florida, for instance, a clandestine FBI team had been operating in true *Miami Vice* style, in a 'stake-out' fronted by a video company called Golde Coaste Specialities Inc. The objective was to covertly infiltrate the Mafia links in the porn trade; the operation was code-named 'Miporn'. On St Valentine's Day 1980 they finally went in to bust the Florida porn network, only to discover that the warehouses were full of illicit copies of mainstream Hollywood movies – 'white films', including (aptly enough) *The Godfather*.[6]

In Britain, FACT was launched with similarly qualified staff. Its initial budget was £750,000. The director-general was Robert Birch, ex-solicitor for Scotland Yard. The chief investigator was Peter Duffy, former commander of the Anti-Terrorist Squad, after serving in the Flying Squad, Serious Crimes Unit, and Fraud Squad. His previous investigations had included the siege of the Iranian Embassy in 1980, and the IRA bombings on Bromley gas-works and the RAF base at Uxbridge.[7]

Other copyright industries soon followed suit, or drastically beefed up existing legal departments. In March 1983 the UK Publishers' Association set up its Campaign Against Book Piracy Unit, with its 108 member publishers each pledging to contribute a percentage of their export revenue to finance it. In July 1984 the Federation Against Software Theft (FAST) was launched with the backing of IBM chairman Donald McLean. For the record industry, the British Phonographic Industry (BPI) stepped up the activities of its own anti-piracy unit, while the International Federation of Phonogram and Videogram Producers (IFPI), founded in 1933 as the music industry's lobby, launched the JAPIG (Joint Anti-Piracy Intelligence Group) in September 1984 to police the international pirate routes from South-East Asia to West Africa.

These new agencies joined the ranks of the booming new security and surveillance businesses that were the growth industry of the 1980s. To combat maritime fraud, the International Maritime

Bureau (IMB) was founded by the International Chamber of Commerce in 1980. By 1985, specifically to investigate counterfeit trade-marked goods, pirated industrial designs, and fashion rip-offs, the Counterfeiting Intelligence Bureau (CIB), under Fraud Squad detective Jack Heslop, was operational. Product counterfeiting was up to 9 per cent of world trade, accounting for $60 *billion* annually.

At the same time, in the banking and finanical sectors, the new computer fraud teams were beginning to patrol the byways of the telephone networks and electronic data routes. The covert 'Tiger teams' set up by the US government to test military defence had been transplanted to watch over civilian commerce. Specialist security agencies also continued to expand, offering expert advice on everything from alarm systems to electronic bugs and scramblers, forgery tracing devices, and the whole paraphernalia of surveillance gadgetry.[8]

The film industry's Federation Against Copyright Theft became the successful model of how enforcement agencies should operate in Europe. 'My first commandment', explained Peter Duffy, 'was "Protect the film print".'

This he did by secretly marking every film print destined for a British cinema. The inspection of any pirated cassette from then on would reveal the cinema from which it had been illegally taken – and, after some spade-work, the staff member who was responsible. Within a year the two major rings in Britain, operating from the Barking Odeon and the Ace, Stoke Newington, had been smashed, with sixteen people awaiting trial for conspiracy to steal copyright and defraud.

By the end of 1984 Duffy was proudly announcing that no film print had been stolen from a British cinema since the unfortunately titled *Never Say Never Again* in August 1983. He didn't exactly have to eat his words, but there continued to be a steady stream of pre-release pirate videos circulating the country. In 1985 there were eighty-eight new release films captured by FACT on cassette – imports from the USA, the Middle East, and South-East Asia.[9]

Inevitably, the pressure on film distributors has been to protect its Achilles' heel, the time gap between the cinema and video releases of new movies: The 'video window', as it is known. The gap has steadily narrowed from a year to six months, and even less in some cases. But it varies in different countries, with some, like France, resisting the trend in order to protect cinema-going and, in turn, their own film industry.

'Disregarding back-to-back copying, you could kill film piracy stone dead by simultaneous release,' admits Duffy:

But I don't see how you'll ever get it. There's just no cohesion within the industry. The marketing strategy for each company is to do its own thing. They say let's have it in that territory for six months, before it goes there. . . . And not only that, but it saves them the cost of producing prints if they stagger releases across the world and use the same prints again and again.

It is not as if the major Hollywood studios are in control anyway:

When you take a film like *Rambo*, you're not dealing with a major for distribution, but a one-man small company called Corocco in California, which has *all* the distribution rights and is making different agreements all over the world.

Against the back-to-back pirates, FACT adopted a different strategy: propaganda. It launched a campaign to advertise its existence, aimed not at the general public, but at the emerging video rental trade. It carried out spot checks across the country and mounted a series of high-profile raids on shops. Its tactic was to win over the video shops to its own side of the battle and isolate the pirates to more marginal outlets – such as mobile vans on housing estates and at factories, and non-specialist corner shops. Within months a network of legitimate dealers emerged, keen to keep the investigators well informed about the illicit competition. Within six months FACT had received over 3,000 letters and telephone calls giving tip-offs about suspect operations.[10] It also cleaned up the cassette duplicating plants, inspecting security arrangements and giving its seal of approval only to those that met its standards. Thereafter, reputable distributors would deal with no one else.

In July 1983, after hard lobbying by the industry behind the scenes, FACT got the legal muscle it wanted: criminal punishments that were a real deterrent. Sir John Eden obtained an amendment to the Copyright Act that increased the penalties for commercial piracy to a maximum fine of £1,000 (soon increased to £2,000 per offending movie) and up to two years' imprisonment. The main significance of the amendment, however, was its search-and-seize provisions that were now available to the police with a warrant. The police no longer had an excuse to ignore the problem, and FACT set about co-operating closely with them. The relationship was nevertheless sometimes controversial.

In May 1985 Newham magistrates' court began hearing allegations of 'gross misconduct', in a case that was to expose some of the seamier aspects of the new enforcement tactics. In particular, it was to bring to light the extraordinary legal powers FACT had acquired, through an anomaly known as 'Anton Pillar orders'.

The Robinson case

A major benefit of the 1983 Amendment Act was gradually to make redundant these notorious and finally discredited search-and-seize procedures adopted by the copyright industries. Named Anton Pillar orders, after the West German electronics company that first obtained them in 1974, they were obtained *ex parte* (in the absence of the defendant) in the civil courts and gave solicitors (acting for copyright owners) the power to enter the business premises and home of suspected pirates, search for illegal copies, and seize material to be used as evidence against them.

The orders' purpose was to prevent a defendant, when informed of impending litigation, from destroying the evidence. They quickly became one of the most powerful orders granted in British civil courts, made in secret and intended for immediate execution. Those against whom they were made had to allow solicitors to enter their premises and seize material. The orders were usually accompanied by injunctions freezing the defendant's assets and bank accounts, preventing him carrying on his business. And all this before a court had heard the full merits of the case.

Ten years after their introduction they were being extensively used by the film and record industry. One firm of London solicitors, Hamlin Slowe, alone executed over 300 of them. Most of the defendants could not afford to defend themselves in lengthy copyright actions and simply went out of business. Others settled out of court, but one, Christopher Robinson, a Luton video dealer, obtained legal aid and decided to fight. The four-year legal wrangling, costing the Motion Picture Association of America which brought the case over £500,000, succeeded in proving that Robinson had dealt in pirated material. But, in an unprecedented judgment, Mr Justice Scott awarded Robinson £10,000 in aggravated damages against the film companies, because of the way their solicitors, Hamlin Slowe, had behaved.

The High Court judge declared that the solicitors had shown a flagrant disregard for the defendant's rights. He found that the film companies' intention had been to close down Robinson's business regardless, even though the orders were meant only to preserve evidence. Some of the material seized in the raid had been kept for nearly three years by the solicitors, 'without a shadow of right' said the judge. And he found that the solicitors had misled the court at the original application for the order, witholding relevant information. The Law Society later held an inquiry.

It was not the only incident of harassment suffered by Robinson, who had had the temerity to challenge the film industry's muscle.

About a month before the trial, he was arrested by Luton police and charged with attempted gross indecency against a ten-year-old boy. Fortunately for Robinson, he happened to be consulting with his counsel at the time of the alleged offences; and three weeks later the charges were dropped.

Robinson also complained that police had entered and searched his house in the middle of the night on two occasions, neither time with a warrant. Also, two private detectives hired by solicitors Hamlin Slowe, both ex-Bedfordshire police officers, had approached his neighbours and acquaintances, including his former wife, asking a mass of questions ranging from his personal finances to his possible connections with prostitution and pornography – none of which led to any charges against him.[11]

The example of FACT and the deterrent effect of tougher criminal penalties had not been lost on the other copyright industries, particularly the computer software firms. They had been lobbying government for similar treatment and in 1985 were rewarded with a similar Copyright (Computer Software) Act, bringing them in line with music and video.

Organized piracy in the backyard of Europe was starting to look containable. But it was also becoming little more than a well-patrolled lagoon compared to the international routes where, traditionally, piracy has always prospered, electronic piracy being no exception: the high seas.

18

The enforcers abroad

We have to identify the enemy and track the flow of goods and cash.
(Joe Palmer, Joint Anti-Piracy Intelligence Group)[1]

In January 1985 Ian Thomas was presented with Tin Pan Alley's insignia of success – a gold disc. Only in this case the award was not for selling, but for *preventing* the sale of a million cassette tapes. Thomas is the director-general of the International Federation of Phonogram and Videogram Producers (IFPI), and this was the climax of an extraordinary undercover operation which had been investigating the trade route in pirate tapes that has sprung up between the Far East (especially Singapore) and West Africa (especially Nigeria).

In September the previous year they had monitored the passage of the tramp steamer *Ping Ding Shan* across the Indian Ocean, around the Cape and north to the port of Cotonou in Benin. This time the agents and customs were waiting. As soon as the ship docked, they moved in and seized 195,000 illegal cassettes, which had somehow been omitted from the cargo manifest.

The operation was so well co-ordinated that the trap was sprung again and again. Between November 1984 and January 1985 the cargoes of another five ships were seized in raids at ports in the Gold Coast, Nigeria, and Cameroon. The total haul amounted to 1,051,000 pirate cassettes with an estimated street value of $4 million.

The scale of the operation can be judged by the fact that it required the close co-operation of the International Maritime Bureau, SACEM (the French composer's body), ICSAC (the International Confederation of Societies of Authors and Composers), the Nigerian representatives of the US-based Black Music Association, and the customs, police, and copyright offices of four countries. It was a sophisticated piece of work, indicative of the covert international operations which enforcement agencies now mount – and the problem they face.

Confronted by the inactivity of governments and the indifference of conventional enforcement agencies like the police, the threatened industries had no choice but to go it alone, establishing international intelligence operations themselves to out-smart the equally co-ordinated networks of the pirates. And co-operation between the different agencies was inevitable, once the patterns of the pirate routes were repeated with familiar regularity. The tape pirates were only following the same footsteps, and deceiving the same customs officials, as those transporting fake books two years before.

Ian Taylor's Campaign Against Book Piracy had already established agents in Hong Kong and Kuala Lumpur. The Hong Kong representative was analysing local intelligence reports collected by private detective agencies and contacts at the docks, and gaining advance information of shipments of pirated books from Taiwan. This paid off in 1983, when the Nigerian Publishers' Association mounted a raid on a ship docking at Port Harcourt, West Africa, acting on information received from Taylor's agent in Hong Kong. The ship had passed through customs at Singapore and Hong Kong, declaring its cargo as 'holy picture books'. When five containers were searched they were found instead to be carrying several million volumes of pirated English textbooks, destined for schools and universities throughout Central Africa.

Both the music and video industries recognized the advantages of permanently collaborating and in September 1984 launched JAPIG (the Joint Anti-Piracy Intelligence Group), financed by the 600 affiliated companies of IFPI.[2] Its headquarters were in London, headed by Joe Palmer, a British lawyer and commercial crime investigator. Its brief was to co-ordinate national copyright organizations and international agencies like the International Maritime Bureau. 'Initially we will look at video and sound recordings,' explained Palmer, 'but we hope to bring in other counterfeit products, such as auto parts and drugs [sic] later.'[3]

It was nevertheless a daunting task, given the limited resources and the web of sea routes that criss-cross along the Equator from the South China Sea to the Ivory Coast, not to mention each port of call *en route* with its own network of merchants and corrupt officials.

Understandably, the agencies have concentrated their efforts on the source of the global traffic, South-East Asia, with a mixture of international lobbying, diplomatic and economic pressure, and where possible direct action. IFPI's first target was the Crown Colony of Hong Kong, where it set up a local office in 1970 and worked hard to persuade the Hong Kong government to take action. A special Copyright Investigation Unit was set up within the Customs and Excise Department in 1973, and three years later criminal penalties of increased fines and imprisonment, together with wider search-and-seize powers were introduced. By 1980 IFPI was claiming to have reduced tape piracy from 98 per cent of the market to less than 5 per cent.[4]

'The success in Hong Kong', according to Gillian Davis, IFPI's legal officer,

> was due to the existence of adequate legal protection of producers. What confronts us now is a world-wide situation in which the effects of technology have been so far-reaching and dramatic that the whole concept of copyright has been put in jeopardy.

No one was pretending that, having plugged up one hole, the flood wasn't pouring forth elsewhere.[5]

Singapore represented quite a gaping hole, and direct action seemed to be caught on a downward spiral of diminishing returns. In 1982 only thirty raids on tape shops had resulted in the seizure of 395,000 tapes. In 1983 seventy-five raids had elicited 156,000. In 1984 eighty-one raids had netted only 23,000. Either the raids were beginning to bite, or, far more likely, retailers were stocking less to minimize losses in the event of one. It remains to be seen whether the proposed new copyright legislation of Singapore, after years of debate and diplomatic horse-trading with western governments (see Chapter 19), turns the tide around.[6]

But perhaps the conviction of Indonesian business man Anthony Dharmawan in May 1986 points to the future strategy of enforcement agencies. He was ensnared by ingenious undercover operatives of the Recording Industry Association of America (RIAA), not at the source of the pirate traffic, but at its ultimate destination.

Dharmawan was arrested at JFK Airport in New York by US customs agents after offering 360,000 illicit recordings for sale and shipping 5,000 counterfeit cassettes to a dummy import/export corporation run by RIAA agents posing as business men. Dharmawan's company in Jakarta, whose counterfeits carried the Joker, Galaxy, King, and Billboard labels, had the capacity to produce over two million infringing tapes per month. He had travelled 12,000 miles straight into the trap, complete with fraudulent documents, listing the counterfeit tapes as blank cassettes. He could expect to receive up to twenty-seven years' gaol and/or a fine of up to $500,000.[7]

Spearheading the world-wide anti-piracy fight for the United States film industry is the multi-million-dollar programme of the Motion Picture Export Association of America (MPEAA). With headquarters in New York, it has twelve film security offices around the world, staffed by investigators working closely with national organizations, like FACT, in over forty countries. It lobbies foreign governments to strengthen copyright laws, introduces security arrangements for film prints, and seeks to find common ground – not always forthcoming on creative or film investment issues – with other national film industries.

In Europe alone, between 1983–4 the combined efforts of film enforcement agencies claim to have recouped £300 million from the pirate video market, the result of 1,195 raids and the seizure of 366,000 cassettes.[8] Increasingly, anti-piracy units are turning to computers for help. Relevant data is now stored on computers in the USA, Britain, Holland, Sweden, West Germany, and Hong Kong. The most comprehensive system is used by the Video Security Foundation in the Netherlands. It has three databanks: a film title index of all new releases; a European video retailers' index; and an index of investigative intelligence compiled with the assistance of Interpol.

As the interests of the different media converge, there has been a parallel concentration of political lobbying and propaganda. First the individual companies in the respective industries recognized the need to fund industry-wide organizations. Then in February 1986 a new collective campaign was launched, when the British 'copyright industries' formed the UK Anti-Piracy Group. All the different producers, publishers, distributors, and software companies in the various media were brought together within the Confederation of Information and Communications Industries (CICI).

The Anti-Piracy Group's first report indicated the strength of the 'information industries' and the copyright lobby, representing 2.6 per cent of gross domestic product and contributing nearly £6 billion a year to the economy. It claimed that the world-wide figure for lost sales due to the piracy of British copyright products was more than £1 billion a year.[9] But as the industries said themselves, enforcement meant nothing unless there were effective laws to enforce. And that required, not covert operations, but up-front political pressure at the highest possible level.

The anti-piracy charter

In 1978 IFPI unveiled a twelve-point international charter on how to combat piracy. The following were required:

- Effective legal protection for producers, preferably by copyright.
- Reciprocal protection for foreign products.
- Adequate civil and criminal remedies.
- Special anti-piracy budgets within the respective industries.
- A central co-ordinating authority or national group.
- Sufficient investigators.
- Specialist anti-piracy lawyers.

- Co-operation of all member companies in the national group.
- Co-operation of authors' societies and performers.
- Regular international communication and exchange of information.
- Co-operation of governments and their agencies.
- Adoption of strict in-house security procedures to protect master-copies.

19

Protecting the markets

> The British government needs to adopt an assertive and forceful
> attitude to ensuring the protection of UK intellectual property.
> Piracy must be treated as a vital trade issue in negotiations with
> offending states rather than a technical matter of limited priority.
>
> (CICI Anti-Piracy Group)[1]

Electronic piracy follows a course of least resistance across the globe.
Like water finding its own level, the centres of international piracy
flourish where the legal protection is weakest.

The alliance of information and media industries now recognizes
that the world-wide promotion of copyright principles is their only
safeguard for the future. To back up this campaign, they are calling
on western governments to exert diplomatic and economic pressure
on those countries where piracy goes unchecked, to ensure that
effective deterrent penalties and vigorous enforcement methods are
introduced.

This is one area of international policy, however, where the
British government has failed to obediently follow the United States
lead. While the Reagan administration continues to identify the
defence of US 'intellectual property rights' as a crucial element in its
economic future, Britain has failed to take a similarly tough stance.

To the US government these rights are seen as a foundation for
successfully exploiting their lead in science and technology, developing global entertainment media, and underpinning their world-wide
advertising strategies for brand-name consumer goods. As with
terrorism and drugs, piracy is threatening the stability and control of
those crucial markets in whole regions of the world.

As W. R. Cornish points out, unlike the USA and Europe, Britain
has preferred to treat each element of intellectual property (patents,
trade marks, copyright, industrial designs) separately, rather than as
different branches of one guiding principle, namely the need to
regulate all forms of unfair competition – be it protectionist trade
barriers, unfair commercial subsidies, or piracy.[2] In the UK,
international copyright issues are dealt with as a technical issue
within the Department of Trade and Industry, or as a source of
rarefied debate within the over-legalistic Industrial Property and
Copyright Department (IPCD).

For the Americans, the issue is not one of culture, but trade. If the USA is buying commodities from the area, those countries must buy American materials in return.

'The British embassies tell you it is a sensitive issue that cannot be tackled head on,' says Ian Taylor of the UK Publishers' Association in an interview; 'that it has to be done informally, discreetly. It's absolute rubbish. The Chinese, Taiwanese, and Malay business men perfectly understand it's just trade.'

That sense of priority in the USA is borne out by the visit to Indonesia in 1986 of Assistant Secretary of State McNair, deputy to George Shultz, whose meetings with six different ministers in the federal government had copyright at the top of every agenda.[3] Meanwhile, explains Taylor,

> Our ambassador in Jakarta assured us he had considerable sympathy for the students who were photocopying books because they couldn't afford materials, and made it pretty clear he thought the piracy of Live Aid cassettes was not something to be taken seriously. But he was very keen on defence sales.

In equal measure, of course, western economic strategies fuel Third World resistance and suspicion. They are seen as 'creaming off' scarce resources in royalty payments to the west in return for vital educational materials and know-how, and as setting the agenda for technological innovation which often pre-empts the needs of developing countries.

The apparently straightforward arguments about unfair competition change their complexion when viewed from Korea, Jamaica, or Pakistan. They are seen in the wider context of economic and cultural imperialism, where the one-way flow of books from North to South, and the narrow, but dominant, range of records and films produced by the transnationals, undermine Third World efforts to maintain their own publishing, film, and music industries. Or when their demands for autonomy, such as proposals within UNESCO for a New World Information Order, are met with blank rejection by the USA and Britain.

New electronic technology demands structural changes within the economies of the smaller nations, as it does in the west, involving a transition from manufacturing to service industries, and capital- rather than labour-intensive production.

But for Professor Irving Horowitz, most Third World nations are simply not prepared to confront such challenges. They seek recourse to pirating inventions, avoiding payment for research and development, and taking short-term options with second-hand and often inappropriate technologies. By 'claiming less-favoured-nation status, they are in all likelihood doomed to underdevelopment'.[4]

Western publishers argue that piracy not only affects their interests but undermines the development of local publishing industries, too. There is little incentive for a Pakistani publisher, they argue, to go to the trouble and risk of publishing a students' textbook by a local author when if it is any good it will be pirated or have to compete with cheaper pirated editions of foreign best-sellers. The end result is a greater dependence on foreign culture and science within developing countries.

Yet western governments have also been reducing cultural aid programmes and limiting the export of hardware (with technology-transfer regulations), both of which could help redress the balance and encourage local industries to compete. In contrast to the extensive aid programmes of the Soviet Union, western governments' support for low-priced books intended for Third World consumption has virtually disappeared, marginalized by the emphasis on market economics.

As Horowitz comments:

> The idea of the free market has been universalized to include nations that simply have no excess capital and few resources to acquire books or journals in a competitive way. The relative flooding of literature in the Third World by the Soviet Union also means that there is an absence of competitive pressure even to purchase from western sources, since books are available often in English for much less, if not gratis, from Soviet sources.

The 'free market' ethos towards the Third World also pervades the music and film industries. As Wallis and Malm document in detail in their book, *Big Sounds from Small People* (1984), small countries are simply regarded as marginal markets and sources of exploitable talent by the handful of western record companies, themselves subsidiaries of larger conglomerates, that dominate the world music markets.[5]

The difficulties of maintaining an indigenous record industry may be exacerbated by piracy; but the same technology also offers the opportunity to produce and distribute new sounds at low cost. Equally, historical factors within the legitimate industry, like western rip-offs of reggae and calypso music, and the difficulties of redistributing royalties back to artists in South African shanty towns, suggest there are more complex reasons than piracy for the problems of local music industries. Significantly, where a local industry does already exist, such as the Indian film industry, developing countries do have an incentive to introduce strong copyright protection, recognizing that their own markets would collapse if they had to compete with pirated foreign works.

The political arguments are considered later (see Chapter 24, 'The Third World'), but it is no surprise to find western publishers, record companies, and computer software exporters claiming that effective action against piracy is unlikely until western governments either threaten to remove trade benefits or provide trade incentives to encourage pirate nations to change their tune.

'Persuading foreign governments to improve their copyright laws through informal contacts is demonstrably less effective than economic pressure,' warns the UK Anti-Piracy Group.[6] To support its case, the APG points to the slow but steady success of the USA in getting Singapore, Indonesia, and Taiwan to take piracy more seriously; this was achieved through diplomatic influence at the highest level and threats to remove the General System of Preference (GSP) trade benefits and commence punitive '301' actions under the US Trade Act.

Far removed from the problems of struggling artists, the issue has become an international game of diplomacy, with many smaller countries quickly picking up the 'rules'. An example of this was the announcement by the Singapore government in 1986 that it would join one of the international copyright conventions on condition it obtained additional benefits under the GSP.

The UK Anti-Piracy Group goes on to demand a series of initiatives to be taken immediately by the British government, including a review of current trade agreements, diplomatic lobbying of offending states, and the threat of trade sanctions. The APG spells out the dangers of letting the USA make all the running:

> In Singapore, Korea, Malaysia, and Taiwan, the Americans are there ahead of us, with negotiating teams already in place to influence the course of new copyright legislation as it passes into law. But the policy of allowing the USA to fight our corner is a dangerous one.
>
> While they are our allies on this issue, they are nevertheless our chief competitors and are hardly likely to give consideration to UK interests when it comes to the small print. In Singapore and Korea, for example, we may well wake up to find copyright laws drafted under exclusively US pressure, that are not at all sympathetic to British interests. The danger is that countries may enter into bilateral agreements instead of joining multilateral conventions.

Such warnings have already proved too late in some cases. After last-minute appeals to Korea's President Cheung by Mrs Thatcher on his visit to the UK in April 1986 (and repeated during her stop-over in Seoul on her way to the Tokyo Summit), Korea has finally agreed to join the Universal Copyright Convention (UCC) in 1987.[7] This will eventually protect British publications, but in the meantime Korea has signed a separate bilateral deal with the Americans giving US publishers retrospective protection for books published ten years before joining the convention!

'Ours will not be protected,' says Taylor. 'We've been completely left out, and it will be another ten years before we can get back into the market.'

That the British lion has been outsmarted by the American hawk in this instance only emphasizes the ambiguity of attempts at international co-operation in the field of information technology. With the protection of 'intellectual property' becoming such a pivotal factor in complex political and economic trade-offs, not to mention the cultural effects within the countries themselves, the simple certainties of copyright seem to evaporate.

On a very practical level, the task of harmonizing the world's copyright laws is enormous. Out of the 157 states affiliated to the United Nations only 90 belong to one or both of the international conventions on copyright – the Berne Convention of 1886 and the Universal Copyright Convention of 1951. These set out the minimum standards for copyright protection which the national laws of each member country must meet, and require each country to protect the works of all other member countries in the same way that it protects its own.[8]

As for the specific international protection of sound recordings, only thirty-one countries are party to the Rome Convention of 1961 which protects producers and performers from unauthorized reproduction of recordings and grants rights to producers to benefit from broadcasting and the performance of music in shops, discos, etc. And only thirty-nine countries have signed the Phonograms Convention of 1971 against the unauthorized duplication of recordings. Less than half the governments in Europe have joined this convention so far.

The countries outside these major conventions are hardly negligible. They included China until last year and still include Indonesia (with a population three times that of France), Singapore, Malaysia, Korea, and all the oil-rich states of the Arabian Gulf.

The major producers and exporters of the west (as well as Japan) are the most protected and most actively engaged in bolstering and formulating new legal remedies to control the effects of technology. As one travels east and south, however, across the major illicit markets of West Africa and the Middle East towards the powerhouse of world piracy in South-East Asia, the level of formal protection gets progressively weaker, and in some cases is non-existent. In part this is a reflection of the historical development of the copyright principle, evolving within different cultures and diverse legal systems.

There is no one uniform set of standards world-wide, but a series of hybrid variants, diverse interpretations of the four basic systems: the Anglo-Saxon system adopted in Britain and the USA and exported to many Commonwealth countries; the French and continental European system, including many of their past colonies; the centralized state system of the Communist bloc; and the modern 'mixed bag' approach of many developing nations. The Arab states of the Middle East have no tradition of copyright. It falls to international copyright organizations like WIPO (the World Intellectual Property Organization), a United Nations agency with 116 member states, to attempt some harmonization between the competing systems.[9]

Against this legal background the activities of the industry intelligence units and anti-piracy groups have produced thick files on the principal trade routes of the pirates. Such intelligence-gathering, however, even when resulting in entrapment and seizures, is only the first step along a very rocky judicial path. As the papers are passed on to local lawyers to take the cases through court, the full complexity of arcane procedures and statute law, with fundamental differences between each neighbouring state, becomes frustratingly apparent.

For example, to ensure copyright protection in Korea and Indonesia, first publication of UK works must take place in those countries, hardly a practical option for British publishers. In Taiwan, as in many other countries, protection is given only to works that have been registered at the relevant government department first. The registration fee per book title in Taiwan is six times the published price – even of high-priced textbooks and limited editions. This applies to computer software, too, requiring the open registration of possibly secret and valuable programmes. Neither Korea nor Indonesia offer protection to foreign works, whilst speedy and efficient court actions are notoriously absent in Singapore, Malaysia, Pakistan, and Nigeria, to mention but a few.

Similar imbalances exist in the administration of legitimate royalties within the international music industry. Different copyright bureaucracies often produce in-built discrimination in favour of western interests within the huge royalty-collecting and distribution societies for composers, publishers, and record companies.

Of the ninety member states of either international copyright convention, less than half – about forty – have anything approaching an effective system for enforcement or the collection of royalties. Membership of copyright conventions hardly guarantees protection. None oblige national governments to honour the principles, there is no mechanism for monitoring whether they fulfil the requirements, and sanctions are not applied to those who don't.

In reality, 75 per cent of the members of the United Nations lack a modern or effective copyright system. As the director-general of the International Confederation of Societies of Authors and Composers (CISAC) put it, 'What would be the reaction of producers of petrol, armaments, cocoa, or wheat if 75 per cent of states received their exports for free?'[10]

Even in Western Europe the response to the modern commercial pirates and calls for new, stiffer criminal penalties have varied considerably. In Finland the maximum term for wilful breach of copyright has just been increased from six months' to two years' imprisonment; in West Germany it's one year (in contrast to sentences of up to ten years for the theft of goods such as cars); in Greece cassette piracy has been made punishable under forgery laws, allowing a sentence of six and a half years in one recent case; in Norway the maximum is just three months, in Portugal three years.

The most dramatic reform to meet the challenge has been in the UK, where the law has been amended twice, in 1982 and 1983, so that now unlimited fines and imprisonment of up to two years can be imposed. The reforms were modelled on changes in US federal law in 1981 which increased prison sentences to a maximum of five years, and fines up to $250,000, for dealing in pirate cassettes.

As for the areas where piracy is of epidemic proportions, the penalties are often woefully lacking. Until recent new legislation passed in February 1987, the average fine for trading in pirate cassettes in Singapore was just £359. This was not much of a deterrent when the estimated loss of potential sales to the UK record industry in that country has been put at over £51 million. In Korea and Pakistan the average fine is £200; in Nigeria the maximum is £78.

Until the recent pressures exerted by the Reagan administration, diplomatic lobbying and specific assistance for drafting more effective laws were left to the international organizations of affected industries such as IFPI and the United Nations agency the World Intellectual Property Organization (WIPO). On its fiftieth anniversary in 1983 IFPI could boast that with its assistance 88 countries had recognized the basic reproduction right in sound recordings and 52 had recognized a performance right. 'IFPI has been consulted by governments planning to enact new copyright legislation and has submitted or commented upon draft laws,' according to IFPI's anniversary brochure. They included India, Indonesia, Jamaica, Malaysia, Philippines, Portugal, Spain, Sri Lanka, Trinidad, and Tobago.[11]

In that year alone, the 'valuable though less glamorous' anti-piracy activity of IFPI in the offices of governments and intergovernmental agencies throughout the world had resulted in four countries enacting entirely new copyright laws: Barbados, Congo, Colombia, and Costa Rica. Seven other countries had increased the penalties for piracy of phonograms or videos, namely Austria, Kenya, Pakistan, Peru, Sweden, the USA, and Uruguay.

After the enforcement success in Hong Kong, IFPI's attention has been turned to Singapore, but with only limited success. 'The Singapore government has not yet reacted with the same vigour as was the case in Hong Kong,' reports IFPI. Whilst the new Copyright Act passed in February 1987 imposes tougher penalties for infringement (distribution of a pirate product now attracts fines of up to $50,000), only limited protection is offered to foreign works, because Singapore has still to join one of the international conventions.

The Singapore law also contains an equally contentious licensing scheme, whereby a new copyright tribunal may grant licences for the production and publication of translations of works on payment of a royalty, but without the explicit permission of the original producer.

In the Middle East, Egypt was chosen by IFPI as a priority area, and recently new laws and stronger penalties have been introduced, backed up with a special police department. Predictably, the Gulf states, 'on the receiving end of 85 per cent of the pirate product exported from Singapore', are the current focus of attention. Likewise the other principal market for the Third World counterfeiters – West Africa, particularly Nigeria.

Yet the challenge to continuing control of the media and information markets is no longer simply one of geography – nor of the speed with which offending countries adopt legislation acceptable to the west. There is a sneaking suspicion, already glimpsed in earlier chapters of this book, that perhaps the law itself is not up to the task imposed on it; that its statutes are out of date, and courts are anyway not the place to fight a revolution. While the information empires defend themselves with the legal tools of an earlier age, dare the corporate lawyers admit that the emperor has no clothes?

The international conventions

In addition to national laws, which vary in detail from country to country, there are two major international conventions in the western world:

The *Berne Convention (1886)* and its later revisions are based on the assumption that copyright is inherent in any creative work. In July 1985 there were seventy-six member nations, including the United Kingdom.

The *Universal Copyright Convention (1952)* was created to bring the United States into the fold, and relies on a registration system. There are seventy-eight member countries. The Americans are now coming round to the view that the Berne system is the better form of protection. Now that the USA has left UNESCO they want to distance themselves from the UCC. They are beginning to realize that when countries like Taiwan join the UCC this does not make it any easier, in practice, for publishers to register foreign works.

20

The levy

Another chevy on the levy?
(Advertisement by Tape Manufacturers' Group)[1]

The record industry claims home taping is killing music. The film industry calls it a cancer. Tape manufacturers say it *increases* sales of LPs and pre-recorded cassettes. And consumer groups say we have already paid for the right, and are entitled to do it when and where we like.

With so many people doing it – though exactly how many depends on whose market research you're prepared to believe – home taping is the most widespread and uncontrollable form of electronic piracy. Its development in the advanced world is every bit as threatening as the organized commercial piracy of the Third World.

Consumer electronics have made it possible, if not inevitable; and one way or another, we are all 'pirates' now. Motivated by convenience rather than profit, home taping has become a way of life along with personal photocopying and back-up copying of computer software. But faced with the impossibility of enforcement, the lawyers have been stuck for an effective response to it. How damaging to copyright owners is the recording of television or radio broadcasts, to play them back later at a more convenient time, as with 'time-shifting'? And is this different from copying records directly onto audio tapes, or simply copying from tape to tape?

Facing the media industries was the dilemma: should private copying be sanctioned without further ado? Or should it be a source of additional revenue for composers, publishers, and record companies?

In 1977 the BPI (British Phonographic Industry), on behalf of the record industry, began campaigning for a levy to be imposed on the sale of blank audio tapes (and later on blank videotapes) and on the recording machines. Not a tax collected by the government, but a levy to be distributed to rights owners. In return, home taping would become legal. The proposal started a relentless battle between contending hardware and software industries, similar to the earlier campaign to ban the machines outright.

The lobbying by both sides was an intense professional operation, targeted not at the public (who could hardly be expected to be impartial) but behind the scenes at Whitehall. It required patience; nine different ministers sat behind the desk at the Department of Trade and Industry between 1977 and 1988.

For the composers, publishers, and record companies there were the powerful royalty-collecting societies: the MCPS, PRS, PPL, and BPI. In the opposite corner, formed 'to provide a united voice of common sense against the levy' – not to mention the commercial interests of Agfa, BASF, Fuji, Kodak, Maxell, Memorex, TDK, 3M, Sony, JVC, and Panasonic – was the Tape Manufacturers' Group (TMG), set up in May 1981. The last three companies in the list were also the principal suppliers of domestic recording equipment. None was based in Britain. Intent on bandying statistics with the BPI, the TMG's main concern was to thwart the levy in Britain, fearing the inevitable knock-on effect in the rest of the EEC.

Applauding or jeering from the sidelines were the National Consumer Council, the Royal National Institute for the Blind, and the press (all against) and the Musicians' Union (for – if they got a slice of the action, their members not automatically protected by copyright, otherwise ...). In the middle, a reluctant minister facing an issue with no political mileage and an embarrassing challenge to the government's sacred cows – fighting inflation, promoting free enterprise, and reducing subsidies to industry.

Yet under the welter of statistics, market research, and moral righteousness, each side knew what was really at stake. It was not the detail of the proposal – how big the levy should be, who should receive it, and who could be exempted from paying it. It was the principle. The music industry could see which way the wind was blowing. 'Why is action to secure a blank tape/hardware royalty necessary without delay?' it asked in its campaign booklet:

> Because the development of ever more sophisticated technology such as compact discs, digital broadcasting, digital cassettes, and so on will immensely facilitate extremely high quality home duplication. Private copying will become an increasingly widespread activity, causing more and more damage to the creators of intellectual property.

If copyright was to survive the information revolution, a new source of revenue would become increasingly important: compensation for private copying. But it opened up a Pandora's box of questions that most governments – and especially a Conservative one – would have preferred to ignore.

Will the real home taper please stand up?

> It used to break my heart
> When I went into your shop
> And you said my records
> Were out of stock –
> So I don't buy your records in your shop,
> I tape 'em all.
>
> (Bow Wow Wow, 'C30, C60, C90')

Who are the home tapers? The published results of rival market research organizations (the British Market Research Bureau for the BPI and National Opinion Polls for the TMG) have come to widely different conclusions. All agree on the size of the tape market – 80 million blank audio tapes were imported into the UK in 1984.[2]

But how are they used? Your guess, or rather statistic, is as good as ours. The BPI say 55 per cent of the adult population use them to copy music. The TMG say that only 22 per cent of the population buy blank tapes at all, for any purpose. The BPI say that 87 per cent of all blank tapes are used to copy pre-recorded music. The TMG counter this by claiming that almost 70 per cent of all copying is of one's own records and cassettes, 38 per cent making compilation cassettes of different music, 57 per cent who prefer handling cassettes rather than records, 26 per cent to prevent damage to their records. For such material one royalty has already been paid, at the time of purchase.[3]

Whatever the extent, clearly private copying of recorded music goes on – as do storing computer programs, making student notes, doing business dictation, recording messages on answerphones, practising with music, speech, and drama, 'time-shifting' radio programmes, and, if one is blind, whatever you would use a pen and paper for, from shopping-lists to recording knitting patterns.[4]

What then was the music industry's case? Originally it rested on the impact of home taping on 'lost record sales'. The crucial element here was how much of the music being copied would otherwise have been bought. Table 20.1 is the result of the BPI's research (BRMB, September 1984).

These results are impressive, until one looks closely. What does the difference between 'very likely' and 'quite likely' mean in practice? After all, one of the record industry's important target markets is 15–19-year-olds, and their tastes are notoriously fickle.

A different presentaton of the findings suggests a less convincing picture – Table 20.2.

Table 20.1 *How likely to have bought copied music (a) (%)*

	From radio	From LPs	From singles
Definitely would have bought it	8	16	18
Very likely	14	15	17
Quite likely	22	20	14
Total	*44*	*51*	*49*
Not very likely	20	10	10
Very unlikely	15	9	10
Definitely not	17	8	11
Total	*52*	*27*	*31*
Already bought it	—	16	14
Not available	2	3	2
Don't know	2	3	4
Total	*100*	*100*	*100*

Table 20.2 *How likely to have bought copied music (b) (%)*

	From radio	From LPs	From singles
Definitely and very likely	22	31	35
Quite likely to Already bought it	76	66	61

Not quite so impressive. The issue, however, was not so much 'lost record sales' as the changing music market as a whole, on which the industry was concerned to keep a grip.[5]

Consumer spending on pre-recorded music has increased from £254 million in 1976 to £548 million in 1984. But this obscures a decline, both in the percentage of total consumer spending that now goes on music (eaten away in part by the rise of home video), down from 0.335 per cent to 0.282 per cent over the same period, and the fall in real terms (taking account of inflation) from £450 million to £329 million. Since the major drop in 1979, however, the level has remained at a constant, slightly rising level.[6]

The picture is one of broad changing patterns in traditional consumption, and the changing sources of pre-recorded music.

'The combined effect of youth unemployment and the decline in the teenage population may well curb total demand for certain types of records,' admits the BPI. 'However, the picture is not full of gloom, growth is forecast for pre-recorded cassettes with the rising ownership of portable and in-car cassette equipment, and the rising market penetration of compact discs.' As for the future, 'It will be of paramount importance to develop and sustain consumer interest and loyalty in the older age groups, particularly amongst 25–34-year-olds.'[7]

This is in line with the current gospel in the music industry – that the future lies with the small stable of 'cross-over artists' – those performers with lasting appeal for the 'yuppie' post-teen consumer market who may otherwise be losing the record-buying habit. This marketing strategy has inevitable consequences for the range and diversity of music produced, since it tends to promote a few big stars, to the detriment of newer or less commercial talent.

The trend began to cast further doubt on the fairness of the levy scheme, which would attempt to distribute royalties according to the level of record sales and airplay time given to particular artists: the market, in other words, that has been moulded by such promotional strategies.

The BPI argue, 'Big hit records make it possible for a whole range of less profitable recordings to be made and for record companies and publishers to invest in and encourage new talent.' But does current music-industry thinking really support that claim?

'Bending the minister's ear'

'It has been a deliberate exercise in low-key lobbying, rather than mounting a huge public campaign,' explains Terri Anderson of the BPI. By 1987 the lobbying reached the ears of Kenneth Clarke, the latest ministerial incumbent at the Department of Trade and Industry, and to the music industry's horror, its ten-year struggle was finally rejected.

Back in 1977 the Whitford Committee considered bringing private copying within the existing 'fair dealing' exceptions to copyright, which allows the free use of literary, dramatic, and musical compositions for research and private study. In the end it recommended a levy on recorders, but not tape, similar to a scheme introduced in West Germany in 1965. The government ignored the suggestion.

Meanwhile, the major record companies were pressing the panic button. Between 1978 and 1983 the real value of record sales plummeted from £446 million to £299 million, a lethal mix of recession, the legacy of punk, and cheap imports from Europe. Small independent record labels were running rings round the multinational monoliths. Yet the finger was pointed fairly and squarely at home taping as the major cause of declining sales.

The statistics began to roll. In 1977 the BPI claimed record companies were losing £15 million worth of sales a year due to the domestic pirates. A year later the figure had jumped to £40 million. By 1980 it was £200 million, and one year after that £365 million (though the government in its 1981 Green Paper cannily pointed out that lost sales, which included the costs of manufacture and distribution, were not the same as lost royalties, and put the figure at £50 million). In 1980 the MCPS (on behalf of composers and publishers) abandoned its voluntary licence scheme which entitled consumers to record what they liked in return for a small annual fee. With only 10,000 subscribers (and a minimal publicity campaign to tell the public of its existence) its abandonment 'was the only effective means of protecting our position', said the MCPS, 'to concentrate all our efforts on the case of a royalty on blank tape'.

The following year Reginald Eyre, a junior minister at the DTI, unveiled the government's Green Paper. It listed eight reasons why the levy was 'inadvisable', and even suggested that home taping might fall outside the proper bounds of copyright law, which should concentrate solely on the commercial sphere. The record industry might have to reconcile itself 'to a situation where its revenue comes mainly from broadcasting and other public performances (such as discos)'.[8]

While the government dragged its feet, Lord Willis introduced a Private Member's Bill in the Lords to impose a levy on recorders in 1983. It lacked government backing and failed.[9]

The levy lobby was not helped by the failure in the US Senate to introduce a similar levy scheme on recorders and blank tape. Nor by the dramatic resurgence in the music industry's own fortunes – thanks to MTV, the 24-hour music cable station in the USA.

The breakthrough in the huge American market for British performers like Duran Duran, the Police, Culture Club, and the Eurythmics, and the world-wide promotional effects of pop videos generally, rocketed British acts to claim 34 per cent of world total sales of pre-recorded music – some $3,865 million worth. The estimated royalties from foreign sales alone of music by British-based companies (including subsidiaries of foreign multi-nationals) was put at nearly $500 million.

The BPI changed their tune. The levy was no longer to compensate directly for 'lost sales', but to recoup 'lost royalties' arising from a new and expanding use of their property. The press were sceptical, and Adrian Berry fumed in the *Daily Telegraph* against the 'rough justice' of the proposal that affected all blank tape purchasers:

It seems reprehensible that people should, in effect, be fined for the 'crime' of buying blank tapes, and even more so that the record companies should pocket the fine. It is rather hard to see why, if the record companies are suffering from injustice, it should be remedied by passing on the injustice to an innocent party.[10]

By February 1985 a new minister was responsible, Geoffrey Pattie, and his consultative document came out in favour of the levy. To legalize private copying without it 'would strike at the roots of the principle of copyright'. Six months later, with a White Paper imminent, the government got cold feet again. This time Leon Brittan was in the hot seat, and a quiet word in the Prime Minister's ear about the effect of the levy on the Retail Price Index scuppered its release.[11]

By the end of 1985 the campaign began to hot up in anticipation of an EEC Green Paper on the issue. Both sides ran advertisements in the press. The BPI claimed that blank taping cost a 24 per cent loss of jobs in four years in the British music industry. The TMG called the levy 'a gift to the greedy'.[12]

John Deacon, director-general of the BPI, announced that without the levy the benefit would go 'into the pockets of the Japanese and other foreign-owned machine and blank-tape importers'. However, it was equally true that much of the levy proceeds would also go abroad, to US multinational record companies, where no levy scheme existed in return.[13]

The BPI had already answered this charge two years earlier in their pamphlet *The Facts about Home Taping* (1984): 'Both the music industry and copyright are international in nature, and it is an extremely insular view to consider depriving rights owners of deserved income simply because they are not UK nationals.'

Two months later Brittan had resigned over Westland and was replaced by Paul Channon at the DTI; the subsequent White Paper came out in favour of a levy again. The enthusiasm did not last long.[14] Eighteen months later, when Kenneth Clarke unveiled the long-awaited Copyright, Designs, and Patents Bill (1987) in the Commons, the levy was proposed a 'dead duck' and had been dropped from the legislation. He declared, 'a new bureaucracy would have been required to collect and distribute the proceeds of the levy at a cost disproportionate to the amount of money concerned. The financial benefit to copyright owners and performers would be outweighed by the adverse effects on consumers, especially visually handicapped people'.[15]

John Deacon, Director-General of the BPI, retorted, 'The government's action is purely politically expedient. What the music industry will be doing now is spending more of its time attempting to protect itself when what it should be doing is looking for expansion and opportunity.'[16]

The government's plans are hardly consistent. The 1987 Copyright Bill legalizes private copying of television and radio broadcasts for 'time-shifting' reasons, but not the direct copying of records, compact discs, audio, or video cassettes. This form of home taping still remains technically illegal.

Is it a tacit recognition, perhaps, of the principle hinted at in the Green Paper of 1981 that copyright law should confine itself to the commercial sphere, and that the music industry should get used to the idea that its revenue in the future will come mainly from broadcasting, 'secondary use' like film and advertising soundtracks, and other licensed public performances, such as shops and discos?

It would appear that the government is becoming resigned to the existence of two 'markets' for copyright works. The first operates between the various branches of the media industries, where the use of material can be monitored, calculated, and translated into fairly accurate royalty payments. The second is an unregulated, unmonitored exchange of pre-recorded works copied from one medium to another, made by millions of private individuals every day of the year.

The proposal by the record industry that a pot of money be levied from consumers of blank tape, which could then be divided 'equitably' in 'compensation' to rights owners, irrespective of actual use of specific works, has been rebuffed by the government for the time being.

But already the music industry is gearing up to try again, this time turning to its latest *bête noire* – the problem of controlling the rental of compact discs, which they fear will be used by consumers to copy onto other media, like audio cassettes or Digital Audio Tape (DAT), with no reduction in sound quality. They see this as a new, increasing use of artists' work, for which they should receive compensation. At the time of writing, their proposal for a levy on such rental has not been included in the 1987 Bill, although the government has indicated its willingness to look at the problem again.

But can the royalty system still be efficient? We no longer live in a world where the market success of an artist or record company is simply reflected by the number of records or tapes sold. It is now a very different, more complex calculation, which includes revenue from broadcaster's airplay, public performance at live concerts or on juke-boxes, the use on soundtracks for films and television commercials and so on. The increasingly sophisticated monitoring by the royalty-collecting societies of these uses *within* the media industries is sufficiently reliable to calculate remuneration.

But attempts to extend monitoring systems outside the entertainment industries themselves, like the levy on consumers, means abandoning the idea of royalties reflecting the actual success of particular works for a round-table carve-up between the principal vested interests – artists, unions, broadcasters, and producers. Relative bargaining strength of the big media institutions, regulated by a Copyright Tribunal, will increasingly determine individual creators' incomes: not all that different, ultimately, from a trade union negotiating wage levels on a collective basis for its members. Which is all very well, but it does undermine the original intention of copyright law, where the individual creator was paramount, and protected by the market from institutional (or state) pressures.

As for the record industry's defence of royalties, the attraction lies in the fact that such a system does not threaten their control or power over the market or the artists themselves. If it was ever proposed to redistribute royalties more equitably, say in accordance with a broader cultural policy to encourage less commercial, minority tastes, the record companies would fiercely resist it.

In some countries, such as Sweden and France, the government has openly recognized the new opportunities for broadening the range of cultural production. The levy schemes on blank tape that they have introduced redistribute all or part of the resulting funds directly into arts subsidy, to less successful, newer artists, regardless of their current 'market appeal': in other words, a 'culture tax'.[17]

It is ironic that piracy should be leading to new forms of state patronage – the very opposite of how philosophers from Locke and Rousseau onwards envisaged the theory of intellectual property developing.

Such trends explain the contradiction at the heart of the British government's policies. Its wish to see information treated as a commodity, governed by market forces and at the same time remain copyright, is a classic case of 'catch-22'. For each new attempt to accommodate the existing system, such as levies on blank tapes, blanket licences for photocopying, and compulsory publishing schemes in developing countries, further dilutes the fundamental principle of copyright – that royalties reflect success in the marketplace.

Electronic technology divorces the use of the 'message' from the purchase of the 'medium' that contains it. When the number of users and quantity of use can no longer be traced simply by looking at market sales of physical objects – LPs, pre-recorded tapes, books, software disks – the calculation of precise royalties becomes impossible. The inevitable trend is away from direct compensation for owners based on actual market success, towards *collective* solutions.

The new funds from levies and licences must be divided according to nominal assessments of use – airplay logs from selected broadcasters, spot checks, and market research. It will also depend on the relative strength of professional organizations negotiating on their members' behalf to fix their contribution or slice of the cake: from consumer councils and university boards to authors' and producers' associations or trades unions. The test will no longer be actual sales but, more nebulously, what is 'fair' or 'equitable'.

The traditional and powerful royalty-collecting societies, most developed in the music industry, are having to modify their own practices and represent their members in such negotiations. But 'defending the rights of their members' is far from straightforward, since the expectations (and likely benefits) of star performers are not the same as the needs of less successful artists. The resulting collective bargaining will often be between two near-monopolies: the collecting societies, on one hand, and the broadcast companies and distributors, on the other.

Indeed, it is the latter, the 'gate-keepers' of the channels of distribution, whose power will grow, choosing what to offer to the public and moulding the market on which royalties will be calculated. The cycle that determines what should then be produced will be in fewer and fewer hands.

In the battle over how these new sources of revenue should be carved up, copyright owners cite the success of collecting societies like the PRS, which has administered the complex distribution of music royalties from public performances since the turn of the century. But home taping presents them with an entirely new problem. It is one thing to administer licence schemes with identifiable institutions, such as concert halls or pubs, but quite another to track down *each member of the audience*.

Similarly, it is one thing to divide up the spoils between a relatively small number of record companies, music publishers, and composers, but more difficult when it comes to the film and television industries, where the number of creative contributors to any one product is considerably greater.

The resulting trend is for producers and publishers to persuade artists to assign their rights to them at the outset, so that royalties can be properly administered and go to one identifiable recipient; and the artists increasingly depend on the institutions to negotiate blanket agreements on their behalf. Both of these undermine the 'personal, individual rights' of creators, based on a free market, that copyright is supposed to protect.

Whether it is the government itself or the new copyright bureaucracies, the trend is towards *political* choices of cultural policy:

whether to recognize the claims of marginal markets, educational users, special interest groups, the disabled, or support non-mainstream authors, composers, and 'independent' producers. Such a development is not without its dangers, as defenders of the copyright system, such as S. M. Stewart in his book *International Copyright* (1983), are keen to point out:

> Once the state becomes the provider of remuneration for creative effort, there is only one short step to making the state or its functionaries, instead of the general public, the arbiters of what is worthy of remuneration and what is not. That is the road towards both artistic and political censorship.[18]

Yet aren't we already one short step from another form of control, equally undemocratic? The paradox is that the new licensing and proposed levy schemes are likely to create 'cultural quangos' whose members, including unaccountable broadcasters and multinational corporations, will be by default the new 'arbiters of what is worthy of renumeration and what is not'.

How removed from state interference will the new licensing authorities be? It is all too likely that the state will be forced to intervene, to set the parameters of the negotiations and supervise the collecting societies, which in turn, almost by definition, will have the power of a monopoly to dominate the market.

The copyright industries hope that the new Copyright Tribunal, designed to arbitrate between conflicting claims, will distance the role of the state in the bargaining process. But it leaves unresolved the rights of those who have no standing at the tribunal – the ordinary consumers. The Copyright Tribunal will not be a forum to question the cultural policies of those who make them.

If the market no longer accurately represents consumer choice, where will the voice of the public be heard? Will there be calls for more direct democratic control of cultural production and broadcasting? How would it work in practice? Such questions have hardly begun to be debated within the political parties.

The Council of Europe concluded its report of the 1982 Symposium by recognizing the growing involvement of the state in cultural policy, and that the choices represented different visions of society. On the one hand, a reliance on the 'free market' to determine the information and culture we receive (increasingly an illusion), and on the other, 'a broader conception of the function of public authorities, associated with the idea of the welfare state in the English-speaking world, and with democratic planning in the Latin world'.[19] No wonder the Conservative government in Britain has changed its mind so many times.

21

Commodity culture

The concept in copyright law has been wrong. We were trying to fit
the problems of new technology into a preconceived scheme dealing
with tangible things, with books and photocopies . . . but none of the
new means of dissemination of information really fall within the pre-
defined categories. We are trying to squeeze the new technology into
these old forms. And frankly, it doesn't fit.

(Ed Cramer, chief executive of BMI, the US royalty-collecting
society)[1]

When the US Congress ratified a wholesale reform of copyright law
in 1976, bringing it up to date with the Xerox photocopier, it was
confident that its fifteen years of deliberation had resolved the issues
for the rest of the twentieth century. Yet only seven years later a
congressional subcommittee was reporting that the premise of
copyright itself was fundamentally threatened.

Joseph Coates, a Washington consultant, informed the committee
that the basis of copyright was the *ability to exercise control*; that in
theory a copyrighted work cannot be reproduced without either
compensation to the author or the author's permission: 'Now with
home computers, video recorders, and backyard dish antennas, the
element of control is lost, and "intellectual property" becomes
intangible if not undefinable.'[2]

The law has certainly tried to keep pace with technological and
economic changes. For instance, it has extended its reach beyond the
cultural and artistic, to cover a much wider realm of 'information' –
provided it has been created with some degree of human ingenuity
and effort. Nowadays, 'literary works' under copyright include
football pools coupons, railway timetables, computer programs that
operate washing-machines, and compilations of computer data. In
the same way, the definition of 'artistic works' has been extended to
include video games, furniture design, and even the spare parts for
cars.

And it protects more than mechanically reproduced works.
To accommodate computer software, basic definitions have been
stretched, such as 'intellectual property' being 'an idea expressed in a
material form' to 'works fixed in any form from which they can in
principle be reproduced'.[3]

Are such developments the sign of a pragmatic and adaptable system, capable of accommodating change? Or do they indicate an outmoded concept, increasingly divorced from its original intention? Has the new Copyright, Designs, and Patents Bill (1987), presented to Parliament as 'a fresh statement of the law on a more logical and consistent basis, taking into account the technological changes of the last thirty years', really established durable principles to withstand the developments of the next thirty?

As each new remedy is introduced to bolster the system, it seems increasingly to be a case of yesterday's battles being fought today, rather than considering a more appropriate, if radical, alternative.

As we have seen with the response to private copying, like the levy on blank tape, the proposed remedies raise as many problems as they purport to solve. In return for legalizing piracy, they seek collective compensation for rights owners. But in the process they reduce the level of individual control that owners have traditionally exercised. The growing introduction of 'blanket licences' to cover everything from photocopying to recording off-air broadcasts, harmonizing the activities of cable and satellite television stations, and limiting the restrictive practices of software firms, increases the trend.

The contradictions are well illustrated by the approach taken to that particular class of worthy 'pirates' who can neither be ignored as hometapers nor be stigmatized as criminals, but who represent the most organized body of unauthorized copiers in the UK: the teachers. As early as 1975 publishers were calling for action against educational authorities to control the use of photocopiers in schools and universities. The extent of multiple copying for classrooms quickly exceeded the existing 'fair dealing' rules in the 1956 Copyright Act, which were designed to allow single copies of published works to be made for private study and research.

But it was not before 1984 that any agreement was reached between the newly created Copyright Licensing Agency (CLA), representing authors and publishers, and local authorities, on what schools could and could not copy.[4] The agreement, for a one-year trial period, was a model of compromise and confusion. Local authorities agreed to pay £350,000 to the CLA in return for permission to make multiple copies within stringent guidelines. Only 5 per cent of a book or one article of a journal was allowed, for use by just one class. The material could not be stocked or reused by another class and had to be destroyed. All existing copies before the scheme began also had to be thrown away.

Furthermore, the licences did not cover all copyright works. Exam papers, sheet music, newspapers, maps, charts, and tables were all excluded, or covered by other licensing schemes with their own codes and guidelines. And any ordinary publisher could decide not to join the CLA scheme, in which case copying their works was still an infringement. For administering the scheme, and in preparation of a permanent arrangement, 10 per cent of schools had to record every copy they made throughout the year, and the CLA promised to mount random checks with inspectors.

It is hardly surprising that teachers complained that the licence scheme meant extra work, constant uncertainty, and the regular loss of vital teaching materials. Resistance also centred on whether the CLA intended to take on less easy targets than education, like government departments, commercial companies, libraries, and high-street copy shops, all of which were equally culpable of unauthorized photocopying.

Teachers objected that this was not compensation but a demand for revenue, claiming that the scheme took no account of all the out-of-print material that was copied, or the free amounts of material still permitted under 'fair dealing'. When universities were approached by the CLA to make a similar agreement, under which publishers would receive 6p a copy for journals and 3p for books, the vice-chancellors refused.

In 1985 the estimate of copying in schools was put at 88 million copies. The licensing arrangements have now been put on a permanent footing, with educational authorities paying roughly £1 million a year to the publishers.[5] The 1987 Copyright Bill gives these three schemes statutory backing, and where a scheme is not in operation allows one per cent of any published work to be photocopied in any given quarter of the year. Certain classes of works remain exempt from the scheme and are subject to other licences; and publishers can still refuse to join the scheme altogether. Consequently, licensing authorities must now indemnify schools for any unintentional infringement caused by copying their works.

But there is also an ominous postscript. The secretary of state reserves powers to order a publisher to join the scheme, if he considers the publisher's refusal 'unreasonable'. The publisher can appeal to the Copyright Tribunal.

It is still not clear how the resulting licence funds can be divided to reflect accurately the actual copies that have been made, and how they will be divided between publishers and individual authors. Both this, and the compulsory proposals suggest that a loosening control of authors' rights is the price to be paid for collective compensation. There are no proposals to extend the scheme to government departments or the corporate sector.

The position is no less confused over the use of video recordings of television broadcasts in schools. The problem is compounded by the far greater number of creative contributors involved in television and film production. Yet the use of audio-visual material in the classroom becomes ever more important. Apart from documentaries and films, which are useful across the curriculum, all types of broadcast material are essential for study and criticism if 'media studies' are to become a major component of contemporary education.

Years of negotiating have produced a web of limited and conflicting licensing schemes. Some of these cover only educational broadcasts; others are more general. But where most broadcast material was still strictly 'out of bounds', schools and representative organizations campaigned for free educational use of audio-visual material.

Vincent Porter of the Central London Polytechnic summed up the feeling of many teachers at a conference organized by the British Universities Film and Video Council, when he said:

> We are not in the entertainment industry; we see film and television as tools to be used alongside books. We need to have access to all films and programmes kids see. If the makers can understand that then maybe we could get together. We are not interested in people who want to make a buck out of education.[6]

Earlier proposals for a levy on blank videotape were welcomed by educational organizations as being the next best thing, allowing unrestricted use of mass media output. But the 1987 Copyright Bill has recognized the particular needs of education and granted free use of broadcast material (where not already covered by a licensing scheme) and allowed the playing of films and videos in the classroom without having to seek the permission of rights owners.

Electronic images

> Who owns the electronic image?
>
> (John Dovey, video-maker)[7]

The wish to criticize and comment on the output of broadcast media is not confined to those working in education. Artists, political groups, and campaigning organizations regularly seek to use television images as the raw material for their own statements. But they have found that copyright can be an effective means of stifling outside criticism and dissent.

As mentioned earlier, there are accepted limitations to the control exercised by copyright owners over their work, in the public interest. Known as 'fair dealing' exemptions, they allow anyone to quote from literary, musical, dramatic, or artistic works for the purposes of criticism or review, or when reporting current events.

Yet until the 1987 Copyright Bill, it was still illegal to quote from television, radio, video, phonograms, or films in the same medium, with very unfair results.

Whether it was to criticize a new movie release or television drama, or to present an alternative interpretation of news coverage, not only had each clip be paid for, but permission had to be granted by the producer or television company concerned. Such permission, of course, was unlikely to be forthcoming to anyone outside the established broadcasting consensus, or perhaps even to anyone who could not promise a sympathetic review.

John Dovey, an independent video-maker, has described his experience of seeking permission to use news clips for a satirical video called *Death Valley Days*, which incorporated a collage of clips recorded off television from films, adverts, news, and soap operas. The resulting 'scratch video' had been bought by Channel 4 for transmission in September 1985:

> We soon discovered that the clearance process is far from being simple – indeed, financial considerations are the last thing that gets discussed. First of all it's necessary to successfully answer the questions, 'Who are you and what kind of programme are you making?'
>
> If you don't come up with a confidence-inspiring line, you'll be refused clearance, no matter what your financial resources amount to. Copyright owners are terrified that producers might make something using their images that might upset, or even nudge, the apple cart. They live in fear of being refused continuing access to current affairs information and footage. Thus continuing access depends entirely upon them playing the game by the rules – 'balance' at all times, respectful treatment of those in authority, otherwise suddenly they don't get passes or camera positions in those vital press conferences.

Nor were the effects confined to those operating outside the industry. Anna Coote, producer of a regular current affairs series in the early days of Channel 4 called *The Friday Alternative*, was commissioned to present a critique of the way television news is selected and presented. Despite a contract with ITN to supply material, each request was subject to detailed scrutiny and the final consent of the ITN editor. Problems arose over criticisms of news coverage of the Falklands War, when footage was refused. A host of minor delays and doubts were used when the producer requested material to illustrate how an interview with Arthur Scargill was edited to omit his own criticisms of ITN; the same happened after a request to examine the assumptions behind Alastair Burnett's report of Leonid Brezhnev's funeral.

The BBC were even more obstructive, refusing permission for clips for several months and offering access only on condition they approved the context. Anna Coote observed:

> We cannot get access to the necessary material without permission from the copyright owners, and we cannot get that without their goodwill, which we are bound to jeopardize every time we criticize them. Our experience suggests that the BBC and ITN are so unaccustomed to criticism that it causes them disproportionate grief.

Proposing the right to quote, she added, 'They should have a real opportunity to acclimatize.'[8] Under the 1987 Copyright Bill, such a 'right to quote' will be granted for the first time, to sound recordings, films, television and radio programmes, for the purposes of criticism or review, or reporting current events, provided the rights owner is sufficiently acknowledged.

Just as electronic technology has enabled consumers to thwart the prevailing distribution markets, so the same technology is beginning to challenge the structure of cultural production. Low-cost video equipment, music synthesizers, and recording systems, or powerful domestic computers, networked via the telephone, all offer the capacity for non-professionals to produce alternative statements, or to re-edit and reinterpret the messages of the mainstream media.

Video is but one recent example of the wider phenomenon that has emerged in all the creative arts since the war, which treats 'work on the image', from William Burroughs's cut-ups to Andy Warhol's canvasses depicting Campbell's soup cans, as a legitimate art form. Its premise is 'the death of the author', and plagiarism, pastiche, and nostalgia epitomize its style.

Not everyone shares the outlook, however, as Warhol found out in 1985 when he changed from using commercial products and publicity photographs as his subjects to the work of other artists. He added lurid new colouring and his signature to reproductions of *The Scream* by Norwegian artist Edvard Munch. The curators at the Munch Museum in Oslo were not amused; for although the artist died in 1944, his works were still in copyright, and would remain so until 1994. When Warhol offered to sell lithographs of his work at Christie's for £30,000 each, the Munch estate, insensitive to the post-modern aesthetic, sued him.

Nevertheless, new technology enables the mischievous and serious 'borrowing' of popular culture to develop beyond reasonable control, throwing copyright's insistence on 'originality' and authorship into further disarray. Where does plagiarism end and a new work begin? Where does the line fall between the right to quote for the purposes of review, referred to above, and the wholesale manipulation and reworking of 'found' images and sounds (that is, someone else's original material), which no doubt the later creator will argue was meant as a 'critique' of the original work? Do creators have 'moral rights' to protect their work against such later exploitation? The Copyright Designs and Patents Bill (1987) introduces the concept of moral rights for the original creator, author, or composer of copyright works, but how effective they will be remains to be seen. Already publishers and record companies are offering new talent a contract which excludes the moral rights clause in the Bill. Only those established artists, who have equal bargaining power to the producers, it seems, will be able to take the benefit of moral rights safeguard.

Not only in the art world, but in industry and commerce, the interaction between copyright works and computers makes such questions unavoidable. As Alistair Kelman writes:

> Computers, when suitably programmed, can enhance detail in photographs, produce statistics from unsorted masses of data, turn shapes drawn on a terminal with a light pen into musical notes, and animate drawings. Whether these new products are to be considered adaptations of existing copyright works, works of joint authorship with the creator of the computer program, or not protected by copyright at all, has still to be fully considered.[9]

The government believes that existing provisions of joint authorship will be adequate, but unravelling the different levels of contribution and assessing the various elements of skill and effort involved in the development of computer-aided designs hardly promise to get easier.

In the meantime, the music industry continues to rely on computers, raising interesting questions of plagiarism with the use and storage of popular 'sound samples' and the copying of musical patterns using MIDI sequencers. Sophisticated sound 'samplers' like the Fairlight or Synclaviar can store and retrieve several samples of sound, including distinctive notes and extracts from popular recordings, and manipulate them into new sound mixes. The sounds are converted to digital memory for storage, then retrieved, converted back to analogue, and played.

When 'Pump up the Volume' by MARRS rose to the top of the British singles charts in September 1987, record producer Peter Waterman claimed they had 'stolen' sounds from his hit 'Roadblock'. In taking legal action against the MARRS's label 4AD, he argued that wholesale 'sampling' (ie: copying) of parts of other people's records was no longer acceptable. The time had come to 'make sampling respectable' he said, pointing out that it was not illegal to take elements of another's sound recording provided you obtained permission first. His own success with disco dance hits had relied heavily on the new electronic music technology – but now it seemed things were getting out of hand.

The key legal issue was whether the sampling of a musical phrase, or even just a particular sound effect, was a 'substantial' part of the original work. Only if it were 'substantial', would a case for infringement hold up. 'I cannot see sampling a bass drum, or a snare drum as substantial', said Waterman, 'but the start of a record or indeed any musical part must for everyone's sakes mean substantial.'[10] Meanwhile, as lawyers and record producers attempt to agree on an acceptable working practice, it is possible to buy a simple but effective sampling machine made by the Japanese company Casio, for about £80 in the High Street.

The final nail in the coffin for sheet-music publishers must surely be the JVC add-on unit to the MIDI sequencer that will automatically draw a musical manuscript on the screen, corresponding to the tune played into it. Once converted into MIDI data, it can be copied, edited, or adapted, and then replayed through the MIDI on any chosen instrument.

It was the problem of legal inconsistency that occupied the minds of the US congressional subcommittee on copyright reform. 'Trying to anticipate change is futile,' observed Ben Compaine of the Harvard Program on Information Resources. 'It's a real swamp. Things grow off each other, and one change creates many changes. Anything you do has to be very flexible and very general, otherwise you'll be back here every three or four years.'

The Democratic congressman from Kentucky, Romano Mazzoli, replied:

> We have to navigate that swamp. We are searching for certain immutable truths that we can incorporate into the law so that we do not discourage inventors but also protect the creative community from being picked to death by schools of piranhas.

The 'immutable truths' have still to manifest themselves. Meanwhile Joseph Coates had the last word on the subject. 'Pull the stopper on the bottle,' he warned, 'and you will have informaton flowing in every direction.'[11]

Part four
The future

22

Alternative futures

Wherever we are, it is but a stage on the way to somewhere else, and whatever we do, however well we do it, it is only a preparation to do something else that shall be different.

(Robert Louis Stevenson)

This book is an account of events which have occurred in the last twenty-five years, most of them within the previous decade, and are still taking place around us. So it can be no more than an interim report. In spite of all the efforts to control piracy, it is steadily spreading. When a centre of operations closes down, the operators move on. The business may be legitimized in one country, but new opportunities are constantly opening up elsewhere. It is difficult enough to guess what form it will take next, let alone predict the outcome. In years to come it may be possible to fit the jigsaw together and come to self-assured conclusions, but it is beyond us at this stage. All we can do is record what is happening and make what sense we can of the story so far.

The first problem is the sheer diversity of piracy, which takes so many forms, mutating from one social system to another as it adapts to the laws of supply and demand. The criminal video gangs in Europe are a world away from the modern shopping precincts in Bahrain, where the same pirate tapes are openly and legitimately on sale.

The stalls of bootleg cassettes one can see in any London street market have something in common with the pirate paperbacks in a Karachi bazaar, but how do they relate to the day-to-day piracy we all indulge in as we go about out normal routine in homes, schools, and offices? Are they random, unrelated phenomena or part of a global pattern? A sign of declining moral standards or the rise of a new and quite different set of ethical values? In order to make sense of so many varied activities, it is necessary to stand back, to put them in a wider perspective, and see if they fit into some kind of historical context. But this is not easy.

In looking for a frame of reference one must take into account the views of the participants themselves. Yet their perception of events is shaped by the roles they play; and because they are so close to the action, the conflict in their attitudes and motives can be as confusing as the other evidence.

Even our own frame of reference in writing this book, which links electronic piracy to the emergence of new 'information technology', is open to question, because everyone has a different view of that this means. For instance, we began by explaining that information – all information – could be regarded as the same thing. But what exactly is it? A form of liquid currency? A natural resource? A commodity or a human right? According to where you stand it can be almost any combination of these, and the implications are different in each case. This is not some casual guessing game, because the answers could have far-reaching consequences in every sphere of human activity for years to come. However, in spite of these reservations, it is possible to make out certain trends in the welter of evidence.

To start with, it is clear that mass-produced information, like pop-music records and tapes, is most susceptible to piracy; other forms, such as up-to-date news and hi-tech information, are fiercely protected and exploited. It would appear that traditional forms of distribution, like publishing, are the most vulnerable; and the new electronic systems are the most secure. The big money is now going on the media transnationals, who are building the new information networks with the same enthusiasm that their predecessors once built the railways.

From this point of view, piracy is one of the symptoms of a business revolution, part of the massive change now taking place in market forces and world economics. But there is also a political element, in the growing role of national governments, which are being dragged in as negotiators, as enforcers, or even, in the Third World, as the protectors of piracy. These responsibilities are new to political theory and provoke different and often contradictory responses. How, for instance, will governments be able to reconcile the duty to defend their national interests with the spread of transnational corporations and a global network which is outside their control?

Another theme that emerges is the sharp contrast in the kinds of piracy in 'advanced' western countries and in the underdeveloped nations of the Third World. In these terms, it is a geopolitical phenomenon which can be described in the language of 'cultural imperialism': the disparity between the 'haves' and 'have-nots' (in information, as in every other sense) and the new frontiers being drawn between North and South.

The common denominator throughout the book is the technology which makes electronic piracy possible. These machines have suddenly emerged from nowhere, as spin-offs from the information revolution, and are changing our lives before we have time to adapt to them. If piracy is an unexpected, but inevitable, part of the process, it raises an entirely different set of questions. Why are these changes occurring so fast? Do we want them? Can we adapt to them or are they out of control? Above all, what happens next?

In the long run this is the only question that matters, and books of this sort are expected to end with a section or chapter of speculations. So it is worth exploring these different interpretations in more detail, because each provides a different scenario for the future.

The 'business scenario' shows how the struggle to control the world's media could be building towards a transnational grid-lock.

The 'political scenario' sets the piracy issue against the struggle for informational sovereignty in which governments are trying to control the souces of information and, if necessary, censor them.

The Third World perspective shows how piracy can give a kick-start to a nation's economy, or trap it in a closed loop of second-hand culture.

Finally, and most ominous of all (a book should have a climax), we take an apprehensive look at where the information revolution could be heading.

But first a word about networks and a curious form of piracy which falls outside the scope of this book but could play an important part in the future: the samizdat.

23

The networks

Any information net is a social system.
(Jacques Valee, *The Network Revolution,* 1982)

Trying to forecast the effects of information technology is a popular game. Everyone has had a shot at it, from journalists to academics; and one of the common themes in the plethora of articles, novels, and theoretical treatises is the idea of decentralization. They argue that the main effect of these new communication systems will be to break down our centralized institutions into a loose federation of local, independent, self-supporting, small-is-beautiful networks.

'The spread of cheap, universal computer power', writes Christoper Evans in *The Mighty Micro* (1982),

> will result in a gradual loosening of the restraints on the movement of information within a society. The world of the 1990s will be dominated not only by cheap electronic data processing, but also by virtually infinite data transmission. With thousands of communication satellites likely to be scattered into orbit by the Space Shuttle in the next ten years or so, person to person radio communication is going to be commonplace in the Westernized world, and global TV transmissions will also become widespread.
>
> This kind of development will encourage lateral communication – the spread of information from human being to human being across the base of the social pyramid.
>
> Characteristically this favours the kind of open society which most of us in the Western world enjoy today, and has just the opposite effect on autocracies – both right and left wing – who like to make sure that all information is handed very firmly downwards. This point has been made forcefully by Tom Stonier, Professor of Science and Society at Bradford University, who argues that the critical point beyond which an autocracy or bureaucracy finds it hard to hold its power is when twenty per cent of its population have telephones. In his view the Soviet Union, and other tightly controlled societies, will be unable to prevent more and more lateral communication of this kind developing and will gradually disintegrate as a consquence.[1]

The idea that the telephone spells the end of totalitarianism may seem a little naïve – especially when it enables the state (or in this case the KGB) to monitor every call – but there is a grain of truth in it. The most striking evidence for this is a form of piracy we have only touched on, but which has already proved to have dramatic results: the political samizdat.

The name 'samizdat' was originally give to the typewritten material circulated among dissident Soviet writers and intellectuals. Newsletters, journals, and even whole novels by writers such as Solzhenitsyn were laboriously typed and retyped, as they passed from hand to hand around the network of contacts. Over the years a whole body of literature has been distributed in this way, as faded, illegal carbon copies without even the acknowledgement of authorship.

The authorities tried to suppress it, but never quite succeeded, and most of it eventually reached the west to provide the only authentic alternative to Soviet propaganda. The system was so successful that 'samizdat' has become the generic term for all underground literature.

Electronic technology has made it even more effective. Although the private ownership of photocopiers (which are the ideal samizdat machines) is strictly licensed, their place has been taken by the micro-computer. The Soviet authorities are keen to educate the younger generation in basic computer science, so the machines are widely available; by using simple word-processor programs it is possible to print out quantities of illicit material.

The advantages over traditional techniques are considerable. It is much faster, the text can be stored on floppy disks (which are easily concealed or wiped out), and electronic printers can produce especially small typeface, which saves on paper. In theory, it is even possible to transmit the material over the phone. The new Soviet policy of *glaznost* (openness) means that censorship is not applied as strictly as it once was. But the dissident networks still exist, and the spread of information technology has given rise to another kind of samizdat, in the form of pirated video cassettes and tapes.

The Soviet authorities admit that there are at least 2 million imported VCRs in the country, mostly Philips machines made under licence in Czechoslovakia, Panasonics from Hungary, and Japanese models brought in from Yugoslavia. In response to demand, the government plans to increase domestic production to 60,000 a year by 1990, but the release of a meagre 300 video titles a year is not enough to satisfy demand.

The cassettes are very expensive by our standards, at about £100 each (they still have to rely on imported Japanese tape), but Muscovites are still prepared to pay up to £310 for unofficial, pirate editions of American movies, even though many of them, like the *Rambo* series, are rabidly anti-communist. As a consequence, the black market thrives, and a new service industry has grown up converting Soviet recorders to VHS and Betamax systems.

The pirate videos reach a wider audience than the political samizdat and could have far-reaching effects. As *Newsweek* recently remarked, 'Even seemingly innocuous Western fare, when viewed in the privacy of people's homes, undermines state control of information and offers previously inaccessible glimpses of the outside world.'[2]

The story is the same throughout Eastern Europe. Only Bulgaria has attempted to stem the tide; in 1985 it introduced the enforced registration of all video equipment brought into the country. In Poland, with the most independent-minded and disaffected population of the eastern bloc, video has been given a direct political twist by the Solidarity underground, who distribute copies of banned movies like Andrzej Wajda's *Man of Iron* and the works of Agnieska Holland, Jerzy Skolimowski, and Czeslaw Milosz, who was awarded the Nobel Prize for literature in 1980 despite being banned in his country. Satirical videos have been produced and circulated by NOWA-Kaseta, an electronic extension of the underground publishers NOWA; and western news reports are smuggled in by *émigré* groups such as Contakt. The Poles, for whom illegal television parties are now a way of life, have coined the term 'magnetizdat' to describe this alternative form of media.

A revolutionary new development is that Poland is the first eastern-bloc country to allow the private use of television satellite dishes. The official press attacks them as ideological pollutants, but the authorities seem reluctant to ban them outright, though the dishes are strictly licensed on condition that the licensee is the only person to watch the programmes. Even their families are forbidden to join them, and to obtain a licence in the first place a person requires an officially 'acceptable' reason, such as a journalist who needs to monitor western media.

Despite these limitations, the trade magazine *Cable and Satellite Europe* estimates that in 1987 there were more than 2,000 satellite dishes in use in Poland, most of them installed since 1986. There is a black market in the smaller dishes which can be concealed in roof spaces and lofts, and many receiving stations act as miniature studios producing video cassettes of western broadcasts, including those from the cable news network.[3]

'Magnetizdat' is not limited to Iron Curtain countries. The new technology is being turned to advantage by many other exiled or oppressed groups around the world. For instance, one of the most striking examples of it was the use of audio cassettes in the Iranian revolution. When the Shah of Iran exiled the Ayatollah Khomeini to France, he was hoping to rid himself of the focus for religious subversion. But the ayatollah fought to retain his influence by recording hundreds of sermons and messages on tape cassettes, which he had smuggled back into the country. There, they were duplicated and passed from hand to hand till they reached every mosque and school in the country.

The tapes not only raised the religious temperature but helped to establish the Shi'ite mullahs as an organized political force. In the months leading up to the fall of the Shah they became an explosive political currency; and the secret police, SAVAK, were run off their feet trying to seize and suppress them. In fact, the voice of the ayatollah was heard by more people during his exile than when he lived in Iran. The information networks he established eventually achieved what no other political party, including the Communists, had been able to – a mass popular uprising.

Ironically, the ayatollah's opponents are now using the same 'magnetizdat' techniques against his own regime, by smuggling in tapes and video cassettes of anti–Khomeini propaganda. Meanwhile, the Iranians are busy spreading the gospel of fundamentalism, in exactly the same way, to Egypt, the Gulf states, and the 18,000 underground mosques operating in the southern USSR.[4]

Throughout the world – from videos of Middle Eastern hostages to the cassettes of nationalist folk songs distributed by the socialist underground in Chile – wherever beliefs or opinions are suppressed, the cameras and recorders are at work.

The lessons have been learned from the effects that nightly television coverage of the Vietnam War had on the United States population in the early 1970s, and publicity is now a major weapon in a guerrilla war. The commanders of insurgent armies recognize that a thirty-second film clip on world-wide networks can be worth more for their cause than guns. It was recently reported, for instance, that a programme is under way in West Germany to train eighty Mujaheddin rebels in the use of video cameras, so that they can cover the war in Afghanistan for television news agencies. Ironically, as is so often the case, although the guerrillas and their backers both recognize the value of this information, their motives in broadcasting it are entirely different.

In the same way, but in a more general sense, the motives of the pirate and the cultural guerrilla are very different. Yet their techniques are identical, and they are both, in their own way, fighting the establishment for the control of information. Apart from their motives, it is difficult to define where one activity begins and the other leaves off. Both ignore (or override) the principles of copyright. Both are used to make (or raise) money. Both are 'illegal' with regard to national laws. Both are networking activities supplying a frustrated public demand.

The only thing which sets them apart in our minds is the motivation – our personal judgement as to whether the means justify the ends – and the perception, from our point of view, of the long-term consequences.

The network conspiracy

> Professor Robert M. Fano of MIT comments on the necessity for democratization of data equipment, saying that the maintenance of a sensible balance of power in society, and hence the maintenance of personal freedom, will in future heavily depend on whether the services of powerful computer systems are made generally available, practically and economically, like electricity and the telephone today.
>
> If, however, not everyone has access to the new information systems, private networks will be started. The beginnings are already being made.
>
> Such a development of information networks and data banks available to radical groups in society would at present seem to be a somewhat adventurous idea. In fact it would merely correspond to the setting up last century of a critical opposition press, which has long been accepted as a matter of course.
>
> (Robert Jungk, *The Everyman Project*, 1976)

The response to unofficial networks is very different in Europe and the USA, where the hierarchies are more tolerant and even connive at them. The Italian writer and academic Umberto Eco, author of *The Name of the Rose*, believes that the traditional hierarchies are mutating and that it is a mistake to believe there is any longer a centralized power behind them. He argues that the authority of states and big business resides in a 'network of micro-powers' and that this 'finespun, widespread cobweb' is more flexible and tenacious than most revolutionaries (and pirates) realize. 'If this cobweb exists,' he writes,

> it is capable of healing its local wounds, precisely because it has no heart, precisely because it is – let us say – a body without organs.
>
> For example: The triumph of photocopying is creating a crisis in the publishing industry. Each of us if he can obtain, at less expense, a photocopy of a very expensive book avoids buying that book. The practice, however, has become institutionalized. Let's say a book of two hundred pages costs twenty dollars. If I copy it in a stationery store at twenty cents a page I spend forty dollars, and this is not economically feasible. If I use a machine that can reduce two pages onto a single sheet, I spend the price of the book. If I go in with some others and make a hundred copies, I cut the cost in half. Then

the operation becomes feasible. If the book is scholarly, and is also two hundred pages long, it will cost forty dollars, then the cost of the photocopy is reduced to a fourth. Thousands of students in this way are paying a fourth of the list price of expensive books. An almost legal form of confiscation, or expropriation.

But the big German and Dutch publishing firms, who bring out scientific works in English, have already adapted to this situation. A two hundred page book now costs fifty dollars. They know full well that they will sell it only to libraries and research teams and the rest will be Xeroxes. They will sell only three thousand copies. But three thousand copies at fifty dollars comes out the same as fifty thousand copies at three dollars (except that production and distribution costs are lower). Further, to protect themselves, they don't pay the authors, claiming that these are scholarly publications destined for public service organizations.

The example is only an example, and it applies exclusively to indispensable scientific works. But it serves to demonstrate that the capacity of the big systems for healing their wounds is considerable. And that, indeed, big systems and subversive groups are often twins, and one produces the other.

That is to say, if the attack on the presumed 'heart' of the system (confident that such a central Power exists) is bound to fail, likewise the peripheral attack on systems that have neither centre nor periphery produces no revolution. At most it guarantees the mutual survival of the players of the game. The big publishing houses are ready to accept the spread of photocopying, as the multinationals can tolerate the phone calls made at their expense, and a good transportation system willingly accepts a fair number of counterfeit tickets – provided the counterfeiters are content with their immediate advantage. It is a more subtle form of 'historic compromise', except that it is technological. It is the new form that the Social Contract is preparing to assume, to the extent that the utopia of revolution is transformed into a scheme of short-range, but permanent, harassment.

(Umberto Eco, *Reports from the Global Village*, 1978)

The name of the net

Sooner or later the networks will have a name. Eco calls them a 'cobweb', and the technical term in systems theory is a 'heterarchy', but we have yet to evolve a simple, familiar phrase that everyone recognizes.

The French have adopted the term *télématique*, which translates as 'telematics' – a serviceable, if uninspired, word and certainly 'better than some of the appalling neologisms coined by others. Among these are such horrors as 'compunications' (by Anthony Oettinger of Harvard University) and 'domonetics' (a combination of 'domicile', 'nexus', and 'electronics') concocted by Allan Kiron, a research scientist at the Patent Office.

Until a name emerges from common usage – as such things do – it is probably easier to call them the networks.

24

The Third World

Our work is in the national interest. We provide the cheap books for Koreans who can't afford the west's prices.
(Park Tae Gun, chairman of FPRA, the Korean book pirates' association)[1]

It comes as something of a surprise that Third World pirates are prepared to defend their activities, yet many of them are. 'I have about 1,000 titles on offer,' admitted Jerome Su, a chinese book pirate in Taiwan:

> and I print about 300 of them myself. I started my own business because I was encouraged by my teachers at university. I know I am infringing foreign copyright and denying profits to publishers and authors. But the west imported our intellectual knowledge a thousand years ago and we never got any royalties for it. Chinese people do not comprehend the copyright idea, it is a western concept.[2]

In a few sentences he summed up the arguments which are common throughout the Third World: education as a human right, the bitter memories of exploitation, and the contradictions inherent in a very different cultural background. It is perfectly true that in 10,000 years of history the Chinese have never had a law of copyright.

A Korean pirate was recently reported as saying 'Books are public property; therefore reprinting them is not piracy. The concept of intellectual property is alien to us'.[3]

This resentment and incomprehension is the background to Third World piracy. It is the other side of the coin, the reverse of the arguments put forward so strongly by the west. It seldom gets a hearing, but it would be a mistake to underestimate the intensity of feeling behind it. Of couse, 'the Third World' is too loose a phrase to cover the diversity of cultures that make up three-quarters of the world's population. Even in terms of piracy they divide into numerous sub-groups.

The newly industrialized countries like Singapore, Taiwan, Hong Kong, and South Korea, for instance, are the main exporters of pirate material, while the largely agrarian, underdeveloped nations of Africa are their main market. But then there are the newly rich nations which have skipped the industrial stage and are trying to buy their way into the information revolution, usually with oil wealth. In some cases, like the Middle Eastern states, they have become vast importers and consumers of pirate material. In others, such as Indonesia, they simply copy what they need for themselves.

Even then there are exceptions. Countries which are large enough to be self-sufficient, like India, make their own rules; and along the fault-lines of geopolitical stress are anarchic states like the Lebanon, where anything goes and the black market is the only stable economic structure.

Yet they have certain factors in common, which colour their perception of events. The main one is a shared experience of centuries of cultural imperialism which has denigrated, and in some cases suppressed, their own culture. Some have succeded in shaking off these foreign influences better than others, but the educational and social systems, and above all the European languages, that were imposed on them still bind them to the west and provide a pipeline for a one-way flow of information, literature, and entertainment.

They still depend on this; indeed, they have no choice, because the overwhelming majority of films and records still come from the same source in the same language. But it forms a deep current of resentment which explains their attitude to piracy. The fact that the profits (and royalties) for this material flow straight back to the west adds insult to injury.

When Lee Kwuan Yew took office as President of the newly independent state of Singapore, he announced that copyright arrangements were just another form of colonial exploitation, and that his country would no longer be paying royalties to western firms. The official attitude has changed since then, but the Indonesians' desperate need for educational material leaves them as dependent as ever on the advanced nations.

'The underlying cause of piracy', according to a recent report by the Asian Group of the International Association of Scholarly Publishers, 'appears to be the wider fact that much of Asia continues to be merely a market for the producer north's products, including its scholarly books.'

Considering the vast backlog of illiteracy left by the colonial powers, it is hardly surprising that the Malaysian Minister of Education should thank God for the photocopier and describe the pirates as 'benefactors of humanity'. It has even been argued that copying devices are a form of alternative or intermediate technology, that the tape-recorder is the cultural equivalent of the plough – a practical low-tech machine that can operate at village level and free poor countries from dependence on sophisticated technology.

The piracy of western material, according to this argument, is the first stage in developing their own distribution and publishing systems. It is seen as the only way that they can challenge the hegemony of the great transnationals and avoid being sucked into their networks until they have time to establish an 'information environment' of their own.

But there is little evidence that this is happening. It is true that the electronics industries of South-East Asia have prospered. The cheap labour exploited by US companies in Taiwan has produced one of the most computer-literate populations in the area, and the sweatshops of Taipei are being replaced by hi-tech computer parks. The same pattern has been repeated in Singapore, where the government recently defined its future as 'the brain centre of the region'.

Piracy was not responsible for this upward mobility, although it certainly helped. The provision of cheap textbooks helped the crash programmes of education which have produced an incredible spread of literacy in the Third World in the last few decades. And it is literacy which produces electronics engineers. At the same time, piracy was the expression of the entrepreneurial skills necessary to change a captive work-force into locally owned, independent industries. But the association was symbiotic rather than seminal, and it is easy to overemphasize its importance. The complex process of dragging a peasant economy into the twenty-first century involves many other social and economic factors.

Also, Singapore and Taiwan are the exceptions. Throughout most of the Third World the effects of piracy have been negative and self-defeating. When Ian Taylor was investigating print piracy in Indonesia, he was dismayed to find that they were still copying out-of-date textbooks from the early 1970s. 'They couldn't even be bothered to copy new editions,' he complained, in an interview.

The reason for this is obvious. When the pirates destroyed the distribution systems of western publishers, they cut off their supply – and there was nothing to copy *except* old books. Like the ancient American cars still kept in running order in Cuba, long after they have been relegated to the scrap heap in other countries, the pirates were forced to recycle their products. It is a closed loop which actually reinforces ties to the west. The schools are forced to depend on out-of-date English language textbooks, and a whole generation is being conditioned to a second-hand, alien culture through pop music and television. Achieving political independence is one thing, but breaking out of this bizarre cycle of self-imposed cultural imperialism could be altogether more difficult.

Culture aid

> We have to bring the entire human race, without exception, up to
> the level of semi-literacy of the average college graduate. This
> represents what may be called the minimum survival level; only if
> we reach it, will we have a chance of seeing the year 2000.
>
> (Arthur C. Clarke)

The need for information and the importance of protecting national
identities, at least in terms of their language, are widely recognized;
but the 'imperialist' countries have responded in very different ways.

The USSR has long had a policy of exporting books, at subsidized
prices, translated into other languages. In 1982 the state publishing
houses turned out 75 million books in languages other than Russian,
and their export levels rose 20 per cent in the decade from 1975 to
1985.

The contrast with the United States could hardly be more
striking. From 1956 to 1976 about 19 million low-priced books were
published in the USA for Third World consumption. From 1976 to
1985 there were none. The US government, which is prepared to
take strong diplomatic action on copyright law and provides massive
subsidies for broadcast propaganda, has apparently abandoned the
printed word. As W. Gordon Graham complained in *Publishers'
Weekly*, 'The United States has lost interest in the book'.

Whether it is regarded as altruism or propaganda, this form of
cultural aid certainly has an effect on piracy. Ian Taylor points to the
marked difference between East and West Africa. In the eastern
states like Nigeria piracy is endemic, whereas in West African states
like Kenya, which benefit from an OECD-sponsored programme
providing cheap textbooks for schools, it is minimal. Subsidized
books undercut the market for cheap copies. At a simple level this
can be seen as 'decriminalizing' piracy. In Willian Saroyan's famous
phrase, 'If you give to a thief, he cannot steal from you and he is no
longer a thief.'

It is a tactic that has been effectively employed with other
problems, such as drug trafficking, where the legalized distribution
of narcotics can change a criminal subculture in a manageable social
phenomenon. But the analogy hardly applies to piracy. To start
with, it is relevant only to the printed word, and only to one
specialized sector of that; it is difficult to imagine comparable
schemes for tapes or video cassettes. Secondly, it is limited in scope
because of the enormous cost and the necessary involvement of so
many governments and international agencies.

As long as the schemes concentrate on the import of textbooks in
the language of the donor country, they are unlikely to encourage the
growth of local publishing. In fact, it is more convincing to describe

it as an attempt to maintain 'informational sovereignty' – a well-intentioned form of cultural colonialism to replace the blatant imperialism of the past.

The advantages of independence can be seen on the Indian subcontinent, in the disparity between Pakistan, where piracy is rife, and India, where it is kept in check by a prosperous publishing industry and established copyright laws. The contrast between an impoverished Third World country entirely dependent on western aid and an independent developing nation already self-sufficient in most resources, including food, is striking. But the critical difference is that for fifty years India has had a flourishing film and music industry, based on Urdu and Hindustani languages, with its own distribution system and an audience of 600 million people. Completely independent of western influences and jealous of its own cultural heritage, this media base has played a vital role in establishing a national identity and, since it is a business, has made sure that its copyright is protected.

This is not to say there is no piracy in India, but it is concentrated on western imports. Outside publishers stand a better chance when seeking redress for their grievances.

The New Information Order

> The underdeveloped should be allowed to make their own choices
> and not have our choices, our technologies, imposed on them.
> (Michael Shallis, *The Silicon Idol*, 1984)

Whenever one focuses on an individual country, it turns out to have particular conditions that make it an exception – and India is no exception. No other country has such a large internal market, and it is unlikely that Mali or Malaysia will develop their own film industry. The majority of the Third World remains a captive audience for western ideas, dependent on hand-outs and pirates who are themselves the unofficial distributors of western ideas; while, above their heads, the transnational corporations are building their networks of satellites and microwave links.

It is this, rather than piracy, which Third World countries regard as the real problem. From their point of view, the copying of a few tapes or textbooks is nothing compared to the threat of this new, all-pervasive cultural imperialism swamping them with a non-stop diet of western advertising and pop videos. Their fears have taken shape in one of the most extraordinary documents ever to be laid before the United Nations. While Britain and the USA are trying to enforce traditional copyright laws, the Third World states have turned to the only international body which provides a forum for such ideas – UNESCO – with a demand for a New Information Order.

The exact nature of this charter is still being debated, and it may never be agreed, let alone implemented, but the concept is challenging. Of the two proposals to make any headway so far, both concern satellite broadcasting. With the backing of the UN Assembly and the International Telecommunications Union, UNESCO is endorsing the right of nations to 'prior consent' over incoming messages, including television programmes, via direct satellite broadcasts. The second more contentious demand is for the control of content, especially when it comes to the kind of advertising the broadcasts carry.

Nothing illustrates the differences of perception better than the incomprehension and hostility of western governments to these proposals. UNESCO itself is already regarded as a hotbed of Marxist trouble-makers. The British, who were originally responsible for its creation, had walked out. For the Americans, who were threatening to cut off its funding, this only confirmed their worst fears and they followed suit. The demands of the New Information Order had appeared, apparently from nowhere, and seemed quite irrelevant to the 'real' issues – though they were puzzled by the wide support for it.

'For the Americans,' writes Herbert Schiller in his book *Information and the Crisis Economy* (1986), 'accustomed as they are to casting Communists as the primary instigators of global, national, and community trouble, this anti-free-flow coalition presents a disconcerting pluralism.'

The idea that the network may have its opponents, that there are people who regard it as actually *reinforcing* the old divisions, may come as a surprise to corporate executives. Yet the evidence is there for them to see on their own southern border, along the only frontier that the USA shares with the Third World. In physical terms it is so dramatic that it can be photographed from earth resources satellites 570 miles out in space. The Landsat and Spot images show the rich orchards of California as a checkerboard of bright red colours to the North, which stop abruptly in a straight line across the continent, to be replaced by the greys and browns of Mexico's impoverished agriculture to the south.

The frontier between the two information environments is less precise, because the media of Mexico are dominated by the bombardment of US television and radio. For the US government it is part of the battle for the 'hearts and minds' of their neighbours. After all, they would argue, the Mexicans like it, and the more they adopt US values, the less inclined they are to adopt communism.

The Mexican government see it differently. The balance of trade is already stacked against them; the consumer spending encouraged by western media fuels inflation; and with 35 million undernourished people to feed, it is no help to watch heavily advertised processed foods replacing the cheaper and more nutritious staples, like corn and beans.

Differences of perception like this bedevil the whole issue of piracy in the Third World. We in the west seem unable to recognize the knock-on effects of our actions, or to see any connection between events in different parts of the global village. This, more than anything, explains the contradictions and questions raised in earlier chapters.

It is said that the Americans lost the war in Vietnam because they were playing checkers (draughts) while the Viet Cong were playing chess – and it is still true today. We will never be able to make sense of the ebb and flow of information – and of side-effects like piracy – until we recognize that it all connects. It is a global phenomenon, everyone is affected by it, and everyone has a right to protect their interests. The most valuable information today is information about other people. Whether we like it or not, a New Information Order is taking shape, and the only question is whether it is negotiated, fought over, or imposed.

The empire strikes back

The concern over copyright in Western publishing terms focuses on the loss of income and profits. This same concern in government circles focuses on the loss of what is deemed to be vital, sometimes confidential, information and ideas. Inevitably, under polarized global conditions, there is a confusion between the objectives of control and copyright, between the denial of access to others and the insistence upon payment for legitimate uses.

This confusion is shared by both sides, since not a few Third World ideologists explicitly propose the right to access without corresponding recognition of the obligation to pay for such uses. But equating human creativity with natural resources is so transparent a falsity that posing the issue in this way only hardens the position of advanced nations, especially the US.

The new information environment threatens to become more rather than less competitive. Those who expect special favours by claiming a less-favoured-nation status are in all likelihood doomed to underdevelopment. But for those nations who seize the opportunity provided by cheap labour markets, who internationalize their services, and compete in culture and in kind on a global scale, the situation is becoming increasingly attractive.

The alternative is a protectionist cultural environment matching a closed economic environment, which leads to a sealed, totalitarian environment, impervious to the larger world.

Stripped of elegant pleas on behalf of the Third World and sledgehammer assaults on the rights of intellectual property in the name of a vague commitment to a mythic socialism, opposition to copyright protection ... sows the seeds of a massive anti–intellectualism. This inevitably spreads to all forms of information where new communications technologies are changing the public's expectations about its rights to use them.

No amount of vague rhetoric can disguise the confluence of evils paraded about as a higher right. The corollary of there being no free lunches is that there are no rights without obligations.

(Professor Irving Louis Horowitz, Rutgers State University, New Jersey, and president of Transaction Publishers, 1986)[4]

25

The matrix

Radio must be changed from a means of distribution to a means of communication. A huge linked system ... capable not only of transmitting but receiving ... which did not isolate the listener but brought about contact. It is a proposal which is, after all, only the natural consequence of technological development, helps towards the propagation of that *other* system.

(Berthold Brecht, *Theory of Radio*, 1932)

The decentralizing effects of technology and the 'democracy' of information are widely seen as a hope for the future. It is an optimism based more on faith than facts, as if the present problems are so complex and daunting that any alternative seems utopian.

Few are prepared to admit that the information revolution will be as divisive as any other, that the changes will be difficult and bring with them extraordinary social tensions and conflicts. Above all, no one is prepared to admit that the centralized institutions will fight back, that they have no intention of dissolving into democratic networks but, on the contrary, will fight to retain their control and privilege in any way they can. Yet this is exactly what they are doing, and with highly effective results.

It is almost a cliché to say that international business organizations are now bigger than many countries, but the scale of their operations and the concentration of their ownership are remarkable. In 1980 the seven largest US microchip manufacturers had a combined turnover of $1,000 million. By 1990 it is expected to be more than $30,000 million. Yet only 15 per cent of their products are distributed on the open market. The bulk of this vast output – 85 per cent of it – is sold to just eighty companies around the world.

The patterns of ownership among the media transnationals are immensely complex. Familiar names, like the *Washington Post* or Twentieth Century Fox, which people take to be independent institutions, are simply parts of a consortium owned by a company which is in turn owned by an even larger corporation. Umberto Eco's 'cobweb' is not just a figure of speech, because many of them own minority shareholdings in each other's corporations, and actually control parts of each other's operations.

Even transnationals themselves are coming together, as if under the force of their own gravity, to form ever larger alliances which between them cover every aspect of the media environment, from the manufacture of computers to the story-line of soap operas.

There are a number of independent players in the game, such as Warners and the Disney group, but out of this complex power struggle three conglomerates are emerging which may one day dominate the entire electronic network. First, there is the alliance of Time Inc., Thorn EMI, Gulf & Western, and MCA (which owns, amongst other things, both Paramount and Universal studios, and the highly succesful Home Box Office pay-television system). Secondly, there is the RCA – General Electric – Coca Cola-Citicorp group (which includes Columbia Pictures and NBC). Finally, there is the combination of CBS, Loews, and the News Corporation (the Rupert Murdoch empire) which extends from newspaper chains to Sky Channel satellite broadcasting and Twentieth Century Fox).

The diversity within each transnational is astonishing. In Britain, Thorn EMI are involved in cable television film production and distribution (including Elstree Studios and a 46 per cent share in Thames Television), defence systems (through Varian Electron and Systron Donner), electronic security systems (Pro-tech, Malco, Datatech, and Nuclear Enterprises), computers (Datasolve, Software Sciences, and Micrologic), telecommunications (with the Swedish giant L. M. Ericsson), and semi-conductors (with the leading UK manufacturer, Inmos).

Through their subsidiaries, each conglomerate owns a major US television network, film studios, and a large stake in the cable satellite systems. They also, almost incidentally, have an investment in the printed word, in the form of several major US publishing houses. Random House is a subsidiary of RCA, Simon & Schuster is owned by Gulf & Western, Holt, Rhinehart & Winston by CBS.[1] The same pattern of ownership showed up in the consortium assembled to run the new British satellite broadcasting. This consists of Thorn EMI (film and electronics), Granada (television production), Pearsons (publishing), and Amstrad (computers), though the latter has since dropped out.

The transnationals control not only the networks, but to a large extent the material that is transmitted over them. If the process continues – and it shows every sign of doing so – we will soon reach the stage where, in Marx's phrase, they will own 'the means of production, distribution, and exchange' of most of the world's information.

Corporations which have made their name in other fields, such as Getty Oil and Westinghouse, are now trying to buy into the system; and the battle of the US 'videotext' system shows that the 'big three' are only too glad to recruit new allies. Videotext (like the Prestel system in the UK, which provides news, financial market reports, and weather details on television screens for subscribers) has been slow to catch on in the USA; but the transnationals are now preparing to carve up the market, and the line-up is revealing.

The three leading contenders are a system called Trintex (proposed by CBS in collaboration with IBM and Sears), another called Covidea (from Time Inc., backed by AT&T and the Bank of America), and a third called CNR (from RCA, this time in partnership with Citicorp and Nynex).

The corporate giants may have lost interest in the traditional means of distributing information, especially in the Third World, but they are determined to control the wiring of the global village. Their new-found power was vividly illustrated by Patricia Thomson, in a recent article for *After Image* magazine. She wrote:

> In the Europe – Siberia pipeline episode, when nation-to-nation pressure did not produce the contract cancellations desired by the US government of European countries, transnational business was called on to produce equivalent results. With a simple change of a computer entry key at the government's request, a US-based corporation could cut off the vital information supply to its foreign subsidiary, thereby effectively paralysing business operations . . . It is such undermining of national autonomy that represents the challenge by these international organizations.[2]

The nature of the alliances is something new. The concentration of power in data banks and electronic finance is worrying enough, but when these corporations join forces with the media transnationals there is cause for serious concern. The scale of their resources means they could soon be dictating the direction of all research and development.

The requirements of the nuclear industry for security and monitoring systems will influence the development of computers, which will, in turn, affect the nature of electronic publishing. The vast multi-language audience created by communications satellites will affect the type of pop music and advertising they sell, and the best clients for this international advertising space are, naturally enough, the transnationals themselves. The dangers of such a closed loop are all too obvious. 'The growth of industrial capitalism', writes Michael Shannon in *The Reuters Factor*,

> is intimately linked with the invention and development of new means of communication. With radio, movies and television there emerges a cultural industry in which all branches of communication are implicated and in which intelligence and information play

second fiddle to the universal levelling of mass consumption ...
shaping populations' consciousness to the needs of increasingly
passive consumption. Thus the economic development of the media
extends and intensifies still further both the information network
and their own cultural net.

The days of the individual inventor or artist may be over, because
they would both be on the payroll. And the future of the world's
communications technology could be decided in half a dozen
corporate boardrooms – just as weapons technology is today.

With the spread of satellite broadcasting they will soon be
counting their potential audience not in hundreds but in thousands
of millions, with a potential influence over their moral and cultural
values comparable to that of the Church in the Middle Ages.
The possibilities for misusing the system are obvious. The media
merchants may claim to be socially responsible and independent, but
the very efficiency of the system is against them. As Jacques Valee
once remarked, 'Show me an efficient information system, and I will
show you an efficient disinformation system.'[3]

As the transnationals continue to buy into each other, they are heading towards a curious (if hypothetical) situation where every company
has a share in every other, in a super-network that spans the globe.

This is the nightmare of systems theorists, a vast hegemony of
information that Alvin Toffler calls a 'matrix' (comparing it to the
'food matrix' and 'transport matrix' he predicts could develop along
similar lines). It would be comparable in economic terms to a major
power bloc, but since its functions would be so closely integrated, it
would be more powerful than any assembly of individual nations. It
would be an autocratic autarky – self-sufficient, self-referring, and
utterly undemocratic.

It would be not only unaccountable, but progressively less
efficient as it increased in size. The level of bureaucracy would rise,
as it spent more time and energy on its own internal organization,
and it might even – from a systems point of view – reach the
dangerous state where, having filled all the available space, it had no
further outside input. In other words, there would no longer be a
market-place to respond to, or an environment into which it could
expand. The matrix itself would be the environment.

This is the point at which capitalist theories grind to a halt,
because the driving force of the market-place depends on competition; and it is our very *inability* to control supply and demand which
generates change. When competition is removed and the markets are
controlled, the system atrophies. The matrix locks solid; change
becomes impossible as it finds itself trapped in an endless cycle of
repetitions.

It sounds like science fiction, but such a situation is perfectly feasible. The record shows that cultural log-jams of this kind have happened before when societies have been deprived of external feedback. It was a similar 'matrix' of religion, monarchy, and state bureaucracy that froze the Chinese culture for centuries; and in Ancient Egypt the same kind of super-hierarchy stopped history in its tracks for 4,000 years.

Fortunately, the transnational 'grid-lock' is only one of many possible futures, and there are other forces at work which could modify the outcome. The effects of decentralization and interactive media (which Brecht was speculating about in 1932, but have still barely been explored), the growth of piracy and samizdat networks, and many other factors could affect the outcome. There are even examples where transnationals have recognized that it is in their own interests to decentralize their organizations and create some kind of internal competition. As the chairman of IBM, John Opel, put it, 'You have to have people free to act, or they become dependent. They don't have to be told; they have to be allowed.'[4]

In the case of IBM, Opel's answer was to set up a group of companies within the organization, but divorced from bureaucracy and company control, whose job was to compete with each other. Between 1979 and 1983 fourteen of these 'independent business units' (IBUs) were given their charters, and the scheme was an immediate success. *Fortune* magazine ran an article entitled 'How to Start Your Business without Leaving IBM', and in 1981 the most successful IBU, Entry Systems, designed the famous IBM personal computer.

However, the 'independence' of such offspring is questionable. It may, in the words of former IBM chairman Frank T. Carey, be a way of 'making an elephant tap-dance'; but beyond a certain level the policy decisions of transnationals (and their conglomerate allies) are centralized. The computer was marketed as an IBM machine, with an IBM label, and it was IBM that profited.

Perhaps the most important check on the growth of transnationals comes, not from the base of the pyramid nor from attempts to decentralize themselves, but from the outside. It comes from the systems they threaten – the national governments of individual states. The international character and global scale of the media corporations makes it impossible for national authorities to ignore them much longer. The TNCs depend on what they call 'trans-border data flow', which makes nonsense of frontiers and national identities. American Express, for instance, has to authorize 250,000 credit-card transactions around the world every day, which involves up to two and half billion messages a year – and that is only a part of one sector of the global money market.

The transnationals exert such an influence on host countries that they can dictate their own terms and sabotage the economy of small nations by withdrawing their investments. They negotiate as equals and are even beginning to establish a quasi-diplomatic status independent of their own governments.

At the moment, an uneasy truce prevails. The TNCs claim to be neutral and apolitical (except for such generalized notions as a belief in democracy) and try to disassociate themselves from accusations of propaganda. At the same time, they collaborate closely on military and space research. The governments regard them (in public, at any rate) as legitimate commercial enterprises, though they are seriously worried about their growing power and influence. There are so many inherent contradictions that conflict was bound to arise sooner or later, and the pretence that national and transnational interests coincide, or even run parallel to each other, looks less and less credible.

The unrestricted flow of money, information, and ideas around the world is not in the interests of individual states. It removes them from their control, weakens their frontiers, and undermines the identity of the state itself. In fact, it raises an entirely new concept in world politics: the concept of 'informational sovereignty'.

This is illustrated, at present, by the struggle of a particularly information-rich country, the USA, to defend its 'frontiers' against a relatively information-poor country, the USSR. The territory they are disputing cannot be found on any map, but is as vital as any physical resource; and the tactics they are developing will change the whole definition of who 'owns' information.

While the transnationals control the networks, the state is attempting to control the information that flows through them by overriding the principles of individual copyright. Whether you describe it as patriotism, censorship, or piracy depends entirely on your point of view.

Too much memory, too little time

> We approach the new technologies with the psychological conditioning and sensory responses of the old. This clash naturally occurs in transitional periods.
> (Marshall McLuhan, *Understanding the Media*, 1973)

It is impossible to forecast what uses the networks will be put to, when the 'wired society' becomes McLuhan's global village. When the first cuneiform script was inscribed on a clay tablet in Sumeria, no one could have imagined that it would one day lead to *Das Kapital* or *Dynasty*. In the same way, the electronic networks will also create their own uses, new forms of gossip and entertainment, new formulas, even new kinds of information.

The networks are still under construction, but there are two major developments on the horizon which may well set the pattern for the next stage in our electronic 'evolution'. The first is a massive leap in our ability to store information. The limiting factor on all previous technology has been the storage capacity of magnetic tapes and disks, but the advent of Digital Audio Tape (DAT) and new kinds of memory chips will change all that. The DAT system, developed jointly by Philips and Sony, depends on a special magnetic coating for tapes and disks that records digital signals with the accuracy of CD records in a fraction of the space.

The difference is of an order of magnitude, and from now on memory – mass memory – will be freely available; the problem will be what to do with it. The manufacturers of small computers will no longer have to fight to cram a single megabyte into their machines. Even games computers will have the memories of today's main frames. Video recorders will provide four hours of colour pictures and stereo from something the size of an audio cassette or smaller. Above all, it will make it easier to produce instant perfect copies of anything. If DAT lives up to expectations, it will provide a pirate's charter.

In a recent address to the Foreign Correspondents' Club in Tokyo, Heinrich von Moltke, director of industrial policy in the European Commission, warned of the dangers. 'It will blur the distinction between private and commercial copies,' he said, 'and it is that distinction on which our copyright laws are based. Digital copying allows an unlimited number of quasi-identical copies. This is entirely new.' In a direct reference to Philips and the Japanese manufacturers, he added:

> They are basing their whole business on copyright, and our copyright is becoming obsolete through new technology. It's clear that technology itself must be dealt with, otherwise a whole segment of our creative economy is threatened. Creativity is the real stimulus to our human life, and we are coming to a situation where our creative people are going to be pushed back into the Middle Ages.

Paradoxically, DAT also offers a unique opportunity to defeat the pirates. Because it requires a whole new generation of recording equipment, it provides the most important chance yet of building in copy protection *at source*. CBS have developed a spoiler system designed especially for DAT, known as Copycode, which works by cutting a notch of frequencies out of the recorded music. When Copycode is built into a recorder, it recognizes this unnatural gap (300 Hz wide and 60 dB deep, centred around the 3.48 Hz frequency) and refuses to record the material. It would be an active or 'double-ended' system, like that used on computer software, and if it were introduced it would undoubtedly be a blow to the pirates and home tapers. In fact, it is probably the last opportunity for many years for the two sides of the industry to agree on a single anti-piracy standard.

History repeats itself in an uncanny fashion, however, and this opportunity, like many previous ones, is slipping away. To start with, DAT has already split into two different and incompatible technologies: the S(stationary)-DAT standard based on traditional recorder technology with a fixed head, and R(rotary)-DAT, a descendant of video technology using a spinning head that scans the tape helically.

Secondly, the problem common to all spoiler systems, the suspicion that they interfere with the quality of the recording, has resurfaced with Copycode. CBS claim that the missing frequencies are undetectable and have demonstrated the system to record company executives at the EMI studios in London, but so far they have not subjected it to the more critical ears of musicians, producers, and journalists. However, studio engineers who have carried out unofficial tests say the effects are clearly noticeable, including a distortion of other frequencies due to phase shifting and a muddying of the stereo image.

Thirdly, and more importantly, the introduction of Copycode requires co-operation between the Japanese, who manufacture the hardware, and the Americans, who produce most of the software: But their traditional rivalry is intensifying against the background of a growing trade war. At a high-level meeting in Vancouver in December 1986 executives of the western record industry proposed to their Japanese counterparts that the CBS spoiler be built into their equipment. The Japanese politely refused, pointing out that, since European governments were proposing to 'legalize' home taping by the introduction of a tape levy, it was unreasonable to expect them to make recorders incapable of recording.

The record industry is now expected to appeal to the Common Market and the US Congress to block the import of DAT copiers by introducing a penalizing tariff barrier.

In a curious way, the second factor may actually cancel out this advantage. It is, quite simply, the speed of transmission and coverage of the network, which makes it possible to distribute more, faster and everywhere. The key word here is 'distribution', because the electronic net will, in due course, enable information to be distributed instantly, as a one-off process, and still make money.

An example of this would be the satellite distribution of, say, a new feature film. The signal would be coded and relayed by cable network to chains of video cinemas using the new high-definition screens which are indistinguishable from film. Allowing for differences in time zones, this kind of link-up would allow a feature film to be transmitted from one machine, in Hollywood or New York, to every cinema in the world.

By compressing the distribution time for a film from ten years to a week, the film industry could bypass the pirates altogether; and once the costs (and profits) had been recouped, they could afford to abandon their copyright. From then on, the film would be in the public domain, and anyone could copy it – as they would probably be doing, anyway.

The principle of 'instant release' (which already forms the basis of much television and radio) could even be applied to books and print, with on-line photocopiers producing instant copies of anything the customers selected, like an information automat.

In the last fifteen years, the apparatus of cultural production of the North American Empire has suffered profound mutations. No sector, be it press, radio, television, cinema or advertising, has escaped. In the course of the process of industrial concentration, the owners of high technology have increasingly become the ones who determine not only the manufacture of hardware and the installation of systems, but also the development of programmes, the content of messages. A field such as education which had not previously been affected by massive industrialization has begun to be colonized by the newcomers. The internationalization of production has posed the problem of the internationalization of cultural merchandise.

(Ian Reinecke, *Electronic Illusions,* 1984)

26

The source

Technological revolutions have always made the ruling classes nervous because they sense, corrrectly, that their power is being undermined. The fears are well founded because each new age ... has affected the power structures and changed the political landscape. Information technology gives new dimensions to governments' worry about loss of control.

(Walter Wriston)[1]

The right of governments to 'confiscate' intellectual property (which was mentioned in Chapter 14, 'The spoilers') has never seriously been challenged. In fact, it is practised, to a greater or lesser extent, in all countries. Where national interests are thought to be at stake, the right of individuals to remuneration, or even credit, for their ideas is brushed aside, expecially in sensitive areas like scientific research and high technology.

This is reasonable enough in time of war, when the suspension of civil liberties (including copyright) may be necessary. But many governments are coming to regard this kind of information as a national resource to be protected at all times, and are determined to control its dissemination and establish what has been described as 'informational sovereignty' over it.

In a report on the future of electronics prepared for the French government by Simon Nora and Alain Minc, the authors spelt it out bluntly:

> Governments have always tended to turn communications into a field of combat over sovereign prerogatives. From now on this area of conflict may be surreptitiously extended, if they do not provide themselves with the means to become a partner in a game where they can no longer be the master.[2]

The warning is well founded, but governments have been slow in coming to terms with it. They still believe in the nation state as the ultimate authority (as, indeed, they are sworn to) and that the transnational networks ultimately owe them allegiance. They are determined to remain the masters of the game, and are not too scrupulous how they do it.

The most dramatic example of this is in the United States, where the government are making strenuous efforts to prevent what they call the 'transfer of technology' to the Soviet Union. A strict embargo has been applied on the export of computers and other electronic equipment, and diplomatic leverage has been applied to their allies to prevent them acting as intermediaries, while at home they exercise extraordinary powers of censorship. In April 1985 the Defense Department prevented the reading of research papers at a symposium by the Society of Photo-Optical Instrumentation Engineers at Arlington, Virginia. They even limited the audience to US citizens who were willing to sign a form promising not to communicate the information overseas, and visitors from NATO countries who could get their embassies to certify that they would comply with export regulations to the eastern bloc.[3]

The main source of US government power lies in the system of funding for research projects in universities and commercial firms. The academic institutions have become so dependent on this that it is now estimated that three out of every four US scientists are working, directly or indirectly, for the government. The government dictates the nature of the work, and every invention, discovery, and idea that comes out of the laboratories is carefully monitored. It is national information, copyright of the US government, and they alone decide what happens to it.

The Doomsday Book

The heart of the system is one of the most extraordinary, and secret, books in the world – the Military Critical Technologies List (MCTL) – which itemizes every project the US government wants classified. An edited summary, known as the Federal Register, is published for reference and as a basis of policy statements, but the MCTL itself contains details of many inventions and discoveries that will never see the light of day.

The MCTL originated in the cold war of the 1950s, when the administration was shocked by the number of 'atom spies' passing secrets to the Soviets. The success of the Soviet space technology in the 1960s only heightened the sense of paranoia, and the MCTL was expanded to cover state-of-the-art developments in almost every science from molecular biology to parapsychology. It now consists of a huge twenty-chapter volume, running to many thousands of pages, subdivided according to the type of technology, and brought up to date by twelve committees that meet every month in Washington.

These committees, known as 'the disciples', consist of representatives of the armed services, the CIA, and transnational corporations such as IBM, AT&T, General Electric, and Intel. They are among the most powerful and influential and best informed groups in the world: the equivalent of a war cabinet, whose task is to plot the USA's strategy in the information revolution.[4] But their remit runs beyond the USA, because the US government is determined to prevent the transfer of technology from other countries, including their NATO allies and Japan. In fact, many believe that a covert attempt to extend this 'informational sovereignty' to Europe is now taking place under cover of the Star Wars programme.

Leaving aside its practical feasibility and political implications, Reagan's Strategic Defense Initiative has two unusual characteristics. The USA has carried out major technological programs before, from the Manhattan Project to the Apollo programme, but never before has such a range of sciences been involved. There is hardly a field of research, from computer codes to holograms and genetic engineering, which does not touch on Star Wars in some way. Secondly, there has never been such an open-ended invitation to other countries to take part, and the US administration has gone to unprecedented lengths to recruit the scientists of European universities and research institutes in the programme.

The SDI proposals were greeted with suspicion and hostility in many quarters. Academics on both side of the Atlantic have organized protest campaigns to emphasize the moral and social issues. Professor Nicholas Macintosh of Cambridge University was speaking for many of his colleagues when he said, in a radio interview, 'It is the duty of scientists, especially those supported by public funds, to tell the public what they are doing and what they find out'.

Governments, for their part, were more concerned about the constitutional implications, especially the issue of 'extraterritoriality' – the long-running argument about the extent to which the USA interferes in other nations' affairs. But at least three countries, the UK, West Germany, and Israel, are now committed to the programme.

In December 1985 Caspar Weinberger and the UK Defence Secretary, Michael Heseltine, signed a memorandum of understanding in Florida; and Heseltine's West German counterpart, Martin Bangemann, followed suit in April 1986. The documents were intended to be secret, but the West German text was leaked to the *Cologne Express*. When the details were published, three facts stood out. First the Transfer of Technology agreement, which accompanies every SDI contract, goes far beyond Star Wars research to cover all 'sensitive technologies'. Secondly, the US Defense Department receives 'unlimited rights' to all models, prototypes, technical data, and software generated by the research. In other words, they retain the right to exploit any spin-off, whether relevant to Star Wars or not. And thirdly, they *alone* have the right to classify any research document as secret, and to suppress its publication.[5]

The SDI documents put the question of intellectual property in a new perspective. Governments may discuss the Berne Copyright Agreement or the New Information Order, but the final paragraph of a letter from the US negotiator, Richard Perle, makes their real attitude quite plain. 'As far as international law is concerned,' he wrote, 'The American government considers the common declaration of principles to be more of a political commitment than a legal document'.

The main focus from the US point of view was to prevent the export of technology from West to East Germany, and the East Germans were predictably scathing. 'The government of the Federal Republic', ran an editorial in *Neues Deutschland*, 'is delivering up to the Defense Department of the USA its sovereign rights including the right of intellectual property in decisive areas of science, technology, and production.'

The British obtained better terms on technology transfer and copyright, but it still meant, for instance, that advanced UK research into computers, which is ahead of the Americans in some respects, would be handed directly to their competitors at IBM and Intel. According to the UK journalist Paul Walton, who has made a special study of SDI, it is 'a crucially flawed agreement' which 'takes little or no account of the way in which the American defence industries operate':

> Even if the issue of intellectual property rights and the ownership of ideas is resolved, unscrupulous US contractors could take and misuse research findings. The only way to prevent enabling technologies from being lost across the Atlantic is for British firms to act as prime contractors. But this is unheard of, and (under the agreement) just one SDI contract will be set aside in which Britain will be in control.
>
> The MCTL will continue to grow and place much otherwise useful research beyond the veil of secrecy. Cases are beginning to emerge in which Europeans, even friendly Britons, are being excluded from the free exchange of scientific ideas with US colleagues who now do work for SDI. Research which is open today, can become closed tomorrow.[6]

SDI is only the beginning. Whether or not the space lasers are ever launched, the US government's long-term strategy is not in doubt. In a recent article in the prestigious *Jane's Defence Weekly*, Paul Watson described the comprehensive study now being carried out by the Pentagon, which involves the vetting of thousands of firms in Europe and Japan: 'In effect, the Americans want the right to classify any technology and any product, (and) every significant technology research laboratory or manufacturer would be on the list.'[7]

This process has only just begun, and the outcome is uncertain. Japan, for instance, will be a more difficult nut to crack, because its electronic firms are engaged in a ruthless trade war with US rivals. But the cards are on the table, the strategy is established, and the US authorities are adamant that it will be extended to other countries. It is no longer just a conflict of interest between pirates and manufacturers, transnationals and governments, the 'haves' against the 'have-nots'. The world's power blocs are now defining their spheres of influence, and a new kind of 'iron curtain' is drawn along the frontiers of information.

The line between piracy and espionage is becoming blurred. When the state decides what can and cannot be known, and the flow of information is controlled by anonymous and unaccountable organizations, the moral issues are reversed. Spies do not necessarily have to act for a 'foreign power'; they can be operating on behalf of the people themselves. There are even circumstances when the crimes mentioned in this book, from piracy and samizdat to un-official computer networks, may be not only justified but morally right.

If the present trends continue, the outlook is ominous. When frontiers are established, sooner or later they must be defended. If information is to become the world's most valuable resource (and ideas, as Buckminster Fuller predicted, are at the greatest economic premium), then sooner or later it will be fought over.

The First World War was fought over geopolitics – the national structure of Europe and the distribution of empires. The outcome of the Second World War was determined by resources – the oil of Russia and the Middle East, and the coal, iron, and steel of Europe. The Third World War may well be about information. It will be a war of a very different kind: conflict between paranoid ideologies, east and west, north and south, between hierarchies and heterarchies, the state and the people. No battles have yet taken place. Indeed, there may be no battles in the usual sense. But the bootleggers and pirates, enforcers and collectors, hackers, spies, counterfeiters, moles, plumbers, censors, and security experts who people this book are already fighting the first skirmishes.

The Miller scenario

Governments are not only seeking to control the sources of information, but are using electronics to reinforce their authority in another way – by gathering information about their own citizens on an unprecedented scale. There is no need to describe the possibilities this raises. The nightmare visions of Kafka and George Orwell are only too familiar to all of us. But what is new about it, today, is that the fantasy is becoming a reality.

It is happening in the Soviet Union, where the newest computers go, not to the military, but to the KGB. It is happening in South Africa, where the apartheid system is run from two large main frames. And, according to Arthur R. Miller, Professor of Law at the University of Michigan, it is happening, right now, in the heart of western democracy.

'Let me start with three basic propositions,' he writes:

First, Americans today are scrutinized, measured, watched, counted, and interrogated by more government agencies, law-enforcement officials, social scientists, and poll takers than at any time in history.

Secondly, probably in no nation on earth is as much individualized information collected, recorded, and disseminated as in the United States.

Thirdly, the information gathering and surveillance activities of the federal government have expanded to such an extent that they are becoming a threat to several of America's basic rights, the rights of privacy, speech, assembly, association, and petition of government.

There is nothing wrong about collecting statistics. Census-taking is one of the oldest hierarchical activities. Governments only became possible with the invention of writing, and one of the first uses of this 'new' technology was to take polls and keep records. As an activity, it has been going on a very long time.

However, electronics has given the state a new and unprecedented capacity for storing and analysing this information. In the form of tax returns, medical histories, criminal records, credit ratings, insurance assessments, licence applications, and welfare forms, every detail of our lives is now recorded on centralized computers, compiled and cross-referenced without our consent, and consulted without our knowledge.

Quite apart from the political consequences, and the threat to individual liberty, it raises interesting questions of copyright. Who does this information belong to? Do you own the copyright on your own life? Or does the state have the right to know more about you than you do yourself? Is it possible to pirate this information (in the way that other records, such as mailing lists, are copied and sold)? And if an outsider manages to steal or misuse the information, who is responsible? How are we to define the crime, or set the punishment?

The moral and legal implications of these new databases are far-reaching. Governments are reluctantly conceding the right of citizens to know what is on their record, provided they ask to see it (in 1984 Britain passed the Data Protection Act); but they are not obliged to tell you in the first place. And knowledge, as Francis Bacon said, is power.

27

The curve

I fear none of the existing machines; what I fear is the extraordinary
rapidity with which they are becoming something very different to
what they are at present. Should not that movement be jealously
watched, and checked while we can still check it?

(Samuel Butler, *The Book of Machines*, 1872)

Much of this book is written in the language of crisis, and we make
no apology for it. If the facts and figures were not serious enough,
the idea that a revolution (information or otherwise) might be taking
place around us gives the subject a sense of urgency. If anything, we
have underplayed the situation. Many of the experts who have
studied it are agreed that, unless we take it very seriously indeed,
and prepare for change, we may not be able to ride the wave.

Even capitalists like Walter Wriston, who are committed to the
spirit of enterprise, are under no illusions as to the scale of the
problem. 'Significant socially beneficial utilization of the new technologies require societal restructuring,' he warns. 'The notion that
humanistic societal change can be introduced incrementally, via the
new technologies, is unrealistic to the point of fantasy.'[1]

Some commentators, like Alvin Toffler, are optimistic that we can
avoid the 'Big Brother' perils of techno-facism; others, like Herbert
Schiller, author of *Information and the Crisis Economy* (1986), have
no doubt what we are in for. 'Surveillance, intervention, and
marketing', he writes, are the near certain outcomes of the utilization
of new communications technologies, domestically and globally.'[2]

This is a grimmer forecast than any we have tried to justify. There
are too many variables at work, including piracy, to be certain that
the networks will develop in this way. For a start, three-quarters of
the world's population are still outside them, and they, too, will have
a say in what happens.

Prediction of any sort is a risky business, because the future
consists of alternative possibilities, radiating out from us like a
set of paths, which increase in number and variety the further ahead
we look. But there is one exception to this – the situation where there
is a clear pattern of events in the past, that lead directly to the
present and are still repeating themselves. When a pattern of this
sort appears on the records, it is only human nature to project its
tracks into the future, to see where we are heading.

The importance of the information revolution is not in doubt. It has been compared to other major turning-points, such as the invention of writing, events which changed everything from the structure of society to the way we view the world. These paradigms in human history form a pattern, like a slow groundswell behind the comings and goings of kings and generals, and have changed our lives more profoundly than any political theory. The information revolution was a long time coming, but the signs were there to read, if we had known how. If the signs are right, and we read them correctly, and we are heading in the direction they seem to indicate – then the outcome is ominous.

The shape of change

> If changes in technology occur at a faster rate than changes in society's institutions or in the public's understanding, the society, to a major extent, is in the grip of the machine.
> (James Martin and Adrian Norman, *The Computerized Society*,
> 1970)

The man credited with discovering the pattern is R. Buckminster Fuller, the American engineer, philosopher, and visionary, the inventor, amongst many other things, of the geodesic dome. In 1942 he set himself the task of discovering whether scientific events occurred in any regular or predictable pattern. He had to select phenomena that were comparable with each other, and while considering this it occurred to him that there was one set of 'pure-science' events which were ideal – the progressive discovery of the ninety-two basic chemical elements.

Ignoring the prehistoric discoveries, such as lead, gold, and iron, he began with the first element to be deliberately extracted from nature – the isolation of arsenic in Italy, in AD 1250. There was then a long period of over 400 years when only two chemicals were discovered, antimony (in 1450) and phosphorus (in 1670). Sixty-two years later came cobalt, and from then on they came thick and fast, through oxygen, silicon, and platinum, until a new element was being discovered every two years.

There were periods when the rate slowed down or speeded up, but when the discoveries were plotted on a graph the overall pattern was an unmistakable curve, shallow at first, but rising more and more steeply until it was almost vertical. It was a familiar shape, one that any scientist would immediately recognize as the pattern of *exponential growth*, where the rate at which things happen increases, at each stage, like compound interest.

Fuller left a space on the graph to see if future discoveries confirmed the predictions. By 1969 he had been able to add ten transuranic elements (unstable radioactive molecules heavier than uranium). Plutonium was number 94, and the list was headed by Lawrencium at 103, each in its appointed place on the curve.

He applied the same technique to other phenomena, such as the time it has taken us to circumnavigate the globe. When Magellan's wooden sailing ships first completed the voyage in 1520, it took them two years. The steamship reduced it to two months; aircraft have reduced it to two days, and satellites to a couple of hours. The periods between each stage, from 350 years, to 65, to 30, flow the same pattern.

It applied not only to inventions, but to the speed at which they were adopted for everyday use. It took 150 years for the steam engine to become commonplace, 50 years for the car, 25 years for radio, 15 years for the transistor, and 5 for the microchip. Fuller's original chart spanned 760 years, but the same exponential curve is apparent over a period of a century, or even a decade. The effect is more marked the closer we come to the present.

In 1950 almost 20 cubic inches were required for a single electronic circuit. A decade later transistors made it possible to pack it in 1 cubic inch. Five years later one could pack 10 circuits in the same space, then 100, then 1,000, until today's microchips can carry up to a million.[3]

Whether one considers the frequency of discoveries or the increased miniaturization and complexity of machines, the same rules apply; and the charts show that they affect every aspect of information technology, from the speed of transmission and volume of flow to our capacity to store the data. We are accumulating more information, analysing it faster, and making use of it sooner all the time – and to do this we need even more information. Or as Toffler put it, 'More diversity and change equals more information, equals more technology to handle the information, leading to still more diversity and change'.[4]

But what, you may ask, is wrong with that? We've done all right so far, the economy depends on it, and many would argue that it brings us increasing prosperity. The problem, quite simply, is that there are no free lunches or, to alter the analogy slightly, for someone to get increasingly rich, someone else has to get increasingly poor.

The rich get rich

It is characteristic of any race which involves exponential acceleration, that the man who gets off first continually pulls away from his opponent.

> It is clear that we are facing a calamitous political stress point. Whether the world survives ... may not depend upon conflicts in the Middle East, Africa, or on the Sino-Soviet frontier, but on the political implications of advanced computer technology.
>
> (Christopher Evans, *The Mighty Micro*, 1982)

There is a terrible determinism about the idea that the rich get rich and the poor get poorer: the idea of the unwinnable contest, where the gap between each competitor steadily widens, where the Third World is forever third, and there is nothing anyone can do about it. But this is to forget one important fact, which makes all the difference to the outcome. The exponential advantage applies across the board, to good and bad alike, and they are not all aiming for the same goal. In fact, there are many different 'races' taking place, which could cancel, or at any rate balance, each other out. The situation is reminiscent of other doomsday theories, such as the Malthusian forecast that the world would be choked by over-population, which made no allowance for education or the development of contraception.

In the centralized and tightly controlled networks, the authorities are well ahead, and time can only reinforce their position. But in the development of decentralized technology it is the general public – us, the pirates – who are in the lead, and as time goes on we will also get further ahead. This sounds like a contradiction, but the two are not necessarily incompatible. It is possible to imagine, at some future date, a stable frontier between them, evolving around the 'moment of release' (referred to in the previous chapter) – the moment when closely guarded private information is set free, to become anyone's to use or copy.

This is roughly how it may work. Once a feature film or software program or digital music recording was released, it would be lost to the networks. The première itself, paid for by an unprecedented audience over a global network, would be their source of income and return on investment. It would be a real-time release, synchronized over a 24-hour or 48-hour period at most, over computer networks, by broadcast transmissions, or through the chains of high-definition video cinemas now being planned. From then on, by common consent (or force of circumstances), it would be second-hand information, in the public domain, to be duplicated or resold like second-hand cars or furniture by anyone who can find a local market for it.

This may seem like a far-fetched scenario. For a start, it would require a massive increase in pay-television and other forms of on-line marketing, but we are talking about twenty or thirty years ahead, when the wired society should be an operational reality – at

least in Europe, America, abd Japan. In fact, it may be forced on us
as the only way to cope with the increasing volume of information
(news, entertainment, and expertise) that will then be flowing
through the system.

Either way, it would allow both the information merchants
and the pirates to prosper, each in their respective spheres. The
exponential race may in the end turn out to be like the caucus race in
Alice in Wonderland, where everyone wins and they all get prizes.
But thirty years ahead, or twenty, or even ten, is a very long-range
forecast. The only safe prediction is that by then everything will
have changed, including our concept of piracy. Today's beliefs and
attitudes will probably seem as quaint as those nervous Victorians
who believed that travelling at more than ten miles an hour could
damage your health. In thirty years' time we will have other things to
worry about, because the exponential curve will have gone off the
top of the chart.

Onwards and upwards

> My forecast for the future is this. Whatever hasn't happened, will
> happen, and no one will be safe from it.
> (J. B. S. Haldane, scientist and philosopher)

The graphs of historical events tend to go up and down with the
fortunes of the country, the cycles of freedom and oppression, or
whatever social statistic one happens to be studying. But Fuller's
graph is different. There are no undulations, no periods of falling
back and recovery. As if it was following some inexorable logic, each
step is an exact, predictable increase over the previous one.

The question is not *what* is happening (it's a straightforward
logarithmic progression), but *why*? How can a mathematical formula
like this apply to such random, and essentially human, activities as
invention and discovery? And why is the whole process apparently
speeding up?

Fuller suggested that it was driven by cycles of war and peace,
with theoretical discoveries being made in peacetime and the application – that is, the realistic technology – emerging from periods of
violent unrest.

There is some truth in this. Necessity really is the mother of
invention, but the cycles are not regular enough to explain the curve.
Wars are not occurring more frequently, and there are many
examples that defy the rule. For instance, the theory of computers
was developed in the Second World War, and most of their
applications came later.

Like other attempts to explain the curve, it is too anthropomorphic.

They start with the assumption that it's our fault, that we deliberately make it happen. The trouble is that we still delude ourselves that we are in charge, that we decide what we want and then invent it, that these developments are a matter of *rational choice*. But this is putting the cart before the horse, and every shred of evidence contradicts it. The one certainty about change is that it takes everyone by surprise, and the long-term results are never what was anticipated. The side-effects overtake our purpose; and the more complicated our plans, the less certain is their outcome. Nothing dates quicker than science fiction, as the threats prove to be advantages and the dreams turn into disasters.

'The trouble with scientific utopias', wrote Kenneth Bolding in *The Image*(1969), 'is that once they are stated they look remarkably like nightmares.'

If we really were in control, we could do something about it; and there is no shortage of advice on that score, including this stern injunction by Gordon Rattray Taylor in his book, *Rethink*:

> It is not men who must adapt to the storms generated by science, but science and technology that must adapt to man. And that adaptation means more than a simple limitation of scientific activity. It means that the scientist must learn to moderate his materialistic and individualistic urges.[5]

Unfortunately, although scientists may be the agents of change, they are not responsible for it, since their work is funded and directed by others. It is estimated that three out of four scientists in the technologically advanced countries are now directly employed by government authorities. So they are, in effect, working for us; it is *our* 'materialistic and individualistic urges' which drive them on.

In fact, this kind of moralizing is as naïve as the Victorian equivalent, which assumed that a lack of science was responsible for the world's ills. If we were in control, it would be possible to do something about it (at least in theory) – but if we were in control, the graph would be a different shape. The ruthless geometry of the curve itself indicates that some other force is at work, something impersonal or at least instinctive, some mechanism or feedback that we are not consciously aware of.

A more likely solution is the self-perpetuating process suggested by Arthur C. Clarke when he wrote, 'the old idea that man invented tools is a misleading half-truth: it would be more accurate to say that tools invented man'.[6]

By reversing the problem like this a different and rather startling mechanism suggests itself. According to this theory, the old paranoia that 'the machines are taking over' is well founded – except that it has already happened. In other words, it is technology, rather than politics and religion, which has been controlling the development of human society for centuries. The politics came later, as a means of deciding how the technology should be controlled and its benefits exploited.

The Industrial Revolution gave rise to capitalism, not the other way round. Marxism was made by the proletariat, but the proletariat were created as a by-product of machines.

There is nothing surprising or disheartening about this. It is just that the unique characteristic of human beings is not reason or imagnative vision but our ability to adapt to circumstances. We are *reactive* organisms, and our genius lies in creating, identifying, and solving problems. When you look at the pattern of inventions and discoveries, it is clear that each generation of technology is designed to solve the problems created by the previous one, in the same way that scientific discoveries emerge as a result of the questions raised by previous discoveries.

'The transforming power of technology', writes Michael Shallis in *The Silicon Idol* (1984),

> has been the essential ingredient in the development of science, rather than vice versa. The application of knowledge has determined what knowledge is to be sought and the realization, by Bacon for example, that the sort of knowledge we call modern and scientific, is sought *in order to* 'effect all things possible'.

So it is that answers produce questions; the more we know, the more there is to discover; and each solution presents new and more complex problems. It is this form of positive feedback which results in Buckminster Fuller's curve rising steeper and steeper, until it eventually reaches the point when it is vertical, instant, and out of control. What happens next, and what if anything we can do about it, is another question. Is there time to pull ourselves together? Or even slow down? Should we give in and hope for the best? Or simply brace ourselves for the shock as we crash through into an entirely different form of society?

The final stage of this scenario is yet to come, but the symptoms are all around us. The signs of stress are appearing in social structures, law, and trade; science is surrendering to sectional political interests, and the information system is overloaded. We have long abandoned any pretence of a game-plan. Strategy has given way to tactics, and our only motive is expediency, as we plan for shorter and shorter periods ahead – from twenty-five years, to ten, to five – impatient of long-term issues and looking for quick, one-off solutions. With no time to establish standards, we are increasingly condemned to live in a world of prototypes, rapidly succeeding each other on the basis of anticipated needs, rather than known problems.

Generations of technology will leapfrog each other, rather than 'evolving' in any meaningful way (the market in computers is already dominated by this phenomenon). The result will be that people's decisions to buy or exchange a product are determined, not by what is available, but by what is *promised*.

We are overcompensating for each change of course, like a driver with a blanked-out windscreen, attempting to steer the vehicle by looking in the rear-view mirror. Year by year, month by month, day by day, the visibility is deteriorating. The horizon shrinks, as we accelerate backwards into a thickening fog. In the long run, it is not greed, arrogance, or political ideology which is at fault, but our fatal optimism.

Notes

1 The party of the first part

1 *Daily Mail*, 22 October 1977.
2 *Guardian*, 11 October 1985.
3 *Billboard* magazine, 9 May 1987.
4 *New York Times*, 27 March 1983.
5 *Guardian*, 11 December 1976.
6 *Daily Telegraph*, 5 June 1985.
7 *Daily Telegraph*, 17 April 1978.
8 *Observer*, 25 August 1985.
9 *Guardian*, 13 June 1985.
10 *Evening Standard*, 23 May 1986.
11 *Guardian*, 1 September 1984.
12 *The Times* 6 August 1975.
13 *Daily Telegraph*, 17 April 1984.
14 *The Times* 17 April 1984.
15 *Guardian*. 27 October 1979.
16 *Daily Mail*, 27 October 1977.
17 *Daily Mail*, 30 June 1979.
18 Ibid.

4 The photocopiers

1 Campaign Against Book Piracy, press release, 1 October 1984.
2 *New York Times*, 30 May 1978, 11 July 1978, 12 July 1978.
3 *Daily Telegraph*, 17 June 1980; *Daily Mail*, 25 June 1980.
4 *Financial Times*, 25 February 1981.
5 *New York Times*, 6 February 1981, 21 March 1981.
6 *Guardian*, 15 January 1983.
7 *Sunday Times*, 17 May 1980.
8 *Sunday Times*, 13 January 1980.

5 The book pirates

1 *The Times*, 22 January 1983.
2 CICI Anti-Piracy Group newsletter, no. 5, October 1984.
3 *Daily Express*, 19 May 1983.
4 *The Times*, 13 April 1983.
5 *Sunday Times*, 2 February 1986.
6 *Daily Telegraph*, 19 March 1982.
7 *Daily Express*, 19 March 1983.
8 *Guardian*, 26 January 1983.
9 *London Daily News*, 9 March 1987.
10 *The Times*, 24 November 1984.
11 *Guardian*, 3 February 1986.
12 *The Times*, 24 November 1984.
13 *Sunday Times*, 2 February 1986.
14 *The Times*, 24 November 1984.
15 *The Times*, 1 July 1985.
16 CICI Anti-Piracy Group report, 1985.
17 *The Bookseller*, 5 July 1986.

6 The tape-recorders

1 *The Guinness Book of Recorded Sound*, 1983.
2 *Sunday Times*, 1 October 1978.
3 *Music and Video Piracy in the EEC*, IFPI, 1985.
4 IFPI figures.

7 The sixth transnational

1 *Sunday Times*, 1 October 1978.
2 *The Times*, 22 August 1985.
3 CICI Anti-Piracy Group report, 1985.
4 *Sunday Times*, 1 December 1984; *The Times*, 11 January 1985; *Business Times*, 4 January 1985; *Singapore Monthly*, 3 January 1985.
5 *Guardian*, 20 December 1985.
6 RIAA, press release, February 1985.

8 Home movies

1 *New York Herald Tribune*, 26 February 1975.
2 IFPI, *Video Newsletter*, April 1985.

3 *Video Week*, 24 December 1984.
4 *Video Trade Weekly*, 5 August 1985.
5 *Video Week*, 2 December 1985.
6 Economist Intelligence Unit, *Home Video Revolution in Western Europe*, May 1983.
7 *Financial Times*, 1 March 1986.
8 *Media Law*, vol. 1, no. 13, October 1983.
9 *New York Herald Tribune*, 26 February 1975.

9 The video game

1 Wolfgang Roehl, in *Fernsehen/Video* magazine, July 1985.
2 *Screen International*, 9 February 1985; *Variety*, 24 March 1985.
3 *Screen International*, 4 May 1985; *Video Business*, 6 May 1985.
4 *The Times*, 22 October 1982.
5 *Video Week*, 25 February 1985; Fact, press releases, 7 February 1984, 10 March 1985, 3 March 1986.
6 MPEAA, news release, 8 July 1985.
7 *Financial Times*, 4 March 1986; *Screen International*, 25 January 1986.
8 *The Times*, 21 June 1983; *Daily Telegraph*, 20 June 1983.
9 *Screen International*, 16 February 1985; *Daily Telegraph*, 7 February 1985.
10 *Video Trade Weekly*, 30 March 1984.
11 *Northern Echo*, 19 January 1985.
12 *Guardian*, 16 September 1985.
13 *Screen International*, 3 November 1984; *Audio Visual*, December 1984.
14 *Screen International*, 16 March 1985.
15 *Sunday Times*, 5 May 1985.

10 The chip forgers

1 *New York Times*, 23 October 1983.
2 *New York Times*, 3 May 1983.
3 *Observer*, 17 March 1983.
4 *The Times*, 11 September 1984.
5 *New York Times*, 5 July 1983.
6 *New York Times*, 29 February 1984.
7 Ibid.
8 *New York Times*, 1 February 1984.
9 *New Scientist*, 30 May 1985.
10 *Byte* magazine, vol. 8, no. 11, November 1983.

11 The softlifters

1 *Your Computer* magazine, November 1984.
2 Ibid.
3 *Daily Telegraph*, 3 June 1985.
4 *Sinclair User* magazine, October 1985.
5 Ibid
6 Ibid
7 *Guardian*, 17 May 1984.
8 *The Times*, 4 July 1984; *Guardian*, 15 February 1985.
9 *Sunday Times*, 28 October 1984; Anne and Ian Staines. *Piracy of Computer Software in the UK*, Newcastle Polytechnic, 1984.

12 Stealing the system

1 BBC Television News, 18 July 1985.
2 *The Times*, 18 July 1985.
3 *Telelink* magazine, vol 1, no. 10, May/June 1986.
4 Ulric Coker, in *Telelink* magazine, no. 5, March 1985.
5 Bill Landreth, *Out of the Inner Circle*, Microsoft/Penguin, 1985; there are numerous sources of information on computer security and sabotage, but this is one of the most concise and readable.
6 *Guardian*, 11 January 1977.
7 *Daily Telegraph*, 21 September 1983.
8 Ibid.
9 Survey of Texas cable operations, 1983. Quoted in Showtime/Music Box (1986) 'Combat kit' (PR handout).
10 *Financial Times*, 11 November 1986.
11 *The Times*, 5 June 1985.
12 *New York Times*, 25 September 1983.
13 *Observer*, 2 June 1985.

13 The battle of the machines

1 *New York Times*, 21 October 1981.
2 *The Times*, 13 July 1980.
3 *Financial Times*, 25 June 1983; *The Times*, 30 September 1985.

14 The spoilers

1 *The Times*, 26 February 1981; *Sinclair User* magazine, no. 43, October 1985.

2 *Sunday Times*, 8 August 1985.
3 *Sunday Telegraph*, 3 December 1978.
4 *Music Week*, 8 June 1985.
5 *Sunday Times*, 1980.
6 *New Scientist*, 30 May 1985.
7 *Music Week*, 28 July 1984.
8 *Which Video?* magazine, September 1984.
9 *Video Week*, 23 March 1987.
10 *The Times*, 17 March 1984; *Guardian*, 17 May 1984.
11 *Video Week*, 8 March 1984.

15 The dongles

1 *New Society*, 7 March 1985.
2 *Sinclair User* magazine, no. 43, October 1985.
3 *Guardian*, 17 August 1984.
4 *Guardian*, 14 August 1986.
5 Ibid.

16 Sealing the system

1 *Security and Protection* magazine, June 1985.
2 *Telelink* magazine, May 1985.
3 *The Times*, 18 February 1984.
4 *Telelink* magazine, July 1985.
5 *New Scientist*, 16 July 1987.
6 Ibid.
7 *New Scientist*, 23 March 1985.
8 *Observer*, 2 June 1985.

17 The enforcers

1 Stemra-Buma, annual report, 1985.
2 *Financial Times*, 21 September 1982.
3 *The Times*, 25 October 1982.
4 Green Paper, *Reform of the Law Relating to Copyright*, Cmnd 8302, HMSO, 1981.
5 *Daily Telegraph*, 5 March 1982.
6 *The Times*, 29 April 1980.
7 *Daily Express*, 3 January 1983; *New Standard* 10 January 1983.
8 *Security and Protection* magazine, June 1985.

9 FACT, press release, December 1984.
10 FACT, press release, September 1983.
11 *Sunday Times*, 16 December 1984; *Sunday Times*, 26 June 1985; *Guardian*, 17 February 1986; *Video Week*, 6 July 1987.

18 The enforcers abroad

1 *Billboard*, 5 January 1985, 9 February 1985; *Financial Times*, 24 September 1984; IFPI, press release, February 1985.
2 Publishers' Association, anti-piracy newsletter, October 1984.
3 Ibid.
4 IFPI, newsletters, 1984–6; 'IFPI: the first fifty years', *Billboard*, 11 June 1983.
5 Gillian Davies, *Piracy of Phonograms*, IFPI, 1984.
6 *Straits Times*, 5 February 1985; *Business Times*, 26 February 1985; *Straits Times*, 7 February 1986.
7 RIAA, news release, 10 June 1986.
8 MPEAA, conference notes, June 1985.
9 *International Piracy – the Threat to British Copyright Industries*, PA/ IFPI, 1986; *Audio Visual*, December 1984; CICI, news release, 3 February 1986.

19 Protecting the markets

1 *International Piracy – the Threat to British Copyright Industries*, PA/ IFPI, 1986.
2 W.R. Cornish, *Intellectual Property*, Sweet & Maxwell, 1985.
3 *Financial Times*, 17 June 1986.
4 Professor I. L. Horowitz, 'Expropriating ideas: the politics of global publishing', *The Bookseller*, 2 August 1986.
5 Roger Wallis and Krister Malm, *Big Sounds from Small People*, Constable, 1984.
6 *International Piracy – the Threat to British Copyright Industries*, PA/ IFPI, 1986.
7 *Straits Times*, 1 May 1986; *Financial Times*, 5 September 1985, 28 April 1986.
8 S. M. Stewart, *International Copyright and Neighbouring Rights*, Butterworth, 1983; *International Conventions*, IFPI, 1986; *Extent of Piracy of Sound Recordings Worldwide*, IFPI Secretariat, 1984.
9 WIPO Forum on Piracy of Sound and Audiovisual Recordings, Geneva, 25 March 1981.
10 *Performing Rights Yearbook*, (PRS, 1984–5, 1985–6.
11 'IFPI: the first fifty years', *Billboard*, 11 June 1983.

20 The levy

1 TMG advertisement, *The Times*, 14 June 1986.
2 *The Facts about Home Taping*, BPI, November 1984; *The Case for a Home Taping Levy*, IFPI, 1984; *The Case against Levies on Blank Recording Tape*, European Tape Industries Confederation, February 1984; *Illegal Taping – the Facts*, Tape Manufacturers Group,
3 *Recording and Rental of Audio and Video Copyright Material*, Cmnd 9445, HMSO 1983.
4 Royal National Institute for the Blind, press release, April 1985; National Consumer Council, press releases, 30 April and 2 May 1985.
5 *Response to H M Government Consultative Document (Cmnd 9445)*, BPI, 30 April 1985.
6 *The Case against Levies on Blank Recording Tape*, European Tape Industries Confederation, February 1984; *Illegal Taping – the facts*, Tape Manufacturers Group,
7 British Phonographic Industry, *Yearbook*, 1984–6.
8 Green Paper, *Reform of the Law Relating to Copyright*, Cmnd 8302, HMSO, 1981.
9 *Daily Telegraph*, 7 May 1983.
10 *Daily Telegraph*, 21 January 1985.
11 *Guardian*, 20 February 1985.
12 *Music Week*, 23 November 1985.
13 *The Times*, 8 November 1985.
14 White Paper, *Intellectual Property and Innovation*, Cmnd 9712, HMSO, 1986.
15 *Music Week*, 7 November 1987.
16 *Music Week*, 14 November 1987.
17. Vincent Porter, *Proposal for Levy on Audio and Video Recording and the Funding of the Arts*, vol. 4, European Intellectual Property Review, 1981; Vincent Porter and Bridget Czarnota, *UK Reform of Copyright Legislation – Legal Principles or Political Pragmatism*, vol. 6, European Intellectual Property Review, 1985.
18 S.M. Stewart, *International Copyright and Neighbouring Rights*, Butterworth, 1983.
19 Quoted in Roger Wallis and Krister Malm, *Big Sounds from Small People*, Constable, 1984.

21 Commodity culture

1 Roger Wallis and Krister Malm, *Big Sounds from Small People*, Constable, 1984.
2 *New York Times*, 18 January 1984.
3 White Paper, *Intellectual Property and Innovation*, Cmnd 9712, HMSO, 1986.

4 *Guardian*, 4 December 1984.
5 *Guardian*, 22 January 1985.
6 *Guardian*, 15 July 1985.
7 John Dovey, 'Copyright as censorship – notes on *Death Valley Days*'; *Screen*, vol. 27, no. 2, March/April 1986.
8 Anna Coote, 'Freedom to quote', *Sunday Times*, 23 July 1983.
9 *The Times*, 6 June 1984; *Music Week*, 17 October 1987; *New York Times*, 18 January 1987.

23 The networks

1 Christopher Evans, *The Mighty Micro*, Gollancz, 1982.
2 'Computers and the Kremlin', *Newsweek*, 18 August 1986.
3 Charles Paul Freund, 'Video samizdat', *Village Voice*.
4 *Sunday Times*, 31 May 1987, quoting the Soviet journal *Literaturnaya Gazeta*.

24 The Third World

1 *Sunday Times*, 2 February 1986.
2 Ibid.
3 Ibid.
4 *The Bookseller*, 2 August 1986.

25 The matrix

1 'The information business', *Business Week*, 25 August 1986.
2 Patricia Thomson, 'World Information Inc.', *After Image* magazine, summer 1985.
3 Jacques Valee, *The Network Revolution*, Penguin, 1982.
4 *Byte* magazine, vol. 8, no. 11, November 1983.

26 The source

1 Channel Four Television, 27 August 1986.
2 Simon Nora and Alain Minc, *The Computerization of Society*, MIT Press, 1980.
3 *New Scientist*, 18 March 1985.
4 Paul Watson, 'Top secret SDI technologies ban?', *Jane's Defence Weekly*, 15 February 1986.

5 Paragraph 7.2 of the SDI agreement between Bonn and Washington specifically states: 'The Department of Defense of the United States will allocate the classsification of every contract and every implementation agreement. In the case of classification questions which are not unequivocably regulated ... these questions can be discussed between the parties. The final authority of the classification ... lies however with the Department of Defense of the United States'.
6 Paul Walton, 'Star Wars – where's the beef?', End Star Wars Appeal, 15 May 1986.
7. Ibid.

27 The curve

1 Walter Wriston, Channel Four Television, 27 August 1986.
2 Herbert I. Schiller, *Information and the Crisis Economy*, Ablex Publishing Co., Norwood : NJ, 1985.
3 James Martin and Adrian Norman, *The Computerized Society*, Telecom Library, 1970.
4 Alvin Toffler, *Previews and Premises*, Pan, 1984.
5 Gordon Rattray Taylor, *Rethink*.
6 Quoted in Martin and Norman, op. cit.

Select bibliography

Boulding, Kenneth E. (1956) *The Image*, East Lansing, MI: University of Michigan Press.

Brett, Hugh and Perry, Lawrence (eds) (1981) *Legal Protection of Computer Programmes*, ESC.

Burnham, David (1983) *The Rise of the Computer State*, London: Weidenfeld.

Cornish, W. R. (1985) *Intellectual Property*, London: Sweet & Maxwell.

Eco, Umberto (1986) *Faith in Fakes*, London: Secker.

Evans, Christopher (1982) *The Mighty Micro*, London: Gollancz.

Flint, Michael F. (1985) *User's Guide to Copyright*, London: Butterworth.

Fuller, R. Buckminster (1981) *Crisis Path*, London: Hutchinson.

—— (1973) *Nine Chains to the Moon*, London: Cape; first published 1938.

HMSO (1980) *Copyright and Design Law*, Cmnd 6732.

—— (1986) *Intellectual Property and Innovation*, Cmnd 9712.

—— (1983) *Recording and Rental of Audio and Video Copyright Material*, Cmnd 9445.

Jungk, Robert (1976) *The Everyman Project*, London: Thames & Hudson.

Knops, Karry (1985) 'The information wars', *Communications Quarterly*, summer.

Lahore, J. (1984) *Information Technology: The Challenge to Copyright*, London: Sweet & Maxwell.

Landreth, Bill (1985) *Out of the Inner Circle: A Hacker's Guide to Computer Security*, Harmondsworth: Microsoft/Penguin.

Large, Peter (1984) *The Micro Revolution Revisited*, London: Frances Pinter.

McFarlane, Gavin (1982) *Practical Introduction to Copyright*, New York: McGraw-Hill.

McLuhan, Marshall (1964) *Understanding Media*, New York: McGraw-Hill.

Martin, James and Norman, Adrian (1970) *The Computerized Society*, London: Telecom Library.

Mattelart, Armand (1979) *Multinational Corporations and the Control of Culture*, Brighton: Harvester Press.

Nora, Simon and Minc, Alain (1980) *The Computerization of Society*, Cambridge, MA: MIT Press.

Ploman, Edward W. and Hamilton, L. Clark (1980) *Copyright: Intellectual Property in the Information Age*, London: Routledge and Kegan Paul.

Radical Science Collective (ed.) (1985) *Making Waves*, London: Free Association Books.

Reinecke, Ian (1984) *Electronic Illusions*, Harmondsworth: Penguin.

Robertson, Geoffrey and Nicol, A.G. (1984) *Media Law*, Harlow: Oyez/Longman.

Schiller, Herbert I. (1986) *Information and the Crisis Economy*, Oxford: Oxford University Press.

Shannon, Michael, *The Reuters Factor*.

Shallis, Michael (1984) *The Silicon Idol*, Oxford: Oxford University Press.

Sizer, R. and Newman, P. (1984) *The Data Protection Act: A Practical Guide for Managers and Professionals*, Aldershot: Gower.

Sklair, Leslie (1973) *Organized Knowledge*, London: Granada.

Stewart, S. M. (1983) *International Copyright and Neighbouring Rights*, London: Butterworth.

Thomas, Denis (1978) *Copyright and the Creative Artist*.

Toffler, Alvin, (1970) *Future Shock*, London: Bodley Head.

—— (1981) *The Third Wave*, London: Bantam.

—— (1984) *Previews and Premises*, London: Pan.

Valee, Jacques (1982) *The Network Revolution*, Harmondsworth: Penguin.

Wallis, Roger and Malm, Krister (1984) *Big Sounds from Small People*, London: Constable.

Index